THE TRANSFORMIN⟨...⟩RK

John, from Alec,
in gratitude for
your friendship

THE
TRANSFORMING
OF THE KIRK

Victorian Scotlands Religious Revolution

A.C. CHEYNE

THE SAINT ANDREW PRESS : EDINBURGH

First published in 1983 by
THE SAINT ANDREW PRESS
121 George Street, Edinburgh EH2 4YN

Copyright © A. C. Cheyne 1983

ISBN 0 7152 0545 5

Printed in Great Britain by Bell and Bain Ltd., Glasgow

Contents

Preface

I am grateful to the Chalmers Trustees for honouring me with the invitation to deliver the lectures which form the substance of this book, and for waiting so patiently for their appearance in print.

It is a pleasure to acknowledge the many kindnesses extended to me by the Principal of Trinity College, Glasgow, the Revd. Professor Allan D. Galloway, the Master of Christ's College, Aberdeen, the Revd. Professor James S. McEwen, and their colleagues during my visits to Glasgow and Aberdeen in the autumn of 1976 for the delivery of the Chalmers Lectures.

The material which follows will also be familiar to those who attended the Thomas Burns Lectures which it was my privilege to deliver in Knox College, Dunedin during the month of July, 1980. I am glad to be able to express my gratitude to the Revd. Principal Frank Nichol, the Revd. Professor Maurice Andrew, the Very Revd. Professor Ian Breward, and all who made my stay in New Zealand such a refreshing and heart-warming experience.

That the book has at last been brought to completion is due in no small measure to the encouragement of fellow-teachers and students at New College, Edinburgh whose friendship over the years has been a constant stimulus and delight, to the assistance of the Library staff there, to the expertise of my superbly competent secretary, Miss May Hocking, and to the unfailing support of my brother and his wife and (above all) of my sister. I offer sincere thanks to them all.

My chief debt is recorded in the dedication.

New College, Edinburgh
May, 1982

I

Prelude: Before the Revolution

That the nineteenth century was "pre-eminently a century of revolutions"[1] (as George Kitson Clark described it in his 1960 Ford Lectures at Oxford) has become almost a truism among historians. Certainly most writers of Church history would not hesitate to use the phrase. Both Alec Vidler the Anglican and Henri Daniel-Rops the French Catholic chose *The Church in an Age of Revolution* as an appropriate title for their introductory studies of the period; and Kenneth Latourette the American Baptist was obviously thinking on similar lines when he called his massive five-volume survey *Christianity in a Revolutionary Age*. Either one of these titles would suit the present work, for the nineteenth century in Scotland was no less revolutionary than the nineteenth century elsewhere in the Christian West.

In Scotland as in England, France, Germany, Italy and the United States of America, the environment of the Churches underwent a dramatic and fundamental change during the Victorian age – and churchmen were as keenly aware of the fact as everyone else. Marcus Dods, the newly-appointed professor of New Testament at New College, Edinburgh (the leading seminary of the Free Church of Scotland), declared in 1889 that "It might be difficult to lay one's finger on any half-century in the world's history during which changes so rapid, so profound, so fruitful, and so permanent have taken place as

those which the past generation has seen." He continued:
"Every department of human thought and activity has felt the
touch of the new influences. The past fifty years have exhibited
many faults; but stagnation, contentment with things as they
are, has not been one of them. Nothing is today as it was fifty
years ago. Machinery daily accomplishes what the past
generation relegated to fairy-land or a remote and scarcely
believed-in future. Domestic life, commerce, art, literature,
medicine, education, all that touches the physical condition of
man has been facilitated, accelerated, improved by new
methods, by methods which because they are not empiric but
scientific, give promise of, and lay the foundations for, sure
and indefinitely growing progress in time to come. In politics,
perhaps the revolution is even more striking."[2] Only two years
earlier, the statesmanlike Robert Rainy had urged the Free
Church, of which he was then Moderator, to realise that it was
passing through "one of those times of rapid and remarkable
movement which are critical in human history."[3]

But of course it was not only *around* but also *within* the
Churches that the many-faceted Victorian revolution took
place. They as well as their setting underwent a sweeping and
– so far as we can tell – permanent transformation. In the
volume already referred to, Vidler notes "how recalcitrant they
were to change, how blind or short-sighted in the day of
visitation, how disposed to stone or silence or jettison the
would-be prophets or reformers in their midst, and how
lacking in the imaginative compassion and sensitive humanity
that might have given them a sure standing in the hearts of
peoples when they were deprived of earthly privileges and the
active support of governments." He also suggests, however,
and surely with justice, that "the Churches would not have
been able to survive, except as monuments on the margin of
society, unless they had to some extent changed with the times
and adjusted their teaching and practice to the new climate of
thought and the new structures of society."[4] From a somewhat

different point of view, the late-Victorian Professor Dods apparently came to a similar conclusion. "If it were true", he continued in the 1889 inaugural lecture (whose title, incidentally, was "Recent Progress in Theology"), "that theology has made no growth during this auspicious season, this were a scandal, to be whispered in corners and bewailed in private, not to be trumpeted at the house-tops." But such, he believed, was far from being the case. "That theology has not participated in the general movement no one will affirm"; while as far as his own discipline was concerned he would argue that "the past fifty years have done more to promote the understanding of the New Testament than all the other Christian half-centuries put together."[5] Despite the somewhat uncritical flavour of the professor's remarks, it is hardly possible to deny their main point, and what he says of theology might well be extended to cover many other areas of Christian concern or activity at the time of which he spoke.

Looking back, then, at the life of Scottish Presbyterianism during the nineteenth century, we see that while some of the most important changes that occurred were forced upon it by a rapidly altering environment, others resulted not just from external pressures but from a vigorous and thoroughgoing reappraisal of the entire range of inherited faith and practice – a reappraisal which was to have very considerable implications for both Church and world. In the pages which follow I hope to deal particularly with four main aspects of Scotland's religious revolution: what might be called the Biblical aspect (how Scotsmen came to read and understand the Scriptures of the Old and New Testaments), the confessional aspect (how they viewed their historic statement of belief, the Westminster Confession), the liturgical aspect (how they worshipped God), and the social aspect (their approach to the problems of community life, and the personal life-style which they tended to favour). In each case it will be found that while change was clearly evident throughout the years between the conflict with

Napoleon and the outbreak of the First World War, the tempo of change grew perceptibly faster, and the controversies occasioned by it infinitely more intense, during the tumultuous half-century which may be said to have begun with Darwin's *Origin of Species* in 1859 and ended with Lloyd George's challenge to the House of Lords at the close of the Edwardian period. I intend to concentrate my attention on these later decades. In the final chapter, however, I will advance beyond them into the new world of the nineteen-twenties, thirties and forties, while in the rest of this one I propose to survey, quite briefly, the condition of Scottish religion before the main force of the revolutionary storm had broken upon it.

Since the seventeenth century, Scottish theology has always been like an ellipse with two foci: Holy Scripture, which Presbyterians of every stripe acknowledged (in a favourite, much-used phrase) as the Church's "supreme rule of faith and life", and the Westminster Confession of Faith, which they liked to call its "principal subordinate standard". In a study such as this, priority of treatment might well be given to the history of the Confession, on the ground that it was their Confessional stance which determined men's view of the Bible and their use of it. On the whole, however, it seems best to begin an examination of the Victorians' theological inheritance by considering what they were always careful to describe as the supreme authority in all matters of faith – the Bible itself.

"Faith", declared Scotland's pre-eminent reformer, John Knox, "hath both her beginning and continuance by the Word of God."[6] It was in order to "maintain, set forward, and establish the most blessed Word of God"[7] that the Protestant Lords of the Congregation banded themselves together in a covenant whose eventual outcome was the overthrow of the Roman Church in their land; and the authors of the Scots Confession of 1560 pledged themselves to amend anything in their production which was demonstrably "repugnand" to God's Holy Word.[8] Succeeding generations saw Scripture being appealed to as the ultimate authority for everything in the life of the Church – and almost everything in the life of the nation as well. In the sixteen-forties, the Westminster Confession gave weighty utterance to what had by then become the accepted doctrine. Its opening chapter, "Of the Holy Scriptures", related how – natural knowledge of God's existence and character being inadequate for salvation – it had pleased the Almighty to make a supernatural revelation of Himself and His purposes, and in due course to commit that revelation to writing: the Scriptures of the Old and New Testaments. These (in their original languages) being "immediately inspired by God" and kept pure and "authentical" by His providence, were self-evidently divine and therefore authoritative for both individuals and Churches – though only their author, the Holy Spirit, could bring their message home to men and adjudicate in all controversies as to their meaning.[9] So the Divines; and as far as we can tell most Scottish believers between 1650 and 1800 were little inclined to question the infallibility of Scripture's pronouncements or even the Almighty's personal responsibility for every syllable contained therein. Sceptical views were not unknown, needless to say, especially in the age of Enlightenment. But they hardly percolated down to the ordinary man; and the coming of the Evangelical Revival, with all its ardour and intransigency, served only to reinforce the traditional attitude.

A more embattled age was on its way, however. Premonitory rumbles of the approaching storm can be heard during the bitter Apocrypha Controversy of the eighteen-twenties, whose virulence was perhaps partly due to the unsettling effect which German criticism in the age of Schleiermacher had upon the British scene. One pamphlet produced at that time, and considered worthy of republication more than half a century later, was *Remarks on the Bible*

(1828), by the Reverend Marcus Dods of Belford, father of the future professor of New Testament at New College. It sounded a new note, at once more combative and more defensive. The enemy, clearly, was all those – and they seem to have been quite numerous – who in one way or another sought to set bounds to the divine inspiration of Holy Scripture. "The common position", Dods wrote disapprovingly, "is, that the inspired writers were so superintended by the Spirit of God as to prevent them from falling into any material error, and that in some instances they had things revealed to them which they could not have known except by revelation of God, but that in most instances they were left to collect their knowledge from the ordinary sources of information, to select and arrange their materials, to digest their arguments, to gather their illustrations from the resources of their minds, and to clothe the whole in language of their choosing. It is said that when they speak of things of a moral and religious nature, they were so superintended as to be secured from error, but that when they mention things of a civil or domestic nature there is no occasion to inquire whether they were inspired or not – that in this case, in fact, it would be hazardous to maintain that they were. In order to save us from this hazard, the country is at present deluged with writings, the design of which is just to show us that inspiration is not so very sacred a thing as we have been accustomed to think it, and the effect of which is just to reduce the Holy Scriptures to the level of other pious writings."[10]

The way of thinking thus unsympathetically described had, as we know, a long future ahead of it, and by 1900 it dominated the theological scene, in Scotland as elsewhere. Dods, however, almost certainly spoke for the majority of his contemporaries when he proclaimed it to be malign in both import and influence, and stressed the duty of all right-thinking persons to fight it with every weapon in their power. "Now", he wrote, "while every means is employed with the

most unwearied assiduity to unsettle the minds of the people
on this most important matter, and to lessen their reverence
for Holy Scripture, I conceive that it is every man's duty to
resist the unhallowed attempt, and to do what he can to
prevent England becoming what Germany, by precisely the
same process, has become."[11] The support which he received
should remind us (who are perhaps unduly influenced by our
awareness of the coming "liberal" landslide) that there was
remarkably little evidence, even as late as a generation after
Dods senior issued his pamphlet, of the transformation soon to
be accomplished. After triumphing easily in several notable
heresy cases around 1830, Scotland's religious conservatism
was further reinforced by the Ten Years' Conflict and the
Disruption. It may well have reached its apogee at the official
opening of New College, Edinburgh, the Free Church's
theological show-piece, in 1850.

   As part of the celebrations, the various professors
contributed to an awesome series of lectures on the scope,
content and methodology of their respective disciplines; and in
every case statements were made which either explicitly
affirmed, or at least did not in so many words contradict, the
plenary inspiration and verbal infallibility of the Bible. A
characteristically idiosyncratic and unclassifiable contribution
came from "Rabbi" Duncan, the genial teacher of Hebrew and
Oriental Languages; and James Buchanan, professor of
Systematic Theology, gave no hostages to fortune when he
averred, unexceptionably, that "We are to regard the
Scriptures as a revelation from God designed for the
instruction, and adapted to the capacities, of the human
mind."[12] But their colleagues were more provocative. James
Bannerman of the chair of Apologetical Theology, who was
later to publish a huge treatise on *The Inspiration of the
Scriptures,* warned his hearers of the mounting threat to
orthodoxy. "Recent theories on the subject of inspiration", he
remarked, "have left us in doubt as to what, in the volume of

Scripture, is the wisdom of God, and what is the foolishness of men. It is not now merely the ancient form of the error that meets us in regard to the different degrees and kinds of inspiration attributed to the different parts of the Scriptures of God. But the very distinction itself between what is of God and what is of man has been done away with; the objective revelation is confounded, or, to a great extent, identified, with the subjective belief; and the spiritual intuition or convictions of man are made to occupy the place, and mimic the authority, of an inspiration by God."[13] (One wonders whether the immediate target here was S. T. Coleridge's *Confessions of an Enquiring Spirit,* posthumously published in 1840 and reissued in 1849.) In Bannerman's estimation therefore, one of the most vital questions for beginners in theology was simply this: "Have we a complete, infallible record" of "a supernatural revelation from God?"[14]

Even more unambiguous was New College's exegetical theologian, Alexander Black. "The doctrine of the plenary inspiration of the Word of God', he affirmed, "is one of vital significance, and constitutes the very basis of sound theological study. It does, indeed, seem to involve an express contradiction, to assert that what is professedly regarded as the Word of God, can be otherwise than fully and verbally inspired; and if the minds of the inspired men could be put in possession of the inspired truths in no other way but by the intervention of the appropriate inspired terms by the medium of which the divine ideas were imparted to them, the direct plenary inspired divine authority of the very phraseology of the original Scriptures follows by so necessary consequence as to be merely the statement of the same fact in a different form."[15] As for the ablest member of the professoriate, William Cunningham (principal, and professor of Church History) informed his audience that "God Himself has written the history of His church" – by which he meant the Old Testament; he also referred to "the unerring standard of the

Word of God".[16] For a more extended and illuminating statement of the position which he held then and throughout his teaching career (he died in 1861) we must, however, turn to his posthumous *Theological Lectures*. There we read as follows: "If the Scriptures afford us sufficient grounds for believing, as we are persuaded they do, that the whole Bible was composed, even as to the words of which it consists, through the immediate agency of the Holy Spirit, then it is our imperative duty to receive this doctrine as a portion of God's revealed truth, and to seek continually to apply it for determining our feelings and regulating our conduct in regard to the sacred Scriptures; and then we may be assured of this, that both from the native tendency of this doctrine itself, and the influence it is fitted to exert in guarding us against some of the common sources of error in the interpretation of Scripture, and also from the blessing of God which may be expected to accompany the maintenance of right views of that word which he has magnified above all his works, we will be most fully and certainly guided into all truth, and be led into a correct knowledge of his revealed will, and that the Holy Spirit who dictated the Bible, and whom we honour in recognising him as its author, will pour out upon us most abundantly his enlightening influences."[17]

Such, then, was the view taken of Biblical authority by the Free Church and – without any marked difference – by its sister denominations, the Church of Scotland and the United Presbyterian Church, during the last generation of relative theological peace in Scotland. What of the other great plank in their platform, the Confession?

The Westminster Confession of Faith became the "principal subordinate standard" of the Church of Scotland in 1647, when the General Assembly recorded their approval of it as "most agreeable to the Word of God".[18] But there are various ways of regarding, and applying, a doctrinal standard; and when the Presbyterians won the last round against their enemies in 1690 they began to make increasing use of the Confession, not just as a vital affirmation of faith but as a touchstone of political reliability (against the Jacobites) and as a means of excluding from office those deemed ecclesiastically undesirable (against the Episcopalians). A new harshness and inflexibility developed, reaching its climax in the famous formula of 1711 which had to be subscribed by every minister and licentiate. "I do hereby declare", the wording ran, "that I do sincerely own and believe the whole doctrine contained in the Confession of Faith ... to be the truths of God; and I do own the same as the confession of my faith ... which doctrine ... I am persuaded [is] founded upon the Word of God .... I shall firmly and constantly adhere to the same, and, to the utmost of my power, shall, in my station, assert, maintain, and defend the said doctrine .... And I promise that I shall follow no divisive course from the present establishment in this Church, renouncing all doctrines, tenets and opinions whatsoever, contrary to, or inconsistent with, the said doctrine."[19] It would not be difficult to trace a connection between the rigorous character of these terms – each phrase giving, as it were, another turn to the screw – and the political and religious tension discernible in Scotland during the last years of Queen Anne's reign; but the interesting thing is that although the threat from Jacobites and Episcopalians gradually receded the oath remained unchanged. The obligations concerning the Confession of Faith which had been imposed upon Scotsmen at the beginning of the eighteenth century were still binding at its close.

On the whole, they were not resented. During Principal Robertson's supremacy in the sixties and seventies, some efforts had been made (chiefly through the pages of *The Scots Magazine*) to get rid of clerical subscription, but the great man astutely discouraged all such proposals.[20] The conservative reaction to the French Revolution soon made both parties in the Church more pronouncedly orthodox than ever. Principal

Hill of St. Andrews, the most eminent theological teacher of his age, is reported to have warned students that Calvinism was not for use in the pulpit – yet Thomas Chalmers himself bore witness to the fact that Hill's orthodoxy was "formed in conformity to the Standards" (i.e., the Westminster documents).[21] The same could no doubt have been said about the general run of Moderates. As for the Evangelicals, their devotion to the scholastic Calvinism of Westminster was unimpeachable: one of the most obvious of the enthusiasms which they carried into the Free Church in 1843, it helped to establish that body's early reputation for rigid – not to say immobile – orthodoxy in the early decades of its existence. So while it would be absurd to claim that there were no dissentients from the Confession in the years between William Carstares and George Hill, it is undeniable that they were few indeed. The "Marrow Men's" stress on the unlimited extent of the gospel call and on the free grace of God in the salvation of sinners might earn the condemnation of the General Assembly as an Antinomian modification of predestinarian orthodoxy.[22] The Presbytery of Stranraer might scandalise conservatives by accepting Alexander Gillies for licensing after he had signed the Confession "erroribus exceptis" – errors excepted.[23] And John Witherspoon may not have been altogether wide of the mark when he suggested, in his *Ecclesiastical Characteristics,* that "It is a necessary part of the character of a Moderate man never to speak of the Confession of Faith but with a sneer; to give sly hints that he does not thoroughly believe it; and to make the word orthodoxy a term of contempt and reproach."[24] But on the whole conformity – sometimes reluctant, more often eager and whole-hearted – was the order of the day throughout that period.

Things were to be very different in the new century, which saw the initiation and swift development of a formidable onslaught upon the Westminster fortress. First, the mere outworks (some relatively unimportant chapter or article in the

Confession) were attacked; then, the inner defences (the characteristic doctrines of scholastic Calvinism); ultimately, the central bastion (the assumption that no Church can continue to exist unless its office-bearers are obliged to subscribe to a detailed statement of faith). Rather surprisingly, it was among those staunch traditionalists, the descendants of Erskine's Secession in 1733, that the earliest cracks in the façade of Scotland's confessional orthodoxy appeared during the closing decade of the eighteenth century and the opening decade of the nineteenth. In the questioning atmosphere created by the American and French Revolutions, and against a background of war, social change, and widespread political unrest, majorities in both the Burgher and Anti-Burgher denominations received what they called "new light" upon the age-old problem of the relations between Church and State. After much agonising, their change of mind was embodied in authoritative synodical pronouncements.

The General Associate (or "Burgher") Synod acted first, in 1797. Realising that one chapter of the Confession – XXIII, on "The Civil Magistrate" – might be construed as sanctioning the kind of intermingling, not to say confusion, of the spiritual and the secular which had been taken for granted in the days of the Covenants but was now generally unacceptable, they devised a striking disavowal of any such interpretation. At the licensing or ordination of a minister, so they decreed, the following preamble should be read before the formula that detailed the nature and extent of his commitments to the Confession: "Whereas some parts of the standard books of this Synod have been interpreted as favouring compulsory measures in religion, the Synod hereby declare that they do not require an approbation of any such principle from any candidate for licence or ordination."[25] The Associate (or "Anti-Burgher") Synod followed suit less than ten years later, astutely employing certain phrases from chapter XX of the Confession to elucidate – or was it to amend? – what was causing uneasiness in chapter XXIII. "They approve", the brethren declared, "of no other means of bringing men into the Church, or retaining them in it, than such as are spiritual, or were used by the apostles and other ministers of the Word in the first ages of the Christian Church, persuasion not force, the power of the Gospel not the sword of the civil magistrate, agreeably to that most certain and important doctrine laid down in the Confession itself, chapter XX section 2: 'God alone is the lord of the conscience, and has left it free from the doctrines and commandments of men which are in anything contrary to His Word, or beside it, in matters of faith and worship; so that to believe such doctrines, or obey such commands out of conscience, is to betray true liberty of conscience and reason also.'"[26]

There can be little doubt that this pronouncement betokened the virtual triumph of tolerance and voluntaryism among most, if not all, of the spiritual heirs of Ebenezer Erskine and Adam Gib. Yet in a sense it marked the death of an old order rather than the birth of a new. More significant for the future was another Anti-Burgher statement, made at this same time, which might serve as a kind of text for nearly every criticism levelled against the Confession in succeeding decades. "As no human composure", the Synod testified, "however excellent and well-expressed, can be supposed to contain a full and comprehensive view of divine truth; so, by this adherence, we are not precluded from embracing, upon due deliberation, any further light which may afterwards arise from the Word of God about any article of divine truth."[27] A portentous utterance, this, for it represented an advance in thought from which the mainstream of the Seceding tradition never subsequently departed. Its admission of human fallibility, and still more its appeal from the Church's subordinate to its supreme standard, Holy Scripture (an appeal which was, of course, reminiscent of the phrase already quoted from the preface to the Scots Confession of 1560), lived on in the United

Secession Church of 1820 and in the United Presbyterian Church of 1847. Moreover, the spirit which it embodied may be said to have animated most of the worthier assailants or would-be modifiers of the Confession throughout the Victorian age.

As far as contemporaries were concerned, however, the long-term consequences of the Seceders' enactments were scarcely discernible. What had actually been achieved so far was little more than a questioning of the Confession's eternal validity, and a hedging round of one of its peripheral chapters with fairly drastic qualifications. The Westminster heritage (so it seemed) remained wellnigh intact, and only the very discerning could have predicted the developments of the next few years.

Looking back on the state of Scottish worship before the so-called "liturgical revival" of the later nineteenth century, most modern authorities have inclined to agree with the unfavourable conclusion drawn by Robert Lee of Greyfriars in 1864: "That some considerable alterations are indispensably needed in our modes of conducting public worship is so evident to everyone who is capable of observation, that any attempt to render it more certain or clear may well be dispensed with."[28] In the eighteen-eighties, for example, Robert H. Story opined that "the public services of the Church of Scotland had become", as a result of the combined efforts of Puritans, Moderates and Evangelicals, "probably the baldest and rudest in Christendom".[29] In the first decade of this century, George McCrie, writing from within a very different tradition, asserted that "By the close of the eighteenth century divine service conducted in the churches of Scotland had fallen into a state of lifeless formality and slovenly neglect."[30] And an entire generation of ministers was until recently nurtured on what W. D. Maxwell, in the nineteen-fifties, had to say about the horrors of unreformed Church praise before what he called "the renascence of worship".

What (granting the critics' premises) had gone wrong? Some would contend that the fatal mistake had been made as early as the fifteen-sixties, when Scotland's reformers abandoned the English Book of Common Prayer (frequently used in the years just before and just after the fall of the Roman Church) and adopted instead John Knox's Book of Common Order with its Genevan pedigree. Thereby, so it is argued, they exchanged a fixed liturgy for one which allowed at least a measure of flexibility – and thus gave their approval to a form which diminished congregational participation except in the singing of psalms, pushed the reading of Scripture out to the unregarded fringes of the service, accentuated the hortatory and the didactic at the expense of what was truly worshipful, and – most serious of all – effectually cut the remaining links between Reformed worship and the mainstream Catholic tradition of earlier centuries.

There is a good deal to be said for this argument. In recent years, however, criticism has been directed not so much at the adoption of the Book of Common Order in the sixteenth century as at its abandonment in favour of the Westminster Directory in the seventeenth. For those who are thus minded, the work of the original reformers represents, by and large, the ideal to which Scottish worship should return, and the chief offenders are the Puritan innovators whose influence was in the ascendant even before the Covenanting flood swept away so many old landmarks. These latter, after all, were the men who had refused to kneel for private devotion on entering the pulpit, to say the Lord's Prayer, to sing the doxology at the end of a psalm, to recite the Creed at baptism; who argued against set forms of prayers; and who, suspect of Independency in church government, were charged in general with being of "a sectarian as opposed to a churchly spirit".[31] They did not sweep all before them, of course – even when, in the sixteen-forties, the Westminster Divines set about devising their Directory of Public Worship; but they represented a profoundly significant change of direction within the Scottish Kirk, and when the new book arrived in Edinburgh to receive the approval of the General Assembly it must have been obvious to most intelligent observers that many of the ancient usages permitted or even promoted by Knox's Liturgy had finally been departed from. Nor did the story of (alleged) decline end there. As the years passed and old memories faded, the Directory itself fell into ever greater neglect, while the polarisation of thought and practice produced by the troubles of the later Covenanting period meant that quite a number of characteristically Reformed ways of doing things came to be spurned because of their association with a grossly repressive Episcopalian régime. By the time that Presbyterianism was re-established in 1690, the mould had finally set.

Whether or not we agree at every point with the school who see all this as a tale of virtually uninterrupted declension, at least we can accept what has become an authoritative summary of the situation then and in the age which followed. "Long before the men of the Revolution era had passed away", that scholarly representative of the Scoto-Catholic reaction, Thomas Leishman, tells us, "the amalgam of Reformation tradition and Covenanting usage had hardened into a foundation for the worship of the nation, and was not disturbed for many a year. The eighteenth century was not given to violent change. Silently indeed a great modification of theological opinion went on; but the unwritten code which regulated the forms of the sanctuary was little altered, except by the omissions and negligences of men who had none of the fervour of the former age. Meanwhile the older customs associated with the Common Order ... were laid aside as completely as the book itself."[32] To give just a few instances of what Leishman means, private baptism returned, and private marriages began to be celebrated; the Puritan importation of "lecturing" – a kind of running commentary on the lessons by the minister – continued to exclude the unadorned reading of the Word; the custom of "lining out" the psalms was introduced and gradually canonised; and the protracted Communion services and seasons which had been favoured by the Protesters during the later Stuart period persisted into a very different age. Small wonder that some partisans would go so far as to aver that the slow disintegration of the material fabric of Scotland's ancient churches (a scarcely avoidable feature of those years) was a kind of parable in stone of the steady decay, during the same period, of the authentic Reformed tradition in worship!

Be that as it may, we can be fairly certain about the state of affairs at the beginning of the nineteenth century. Church services, it seems, were quite often ill-ordered, unduly long, dominated by the spoken word, excessively didactic, and over-dependent upon the idiosyncrasies and personal predilections of the minister. They were also, of course, well-attended by our standards, and marked in very many cases by the fervent participation of the worshippers. The buildings in which they took place were sometimes ugly or dingy or in a poor state of repair – though we may not despise the concern which built some five hundred sanctuaries between 1800 and the Disruption, even if quite a few were in a neo-Gothic style which only the eloquence of a Pugin or a Betjeman could induce us to admire today. The praise was confined to psalms and paraphrases, whose occasional grandeur and general faithfulness to the text of the Authorised Version did not altogether atone for their many crudities and infelicities. It was led, without instrumental accompaniment and not always too effectively, by a precentor: were he ignorant or incompetent, the music could be restricted to a small selection of well-worn and sometimes altogether unsuitable tunes. The prayers were on occasion barely distinguishable from the sermon, and liable to last almost as long. They often lacked any obvious sequence of thought, varied distressingly little from week to week, and laid themselves open to the charge of being drawn from what one authority describes as "an unwritten liturgy of stock phrases".[33] Actually to read them was in some quarters considered a heinous offence, while the use of the Lord's Prayer – regarded by the heirs of the Puritans as a lapse into "vain repetitions" – called forth much hostile comment. The custom of "lecturing" encouraged congregations to think that unexpounded Scripture lessons were a waste of time: after all, they could read their Bibles at home! Baptism or marriage in church, "in face of the congregation", had become a rare occurrence. Communion services, though undeniably solemn and elevating occasions, were still insensitively prolonged. At funerals, any kind of religious ceremony, whether in the home or by the graveside, was ruled out through loyalty to both the Book of Common Order and the Directory, as well as through fear of pre-Reformation abuses.

Few were aware, around 1800, that Reformed Scotland had once possessed a liturgy. Even the Directory elicited lip-service rather than whole-hearted obedience. There seems to have been little or no interest, among either ministers or members, in the liturgical practices of other Christian bodies and in the long history of worship stretching back to the days of the primitive Church. Yet in ecclesiastical life, as elsewhere, things are never entirely static. Sometimes unobserved, and often unheeded, new forces were at work within both Church and society – forces which would in due course revolutionise both the form and the content of traditional Scottish worship. Towards the beginning of the new century the tide began to turn.

Nowhere is the revolutionary character of the nineteenth century more evident than in the changes which it witnessed in the attitude of Churches and individual Christians alike to society and its problems. Between 1815 and 1914, the thought of influential Scottish churchmen moved, slowly but inexorably, from a sort of *laissez-faire* individualism to the advocacy of state intervention in the interests of a juster and more equitable social order. In the first half of the period, however, and particularly in the years from the downfall of Napoleon to the onset of mid-Victorian prosperity around 1850, the older point of view almost had the field to itself. This may be seen by comparing the ministries – and the reaction to those ministries – of two exceptionally gifted men, Thomas Chalmers and Patrick Brewster, who both came to West of Scotland parishes in the immediate aftermath of Waterloo.

The Town Council of Glasgow brought Thomas Chalmers to that city's Tron parish in 1815. Some two years later, Patrick Brewster was presented by the Marquis of Abercorn to the second charge of Paisley Abbey. The situation confronting both men could hardly have been more daunting. Scotland's most populous area, already wellnigh overwhelmed by the headlong pace of industrial advance and population growth over recent decades, now faced yet another challenge in the sudden and, for many, painful transition from war to peace. Fortunes were, of course, being made by a few, but abject poverty was the lot of countless thousands more. Taken as a whole, both men's parishioners were just about as pitiable, degraded, and unresponsive to organised religion as any group of comparable size in all Europe. Within five years or so of Chalmers' arrival in the East End of Glasgow, the so-called Radical War suggested that economic distress and governmental inflexibility had brought the entire western lowlands of Scotland to the brink of revolution. Indeed, his whole ministry, both at the Tron and (from 1819 to 1823) in nearby St. John's was carried on in an atmosphere made tense by strikes, marches, riots, treason trials and public executions, the forebodings of the rich and the angry miseries of the poor. Brewster, too, had scarcely begun his work in Paisley when a

great Radical gathering on Meikleriggs Muir degenerated into
a fierce riot: this so alarmed the magistrates that they
persuaded the Government to build a barracks in the town as
a means of keeping the inhabitants in order. In his later years
there, especially from 1835 onwards, what has been described
as "the most chronically depressed of Lowland industrial
centres"[34] continued to be a focal point for every kind of
working-class agitation, including Chartism. Both men, in
other words, faced situations which were well calculated to
arouse fears for the very survival of Christian community life
and civilised society as Scotland had known them. Moreover,
both were of the Evangelical persuasion and strongly in favour
of the "popular" party in the Ten Years' Conflict. There,
however, their agreement ended, for in social attitudes and
policy they were poles apart.

Brewster's views, which he always expressed with breath-
taking forthrightness and lack of ambiguity, perhaps found
their most memorable utterance in words addressed to his
parishioners on the morrow of the Disruption. The conflict
just ended had, as everyone knew, turned on the relations
between Church and State, minister and magistrate. Brewster's
manifesto of June 1843 was concerned with the same subject;
but the way he handled it, and the scale of priorities he laid
down, made clear the gulf which yawned between him and the
vast majority of his fellow-ministers. "It is the duty of
Christian ministers", he declared, "in conformity with the laws
and discipline of the Church of Scotland, and with the practice
of her ancient worthies in her best days, to instruct the
Magistrate in the exercise of his function; and if there shall be
found on the national statute book any enactment at variance
with the law of God – that they denounce such enactment, and
never cease to expose and condemn its iniquity till they have
accomplished its repeal; and if the Christian rights and just
claims of the community are disregarded, or put aside, or if
the faces of the poor are ground by the Master and Ruling

Class, that it is equally the duty of the faithful Ministers of God's Word to vindicate those rights and assert those claims, until they have brought the people to a sense of their Christian obligation to deliver their oppressed fellow subjects, – and that they are bound to reiterate such instruction, till 'every yoke is broken', and all iniquity expelled from the statute book, and all oppression banished from the land." Brewster then added, in a controversial application of the Evangelicals' favourite battle-cry, "The Headship of Christ", to social rather than ecclesiastical affairs: "This assertion and enforcement of the supremacy of the divine law, as the test and criterion of human legislation – this instruction of the National Magistracy for the administration of equal justice to the whole community, is the true practical application of Christ's headship as King of Zion, and Prince of the Kings of the Earth, and is, at once, in strict and beautiful accordance with the principles of Christianity and the laws of the Established Church of Scotland."[35]

Brewster's impressive *apologia* (for that is what it is) may be taken as both a summary and an attempted justification of claims which he had long been making, and would continue to make to the very end of his exceptionally stormy career. Religion and politics, he contended, must not be separated; the underlying cause of poverty and distress was the grossly unequal distribution of the nation's wealth; the most necessary specific for social well-being was "not purity, gentleness, peaceableness, and all that beautiful train of virtues... but only a single virtue, the virtue of *JUSTICE*"; sin was corporate as well as individual and personal; and the selfish rich (at whose door he laid responsibility for many of the nation's current ills) were "guilty in the sight of a Just and Holy God".[36] Not surprisingly, such views made Brewster an ardent supporter of "moral force" Chartism, of a truly national scheme of education, and of a universal, compulsory system of poor relief. They made him an equally enthusiastic opponent of negro slavery, of the fashionable doctrine concerning immutable economic laws, and in particular of Thomas Malthus' deterministic teachings, which he did not scruple to stigmatise as an "Infidel Philosophy".[37] They also brought him, almost inevitably, into frequent collision with both civil and ecclesiastical authority. In 1835, presbytery, synod and General Assembly united to rebuke him for attending a dinner given in honour of the radical Irish patriot, Daniel O'Connell. And in 1842 the Commission of Assembly suspended him for a year because of sermons, preached in a Christian Chartist church in Glasgow, whose "drift and tendency" – according to the prosecution – was "to excite the humbler against the higher classes of society".[38]

But among all the consequences of Brewster's social philosophy the most interesting from our present standpoint is probably the final breach with Thomas Chalmers to which it led him in the year of the Disruption. Despite his obvious sympathy with many of the principles espoused by the Free Church, Brewster ultimately decided not to join the secessionists; and it was a speech by their greatest leader which helped him to make up his mind. Chalmers' opening address as Moderator of the first General Assembly of the Free Church contained a forceful disavowal not only of the anti-Establishment views of contemporary Voluntaries but also of every attitude and action which might constitute a threat to the stability of the existing social order. "There can be no common understanding, for there is no common object, between you and the lovers of mischief", he told the fathers and brethren. "The lessons which you inculcate are all on the side of peace and social order." And he added: "If on the flag of your truly free and constitutional Church you are willing to inscribe that you are no Voluntaries then still more will there be an utter absence of sympathy on your part with the demagogue and agitator of the day – so that in golden characters may be seen and read of all men this other inscription, that you are no anarchists."[39] Rightly interpreting these moderatorial remarks as a denunciation of movements which had long enjoyed his own fervent support, Brewster realised the chasm which separated him from Chalmers and Chalmers' associates. "I ventured", he reported later, "to think it not impossible that I might yet be permitted to cast my lot with the many zealous men who had followed them out of the Establishment. But the door was quickly barred against me by their illustrious Moderator, whose opening speech – cheered to the echo – painfully convinced me that I should have still less freedom, in the FREE Church, than even within the pale of the Establishment; and that wherever my foot might find a resting-place, it could not be among those who, without one dissentient voice, had solemnly denounced the millions of their oppressed countrymen – to whose liberation I had devoted my humble labours, and who were peacefully and constitutionally seeking the redress of their intolerable wrongs – as *anarchists and rebels.*"[40] In a flash, and almost instinctively, Brewster had recognised how essentially conservative, if not reactionary, his great contemporary's social philosophy was; and with the recognition came abhorrence.

Most modern historians, and perhaps most modern churchmen also, tend to sympathise with the minister of Paisley rather than with his Evangelical colleague. In his support they point to various aspects of Chalmers' outlook which strike the twentieth-century mind as uncongenial or even repulsive; but attention is generally concentrated on what he said and did (particularly in the years when he was Brewster's near neighbour on Clydeside) about the immense, mind-boggling problem of poverty. At the time of Chalmers' arrival in Glasgow, an increasingly popular answer to the problem – an answer imported, so it seems, from south of the Border – was to levy a poor-rate on the city's property-owners and distribute the proceeds as "indoor" or "outdoor" relief to the needy. In the eyes of the minister of the Tron this was an altogether deplorable expedient. It betrayed a failure to recognise that the root cause of poverty was irreligion, and by tackling the former while ignoring the latter it offered a palliative rather than a cure. It also undermined the traditional self-respect and self-sufficiency of the Scottish people, and would in the long run lead to an increase rather than a diminution of distress. In opposition to such a baneful expedient, he advocated a return to what he liked to describe as "the principle of locality". We might prefer to call it "the Anstruther solution", for it amounted to a rehabilitation, within the great towns of industrialised Scotland, of the territorial parish as Chalmers had known it in the East Fife village of his boyhood: a manageably small community working and worshipping together, with a church and a school at its centre and a minister and kirk session to attend to both its temporal and its spiritual necessities. Here, he argued, was the basic – he would even have said, the redemptive – unit of Scottish society. Here was the means of national regeneration. Revive it, and reliance could then be placed upon the self-help of the poor, the assistance of relatives, the kindness of neighbours, and the discriminating charity of the rich – all under the supervision of minister and elders – to achieve what could never be looked for from a compulsory, centralised scheme with its multiplication of officials, its impersonality, and its tendency to demoralise the beneficiaries.

Such, then, was Chalmers' remedy for Scotland's ills, worked out during his ministry at the Tron from 1815 to 1819 and applied during the next four years in the newly-created, adjacent parish of St. John's. The "St. John's Experiment" was not only highly publicised: it was also imaginative, courageous, directed by quite phenomenal gifts of leadership, and supported with fervour by men of talent like David Stow and William Collins. For a time at least it seemed to be highly effective, and somewhat inflated claims were made on its behalf. But the voice of criticism was never altogether silent.

Carlyle, for example, argued that the success which Chalmers'
methods enjoyed was due to their author's quite exceptional
gifts rather than their own intrinsic excellence.[41] Professor W.
P. Alison of Edinburgh University suggested that he did not
understand, or take sufficient account of, the environmental
factors in early nineteenth-century poverty – factors which
called for Christian compassion rather than the somewhat
censorious moralism which he sometimes displayed.[42] And of
course the verdict of events (doubtless not unaffected by such
strictures) was equally unfavourable. In 1823, the leading actor
withdrew to a Moral Philosophy chair at St. Andrews. In 1837,
St. John's ceased to be an enclave within the poor law
administration of Glasgow. In 1843, the Disruption
extinguished all hope that official support would ever be given
to an implementation of Chalmers' ideas throughout the
country. In 1845, the Poor Law Amendment Act finally took
responsibility for the care of the poor out of the Church's
hands. Britain had begun its journey away from "the ideal of
parish communities and church-directed social services"[43]
towards the welfare state, and the great experiment was over.

Today, over one hundred and fifty years later, the
criticisms directed against the St. John's project and Chalmers
as a social thinker are many and various. His plans have been
called "speculative and over-confident".[44] His concentration
on the individual and the family, though praised as
foreshadowing the "family casework" approach of our own
time, is seen as blinding him to the wide interdependence –
impersonal but none the less real – of all citizens in a great
commercial and industrial centre like Glasgow. He is accused
(Dr. Lee of Edinburgh's Old Kirk began it in the eighteen-
thirties) of failing to reckon with the new facts of social and
geographical mobility; of encouraging, through the inquisitorial
methods which he recommended to his deacons, the
concealment rather than the relief of poverty; of discriminating
with undue rigour between the deserving and the undeserving

poor. He is written off because of his attachment to a view of economic relations which did not reckon with the emergent world of strikes, lock-outs, booms and slumps; he is denounced for his coolness towards Trade Unions, his paternalism, his amateurism, his bourgeois sentiments and sympathies. His dependence on *laissez-faire* theorists and the gloomy harshness of Malthusianism is noted and deplored: "it may be surmised", writes Stewart Mechie, "that others, neglecting his example and concentrating on his economic teachings, derived from them a positive discouragement to active effort for social betterment."[45]

Perhaps more serious than any of these things, a strange heartlessness seemed to underlie the treatment of poverty worked out by Chalmers and his supporters. Central in the St. John's experiment was the revival of the ancient office of the diaconate; and the instructions which he issued for the guidance of the new deacons (financial administrators) clearly indicate how he hoped to reduce a vast problem to manageable proportions. "When one applies for admittance through his deacon upon our funds" – so ran the memorandum – "the first thing to be inquired into is, if there be any kind of work that he can yet do so as to keep him altogether off" (off the poor roll, that is) "or as to make a partial allowance serve for his necessities; the second, what his relatives and friends are willing to do for him; the third, whether he is a hearer in any dissenting place of worship, and whether its session will contribute to his relief. And if after these previous inquiries it be found that further relief is necessary, then there must be a strict ascertainment of his term of residence in Glasgow, and whether he be yet on the funds of the Town Hospital, or is obtaining relief from any other parish. If upon all these points being ascertained the deacon of the proportion where he resides still conceives him an object for our assistance, he will inquire whether a small temporary aid will meet the occasion, and state this to the first ordinary meeting. But if instead of this he conceives him a fit subject for a regular allowance, he will receive the assistance of another deacon to confirm and complete his inquiries by the next ordinary meeting thereafter, at which time the applicant, if they still think him a fit object, is brought before us, and received upon the fund at such a rate of allowance as upon all the circumstances of the case the meeting of deacons shall judge proper."[46]

Defenders of the St. John's procedure might justifiably argue that no bureacracy can function without guide-lines of the sort indicated, and that while impostors had little chance of obtaining relief under such conditions the genuinely distressed were unlikely to become destitute. Nevertheless one suspects that here more than anywhere else is to be found the explanation for the long-term failure of Chalmers' social philosophy. As Laurance Saunders comments at the close of his invaluable discussion of "The Christian and Civic Economy": "In his understanding of industrial conflict and industrial failure alike Chalmers seemed to exhibit such a contrast between principle and application that many turned away from what seemed to them too much a 'business Christianity'.... Some sought out more satisfying forms of social faith or were caught up by utopian enthusiasms. Others, in hope or in bitterness, adopted a secularism that seemed a blasphemy to the orthodox.... It was only as a workingman achieved success and emerged from his class that Chalmers' rhetoric began to carry with it something of the conviction of experience."[47]

For our present purposes, however, the important point is that in his own day, if not in ours, and for many days to come, it was Thomas Chalmers' approach to the great condition-of-Scotland question, not Patrick Brewster's, that had the sympathy and support of the vast bulk of Scottish churchmen. Chalmers did not lack critics, of course, just as there were supporters for Brewster among the poor. But where policy-making in the Kirk is concerned Chalmers must stand as the representative figure of the early nineteenth century, while Brewster can only be described (in a recent scholar's arresting phrase) as "the unique exception".[48]

The foregoing survey of religious life and thought in Scotland during the period immediately before the nineteenth-century revolution might almost have been entitled "Puritanism: the last phase". The individualistic spirit which had infected social ethics could, admittedly, be accused of departing from the classical Puritan norm. But the prevailing view of the Bible owed a very great deal to the scholastic Calvinism of the seventeenth century; the Confession which ministers, elders and others subscribed on taking office was a Puritan document; and whatever the diversity in forms of worship each and every one bore the imprint of the West-minster Directory. If, moreover, we extended our examination of pre-revolutionary Scottish Christianity to include the life-style of its adherents as well as their theology, worship and social attitudes, we should find once again the same all-pervasive influence. A stress on discipline (both personal and communal), what might be called a kind of this-worldly asceticism, and a profound indebtedness to the Scriptures of the Old Testament: these too are markedly Puritan characteristics – and all of them, it is interesting to note, found their most distinctive expression in that scrupulous observance of the Sabbath for which the Scottish people would be honoured, and laughed at, only a little longer.

Reverence for the Lord's Day was, of course, far from being a new phenomenon; nor was it either distinctively Protestant or exclusively Presbyterian. Medieval church records abound in instances of it, and Grey Graham's valuable, if quirky, study of social life in the eighteenth century notes that "it was upheld as rigorously, and punished as vigorously, in the reign of Episcopacy".[49] Nevertheless the standard text for Scottish Sabbatarianism – Exodus 20: 8–11 apart – came from chapter XXI, paragraphs 7 and 8, of the Westminster Confession; and it was during the Covenanting period of the seventeenth century and the Evangelical ascendancy of the early nineteenth that it and its concomitant, family religion, flourished as never before or since. One lengthy sentence from the Confession supplies the theological rationale. "As it is of the law of nature", we read, "that, in general, a due proportion of time be set apart for the worship of God; so, in His word, by a positive, moral, and perpetual commandment, binding all men in all ages, He hath particularly appointed one day in seven for a sabbath, to be kept holy unto Him: which from the beginning of the world to the resurrection of Christ was the last day of the week; and from the resurrection of Christ was changed into the first day of the week, which in Scripture is called the Lord's Day, and is to be continued to the end of the world, as the Christian Sabbath." But the practical consequences are spelled out in the following phrases, which successive generations of Scots learned to regard as nothing less than a divinely authorised blueprint for their own behaviour: "This sabbath is then kept holy unto the Lord when men, after a due preparing of their hearts, and ordering of their common affairs beforehand, do not only observe an holy rest all the day from their own works, words and thoughts about their worldly employments and recreations; but also are taken up the whole time in public and private exercises of His worship, and in the duties of necessity and mercy."[50]

A reminder that the whole subject of Sabbath observance could arouse strong feelings in the nineteenth century as well as in the twentieth is provided by contemporary testimonies, which also help to recreate the vanished atmosphere of a time when the special character of Sunday played a key role in the weekly rhythm of Scottish life. For an almost horrifying evocation of an early-Victorian Sunday we can hardly do better than turn to the satirical pages of Robert Wallace's *Life and Last Leaves*. Wallace – successively minister of two

Edinburgh parishes, professor of Ecclesiastical History in the University, editor of *The Scotsman*, and member of Parliament – was a child in the eighteen-thirties; and his account is worthy to be set alongside similar pieces in Dickens and in Samuel Butler. "It would be impossible", he tells us, "for me to describe the feeling which was created in my mind by the weekly recurrence of our Sabbatic observances. All of a sudden everything that I had been doing last week had become wicked. Latin, Greek, Mathematics, were now wicked; so were marbles, 'tig', and races; so were walking, except to church, laughing, singing, except psalms, playing the flute, 'fiddle', or any instrument of music, reading newspapers (specially wicked), or anything except the Bible and 'good' books. There was scarcely anything that was safe to do from our rising in the morning until our going to bed at night, except reading the Bible, singing psalms, saying or joining in prayers, hearing sermons preached in church or at home. Breakfast, dinner and tea were permitted, because they were necessary to the execution of the sabbath programme; but even during these meals we were not to speak our own words or think our own thoughts. To me the day was a terror, it was so difficult to keep it perfectly; and I knew the doom of sabbath-breakers…. On Sundays we were usually engaged for fifteen hours in round numbers, directly or indirectly, connected with the special avocations of the day. Of these, fully seven were devoted to exercises of Biblical worship, including the reading of 'good' books, tracts, sermons, and other literature having a Biblical reference; three hours and a half to conversation on the sermons, services, and other religious topics; two hours and a half to preparations for worship, dressing and changing our dress, and walking to and from church; and two hours to meals. I am distributing the conversation, of course, over the journeying and the meals, and allowing each its strict quota."[51]

Even without Wallace's help – the help, surely, of a

caricaturist? – a formidable indictment can be brought against the early nineteenth-century Sabbath. Rooted in a static, mainly agrarian society, it was often a baneful anachronism in the mobile new world of industry and large towns. Its rigid application to modern Scotland of precepts devised for Palestinian Jews in pre-Christian times betokened an attitude which was not only unhistorical but also essentially disloyal to the spirit of the New Testament. It presumed, and indeed enforced by legislation and other more subtle pressures, the general acceptance of an ethos which was becoming increasingly distasteful to many people. It countenanced something like one law for the employing classes (whose conditions of work presented no obstacle to the taking of a regular weekly holiday, and who could find ample scope for recreation in the quiet of their own homes and gardens), and another law for their employees (whose duties, save under exceptionally conscientious Evangelical masters, were pretty much the same on Sundays as on weekdays, and who even if granted leisure time had nowhere suitable to spend it in the cities). Its puritanical banning of all games, not to mention riding or driving, was unreasonable, harsh and sometimes positively ridiculous. It may have borne with special heaviness on children. It fostered hypocrisies and deceptions of every kind. Yet there was another side to the matter. One reputable historian has remarked that "Children will put up with most things when they know that they are loved, and they do not seem generally to have regarded Sunday as 'a day of gloom'." Another reminds us that "For one day in the week, novels and magazines were laid aside and great classical literature like the Bible, *Pilgrim's Progress,* and 'Paradise Lost', besides more secular poetry and history, had a chance of perusal which they no longer enjoy." And a third goes so far as to contend that "the habit of setting apart one rest-day in the week for religion and serious thinking deepened the character of the nation."[52] It is, moreover, worth considering whether an institution like the Evangelical Sabbath could have persisted so long as it did had it not been at least partially successful in meeting the religious and other needs of its time, and had its undeniable defects and abuses not been offset by quite substantial compensating factors.

At any rate, for those impressed by Wallace's account two other contemporary descriptions of a Scottish Sabbath – the first somewhat stylised, the second frankly exceptional – may rectify the balance. In his *Sketches of Religion in the North Highlands,* Angus MacGillivray helps us to reconstruct the scene in Evangelical Strathnaver round about 1800. "They", he tells us, "are up early, for many of them are seven or eight miles from the church. After breakfast and family worship, they are ready to start. At last, the leading Christians leave their houses; all the rest assemble round them, and a portion of Scripture being named, religious conversation begins. The younger people are silent; but they listen with deep interest as one venerable man after another speaks from a full heart about the love of Christ to perishing sinners and the work of the Spirit in the soul. When halfway to church, they sit down to rest, and after singing a few verses to one of their pleasant airs, prayer is offered up for the outpouring of the Spirit, and for a blessing on the Word they are to hear and for Christ's presence with his servant who is about to speak in his name. At last the groups unite, and eight hundred people assemble in the house of God.... When the service is over, the several groups return each to their own hamlets, and after taking the necessary food they meet in the house of one of the leading men. He begins with prayer and praise; he then makes the people repeat all they remember of the sermon they have heard, throwing in practical remarks of his own.... After a portion of the Catechism has been repeated, and the service closed with prayer, the people retire to their own homes to worship God in the family."[53]

For that sense of the numinous with which exuberant

Evangelicalism could invest the Sabbath we turn to John Brown's magical description, from the days of his boyhood around 1820, of a visit by Thomas Chalmers to a remote Border kirk. Even before the service, it seems, the world of nature hinted at the supernatural character of the holy day. "'Calm was all nature as a resting wheel.' The crows, instead of making wing, were impudent and sat still; the cart-horses were standing, knowing the day, at the field-gates, gossiping and gazing, idle and happy; the moor was stretching away in the pale sunlight – vast, dim, melancholy, like a sea; everywhere were to be seen the gathering people, 'sprinklings of blithe company'; the countryside seemed moving to one centre." But it was with the sermon – that climactic moment in every Evangelical Sabbath – and its eloquent meditation on the subject, "Death reigns", that the worshippers were brought to confront dimensions of existence barely glimpsed in their ordinary, weekday lives. "We all had insensibly been drawn out of our seats, and were converging towards the wonderful speaker. And when he sat down, after warning each one of us to remember who it was, and what it was, that followed death on his pale horse ('And I looked, and behold a pale horse; and his name that sat on him was Death, and Hell followed with him' – Revelation 6:8), and how alone we could escape – we all sunk back into our seats. How beautiful to our eyes did the thunderer look – exhausted – but sweet and pure! How he poured out his soul before his God in giving thanks for sending the Abolisher of Death! Then, a short psalm, and all was ended. We went home quieter than we came; we did not recount the foals with their long legs, and roguish eyes, and their sedate mothers; we did not speculate upon whose dog *that* was, and whether *that* was a crow or a man in the dim moor, – we thought of other things. That voice, that face; those great, simple, living thoughts; those floods of resistless eloquence; that piercing, shattering voice, – 'that tremendous necessity'."[54]

"We thought of other things." There, in a phrase, is encapsulated the intention – and, at times, the achievement – of the old Sabbatarianism. One cannot help feeling that there is room today for some reappraisal of it, though the historian's verdict will in the last resort be influenced as much by his own religious convictions, or lack of them, as by anything else. The same may also be true of those other aspects of pre-revolutionary religion (theology, worship, and social attitudes) with which we have been concerning ourselves, and whose destruction or transformation now falls to be examined.

Notes to Chapter I

1. G. Kitson Clark, *The Making of Victorian England* (London, 1962), p. 276.
2. M. Dods, "Recent Progress in Theology" (Edinburgh, 1889), p. 6.
3. *Proceedings and Debates of the General Assembly of the Free Church of Scotland, 1887* (Edinburgh, 1887), p. 5.
4. A. R. Vidler, *The Church in an Age of Revolution: 1789 to the present day* (London, 1962), p. 270.
5. M. Dods, "Recent Progress", pp. 6–7 and 18.
6. D. Laing (ed.), *The Works of John Knox,* vol. IV (Wodrow Society, Edinburgh, 1855), p. 135.
7. D. Laing (ed.), *The Works of John Knox,* vol. I (Wodrow Society, Edinburgh, 1846), p. 273.
8. G. D. Henderson (ed.), *The Scots Confession 1560* (Edinburgh, 1960), p. 32.
9. Westminster Confession of Faith, ch. I, paras. 8 and 10, in *A Collection of Confessions of Faith* (Edinburgh, 1719), p. 7.
10. M. Dods, *Remarks on the Bible, in a Letter to the Corresponding Board, Edinburgh* (Edinburgh, 1828), p. 21.
11. M. Dods, *Remarks,* p. 30.
12. *Inauguration of the New College of the Free Church, Edinburgh, November, 1850, with Introductory Lectures on Theology, Philosophy, Natural Science* (London, 1851), p. 87.
13. ibid., p. 110.
14. ibid., p. 104.
15. ibid., p. 147.
16. ibid., pp. 65 and 68.
17. W. Cunningham, *Theological Lectures on Subjects connected with Natural Theology, Evidences of Christianity, The Canon and Inspiration of Scripture* (London, 1878), p. 409.
18. *Acts of the General Assembly of the Church of Scotland, 1638–1842* (Edinburgh, 1843), p. 158.
19. ibid., p. 456.
20. D. Stewart, *Account of the Life and Writings of William Robertson* (London, 1802), pp. 297–8.
21. J. H. S. Burleigh, *A Church History of Scotland* (London, 1960), pp. 307–8.
22. *Acts of the General Assembly,* pp. 534–6, 548–56.
23. A. L. Drummond and J. Bulloch, *The Church of Scotland, 1688–1843: The Age of the Moderates* (Edinburgh, 1973), p. 110.
24. *The Works of John Witherspoon* (Edinburgh, 1805), vol. VI, p. 162.
25. J. McKerrow, *History of the Secession Church* (Edinburgh, 1839), vol. II, pp. 316–7.

26. ibid., pp. 46–7.
27. ibid., p. 125.
28. R. Lee, *The Reform of the Church of Scotland in Worship, Government, and Doctrine. Part I. Worship* (Edinburgh, 1866), p. 44.
29. R. H. Story, *The Reformed Ritual in Scotland* (*The Lee Lecture for 1886*) (Edinburgh, 1886), p. 36.
30. G. C. McCrie, *The Public Worship of Presbyterian Scotland* (Edinburgh, 1892), p. 310.
31. G. W. Sprott (ed.), *The Book of Common Order of the Church of Scotland commonly known as Knox's Liturgy* (Edinburgh, 1868), p. lxiii.
32. T. Leishman, "The Ritual of the Church", in R. H. Story (ed.), *The Church of Scotland, Past and Present* (London, n.d.), vol. V, p. 404.
33. A. K. Robertson, "The Revival of Church Worship in the Church of Scotland from Dr. Robert Lee (1804–1867) to Dr. H. J. Wotherspoon (1850–1930)" (Edinburgh University Ph.D. thesis, 1956), p. 102.
34. W. H. Marwick, *Economic Developments in Victorian Scotland* (Clifton, 1973), p. 125.
35. D. C. Smith, "The Failure and Recovery of Social Criticism in the Scottish Church, 1830–1950" (Edinburgh University Ph.D. thesis, 1963), p. 218.
36. ibid., pp. 228 and 222.
37. ibid., p. 226.
38. ibid., p. 223 n. 2.
39. S. Mechie, *The Church and Scottish Social Development, 1780–1870* (London, 1960), p. 113.
40. Smith, "Failure and Recovery", p. 227.
41. W. Hanna, *Memoirs of the Life and Writings of Thomas Chalmers*, vol. IV (Edinburgh, 1852), p. 201.
42. Mechie, *Social Development*, esp. pp. 72–4.
43. S. J. Brown, "The Disruption and Urban Property", *Records of the Scottish Church History Society*, vol. XX pt. 1 (1978), p. 88.
44. L. J. Saunders, *Scottish Democracy 1815–1840. The Social and Intellectual Background* (Edinburgh, 1950), p. 217.
45. Mechie, *Social Development*, p. 57.
46. W. Hanna, *Memoirs of the Life and Writings of Thomas Chalmers*, vol. II (Edinburgh, 1850), p. 299.
47. Saunders, *Scottish Democracy*, p. 221.
48. Smith, "Failure and Recovery", title of ch. 6.
49. H. G. Graham, *The Social Life of Scotland in the Eighteenth Century* (London, 1937), p. 314.
50. Westminster Confession, ch. XXI, paras. 7 and 8, in *Collection of Confessions*, vol I, pp. 115–7.
51. J. C. Smith and W. Wallace (eds.), *Robert Wallace: Life and Last Leaves* (London, 1903), pp. 48–9 and 59.
52. C. Smyth, *The Church and the Nation: Six Studies in the Anglican Tradition* (London, 1962), p. 140. The other historians referred to by Smyth are G. M. Trevelyan and R. C. K. Ensor.
53. A. Macgillivray, "Sketches of Religion and Revivals of Religion in the North Highlands during Last Century" (Edinburgh, 1859), p. 28.
54. J. Brown, *Horae Subsecivae* (new 3-vol. edn., London, 1908), 2nd Series, pp. 143–6.

II

The Biblical Revolution

All the major Presbyterian denominations of Scotland helped to bring about the nineteenth-century revolution in attitudes to the Bible, but it was the Free Church which played the leading part. Why was this so? Historians have suggested various answers, but one of the most interesting is to be found in Richard A. Riesen's article, "'Higher Criticism' in the Free Church Fathers", which appeared in the *Records of the Scottish Church History Society* for 1979.

In the course of his paper, Riesen argues that responsibility for transforming "the strictest evangelical body in Christendom" into one which seemed "to go further than any other in setting forth revolutionary conceptions of the Bible" rested at least in part with the Free Church Fathers themselves – "not only because they provided the hard doctrine for their successors to react to, but because in their defence of the traditional theories they sometimes asked 'critical' questions and gave 'critical' answers or, what often has the same effect, gave inadequate answers or none at all, thus perhaps accelerating the very process they intended to arrest".[1] At the close of a difficult but rewarding survey of the writings of such orthodox apologists as Robert S. Candlish, William Cunningham and James Bannerman, Riesen concludes: "There were only a few tactical options open to the traditionalists. One was simply to repudiate the hostile forces, to argue that the battle was pre-eminently spiritual, that the truth could be seen only by the eye of faith and probably never completely in this life. The other was to engage them, to contest every issue on its own ground, answering blow for blow, and sometimes allowing one's position to be vulnerable or even modifiable in order to secure its defence. The traditionalists took both options. Their spirituality required that they take the first, their rationality required that they take the second. But insofar as they took the second they admitted that criticism was with them, if only as an evil to be checked. In other words they joined the battle. Perhaps neither their faith nor their theology would allow them to do otherwise. But the defence of the doctrine of inspiration itself proved to be a double-edged sword. Believing may have fostered believing criticism."[2]

Riesen's article suggests the thought that faith and criticism were perhaps less widely separated from each other in the early-Victorian period than either uncritical believers or critical unbelievers would have cared to admit. Be that as it may, there is no gainsaying the fact that the story of Scotland's Biblical revolution is inextricably bound up with the careers of two Free Church scholars, Andrew Bruce Davidson and William Robertson Smith.

Davidson, who was a crofter's son from the Buchan district of Aberdeenshire, went up to New College, Edinburgh, as a divinity student in October 1852. In 1858, he became tutor in Hebrew there, and five years later – when in his early thirties – he was appointed colleague and successor to his old teacher, "Rabbi" Duncan. At his induction to the chair, some "words of counsel and encouragement" were addressed to him by Dr. Garden Blaikie, then minister of Pilrig Free Church and later a professor in the same college. These may, as Davidson's biographer remarks, have been "somewhat rhetorical", but in the light of what the new professor actually did during the next forty years or so their appropriateness is startling enough. "It is solemn," Blaikie said, "it is almost overpowering, to think of all the influence, for good or for evil, that goes out from a theological classroom. The influence *you* exert may tell upon numberless persons in numberless ways."

Blaikie then went on: "Your great work is the opening up exegetically of the Old Testament scriptures. How are the statements of the Bible to be reconciled with modern science, that we may not be thrown into a fever of alarm each time that science comes out with some new and startling discovery? How are we to adjust the human and the divine elements in the inspired volume so as to separate that which is divine and immutable?... To aid in raising exegesis to its own place of supremacy, to bring out the true purport and meaning of obscurer portions of the Old Testament, to remove the temptation to spiritualise and allegorise, and otherwise twist and torture the sacred Word, will be a service to the cause of truth. There may be more of God's mind to be yet brought out of the Scripture than many think. It is not progress in theology, but revolution in theology, that we have reason to deprecate. To allow a reasonable latitude for progress and the modification of present views is the way to prevent revolution; sternly to refuse such a latitude is the way to hasten it."[3]

Young Davidson soon showed that this advice was very much in line with his own convictions; and so successful was he in acting upon them that he was described, some time after his death in 1902 and with little or no hyperbole, as "the finest scholar and teacher of his land and time".[4]

He was, without question, a supremely effective teacher, whose lectures (like those of a Gilbert Murray, a Herbert Grierson, or a Dover Wilson) could bring the literature of a distant age suddenly and electrifyingly to life and alter for ever his students' attitude to and treatment of it. "On the great lecture days", wrote one of them, "when the theme might be Saul or Elijah, Amos or Hosea or Jeremiah, the First or Second Isaiah, many of us came down from the top-storey classroom to the Common Hall moved with feelings of pity and awe, thrilled with aspirations of faith and hope, such as never held us even in witnessing the grandest dramas of heroic human passion in conflict with fate.... On those days I always found it good to have a walk round Arthur's Seat, and if a high wind was roaring in Samson's Ribs and the Salisbury Crags, so much the better. It harmonised with the tempest of the mind."[5] And another testified even more revealingly: "We scarcely realised that traditional notions were being questioned; rather we became conscious of a new perspective, outlined with caution and reverence, which in its main features appeared self-evident.... There were many details of the critical discussion to which Dr. Davidson never referred. But in an almost furtive manner he would suggest certain broad fundamental ideas, which fermented in our minds all the more pervasively because he refrained from promulgating them as dogmas. He assumed and emphasized what was vital in contemporary criticism, not endeavouring so much to demonstrate its value as rather to indicate its fitness for elucidating the entire scheme of the history or literature of Israel."[6]

Davidson was also, of course, a distinguished grammarian: author of a work on *Hebrew Accentuation*, a famous *Introductory Hebrew Grammar* (which for some of us remains not only an introduction but a conclusion), and a *Hebrew Syntax* which, we are told, "reveals, incidentally and without any ostentation, a knowledge of the comparative syntax of Syriac and Aramaic, Arabic, Ethiopic and Assyrian".[7] And he was an exegete and expositor of quite exceptional powers, whose early Commentary on Job was described by a later expert as "the first really scientific commentary on the Old Testament in the English language".[8]

But from our present viewpoint Davidson's chief significance is two-fold. In the first place, he studied the Bible with the tools of historical and literary criticism. John Duncan, his predecessor (and colleague in the years before 1870), was the last of the old school. A notable linguist – it was said of him and another New College professor of the period that they could have *talked* their way to the Great Wall of China – and a theologian of no mean quality, a mystic and something of a saint, he was a disaster as a teacher. "He taught no Hebrew", says Taylor Innes, "and little of the Old Testament as the Old Testament was historically delivered. And Davidson, called in at first to supply the former defect, had to face the problem raised by the latter. Vast as his reverence for Duncan was, Davidson neither could nor would take the same line. And he saw, apparently from the first, that another line was open. For him the historical delivery of the Old Testament was authoritative as truly as the contents; and the divine meaning was not to be ascertained without a critical knowledge of the original speakers and circumstances. Upon that basis, modest and humble though it was, great doctrinal superstructures might be raised. But the critical, which is the divine, basis of fact must first be laid. He put it that – 'Criticism is the effort of exegesis to be historical. The effort can never be more than partially successful. But... it gives us the right idea of Scripture, which is the reflection of the presence of the living God in human history.'"[9]

Davidson's developing critical position may be illustrated by brief extracts from his writings over a period of thirty years. In 1861, he made his first important contribution to theological literature: a review article in the *British and Foreign Evangelical Review*. Expressing his disappointment with a recent volume on the Pentateuch, he remarked of the author: "[He] has not seen or seized this fact, that revelation is a process.... He has missed the admirable opportunity he had of giving us what we never yet have had, at least the sketch of a historical theology of the Old Testament. No such historic theology is possible under his theory. For, by dissevering revelation from its immediate relation to man, its historic unity is broken up; it can, at most, be sporadic flashes of the Divine, of which we can neither see the immediate cause nor the general connection.... Revelation is a thing given by God to men, but given so as to work itself out through men, and it conforms rigidly to the usual laws of history and progress; there is nothing disjointed or isolated in it, and where we find passages clearly Messianic, apparently disconnected, we must explain them by the general modes of thought and life of the people into which they fitted, and out of which they sprung."[10] James Strahan comments, helpfully, on that review: "The scholar's own life-work is thus clearly outlined. Old Testament theology, he saw, must be made historical."[11]

Towards the end of the seventies, during the first phase of the Robertson Smith case, Davidson wrote another article for the *British and Foreign Evangelical Review* – this time on that storm-centre of theological debate, the book of Deuteronomy. After referring to the by then familiar arguments for the critical theory of its relatively late date, he continued: "Of course there are arguments on the other side; but there are many candid minds, especially those accustomed to historical criticism, which feel the considerations just mentioned to be irresistible arguments for assigning Deuteronomy to the historical period with which it exhibits such close connection."[12] This was the article which prompted Edinburgh Presbytery to call (without success, incidentally) for an inquiry into the theological teaching of the Colleges, and on which Robertson Smith's biographers remarked, justifiably enough: "It is clear, although he does not say it in so many words, that the scholarly reviewer disbelieves in the Mosaic authorship of Deuteronomy; and his conclusion is... that the facts in the history of redemption are left entirely untouched by the most advanced critical theories."[13]

Finally, in the *Critical Review* of 1891 Davidson wrote as follows: "A theology of the Old Testament... is really an impossibility, because the Old Testament is not a homogeneous whole. We see the religious truths or beliefs presented there coming into existence in connection with historical events extending over a thousand years. Instead of an Old Testament theology, the utmost that can be given is, a historical view of the religion of Israel; or, of the religion of Revelation during the Old Testament period. The truths can neither be exhibited nor understood apart from the history."[14]

Davidson must certainly be ranked among the critics – among the greatest of them, indeed. But he must also, and with equal assurance, be ranked among the believers. It seems to have been the unanimous verdict of the students that his teaching was so positive and constructive that they left New College "stabilised, strengthened, settled in their faith". As one of them put the matter: "One thing that struck me forcibly was the ludicrous nature of the idea that Davidson exerted 'an unsettling tendency', to use the famous phrase of the Robertson Smith case. He indeed gave us a new, and, as I believe, a true way of looking at Scripture, but he made me feel that it was a revelation of God in a way I had never grasped before. He was conservative of all that really mattered, and I am certain that, so far from unsettling, he confirmed the faith of many a young man."[15]

There is, then, no reason to disagree with the verdict passed upon Davidson by the most balanced and perceptive of his interpreters (even Robertson Smith not excepted), the Old Testament scholar who wrote his biography. "In the whole Critical Movement", says James Strahan, "he saw things in their true proportions. He never put Historical Criticism first. To him it was only the handmaid of religion. There had been myriads of true Christians before Criticism was heard of, and there will be myriads more when Criticism is no startling novelty, but the merest educational commonplace. And while he knew that he was rendering a great service to the Word of God by introducing more accurate and scientific methods of interpretation, he never forgot that the real and abiding value of the Bible lies in its message, or that its inspiration is first and best demonstrated by its immemorial saving power in the lives of men.... He lived through an age of brilliant criticism, and the career of the crofter's child who became the finest scholar and teacher of his land and time may be called brilliant. But the light of all his seeing was a light that never was on sea or land, save in the Life which is, as he believed, the light of all worlds."[16]

In 1866, only three years after Davidson had entered upon his duties as professor of Old Testament at New College, he told a friend – James Duguid – that "he had a little fellow in his class far ahead of any other student he ever had in any of his classes. He started questions of his own, and he investigated them for himself in a way no other young man could have done." (Duguid, incidentally, added that "That conviction remained with Davidson through life.")[17] The little fellow was, of course, William Robertson Smith, the only scholar in nineteenth-century Scotland whose brilliance outshone that of Davidson himself: a man with very strong claims to be regarded as his country's most influential modern churchman – claims only contestable, it may be supposed, by Thomas Chalmers or David Livingstone.

Smith's father was an Aberdeen schoolmaster who had entered the ministry in the wake of the Disruption, and young William was educated at home (the Free Church manse of Keig, in upper Donside) in an atmosphere of evangelical piety and intellectual rigour which arguably set the tone of his entire life. He went on to a brilliant career at the University of Aberdeen, early displaying the astonishing intellectual versatility which was to make him a serious contender for academic appointments in mathematics, natural philosophy, and logic, as well as in his own chosen field of Old Testament and Semitic languages. Rejecting all attempts to deflect him from his chosen vocation, the ministry of the Free Church of Scotland, he entered New College for the theological part of his training. Davidson captured him for research in Old Testament. Summer semesters on the Continent exposed him to the avant-garde teaching of scholars like Richard Rothe, Julius Wellhausen, and Albrecht Ritschl. It became clear that he was destined for academic life. Before his twenty-fourth birthday, the General Assembly appointed him to the chair of Hebrew and Old Testament in the Free Church College at Aberdeen.

Smith's highly significant inaugural lecture, entitled "What History teaches us to seek in the Bible", was in essence a plea for the historical rather than the dogmatic approach' to Scripture, and reflected the critical, evolutionary attitude which he had acquired from Davidson's lectures, German seminar rooms, and his own very wide reading. "We must", he told his hearers, "let the Bible speak for itself. Our notions of the origin, the purpose, the character of the Scripture books must be drawn, not from vain traditions, but from a historical study of the books themselves." He added the comment (which echoes and re-echoes in all his subsequent writings) that "This process can be dangerous to faith only when it is begun without faith – when we forget that the Bible history is no profane history but the story of God's saving self-manifestation."[18] Rather surprisingly, little or no stir was caused in religious circles by this forthright statement of what was still an unfamiliar position; and for the next five years the young professor was allowed to develop his ideas in peace. A change came in December 1875, however, when the *Encyclopaedia Britannica* brought out volume three of its new ninth edition. Contained therein was an article by Robertson Smith on the Bible which led to heresy proceedings against him in the church courts and eventually to his deposition from the Aberdeen chair.

An early draft of this notorious article came into the possession of one of Smith's biographers, and from it we gain some valuable glimpses of both the critical standpoint and the religious convictions of the author. Where criticism was concerned, he referred approvingly to "the well-known Protestant principle" that "the Bible is to be interpreted by the same methods as other books" (a phrase which is reminiscent of words used by Benjamin Jowett in 1860 in *Essays and Reviews*). As he saw it, this was a principle which implied that "the authors of Scripture wrote under the usual psychological conditions on which the laws of hermeneutics are calculated". He also contended that "the text of the Bible (especially of the New Testament) has experienced the same fortunes and must be corrected by the same kind of criticism as any other ancient text", and agreed with those eighteenth-century scholars who (as he put it) held that "the same principles which compel us to give up the traditional exegesis for a method which allows the Bible to declare its own meaning by the aid of a rational hermeneutic, demand also that traditional views as to the origin and composition of the Bible books be tested by the evidence which the books themselves offer to the judicious critic."[19]

As for Smith's religious position, this same draft article contained a frank avowal that his account of the origin, collection and transmission of the Biblical writings proceeded not from rationalistic presuppositions but from what he called "a recognition of the unique religious value of the Bible as the record of a unique and supernatural Revelation."[20] Years later, an exile in Cambridge, he told a friend that "he would give up everything without a moment's hesitation to get back to his work of teaching in the Free Church." And another friend relates that in the days before his tragically premature death his mind reverted several times to his unfinished Aberdeen lectures, and always with one dominant longing: to be able "to complete his argument". "His argument, remember," Strahan adds, "for a distinctive Hebrew and Christian revelation. If there be anything in Scaliger or Casaubon to equal that, I do not know of it."[21]

On the basis of the critical principles just indicated, Smith's published article assumed that the Scripture narratives which we now possess are not the originals but later, edited versions of accounts dating from various periods in Jewish history. In particular, it contended that the "Mosaic" legislation had first been promulgated, if not actually composed, during Israel's exile in Babylon (hundreds of years after Moses) and under the influence of the great eighth-century prophets; its attribution to Moses was not fraudulent, of course, but simply in accord with the recognised literary conventions of the age. The article also suggested that most of the psalms had not been written by David, eliminated much of the predictive element in the prophets, and denied authorship of the Gospels to the evangelists whose names they bear. In sum, it required no extraordinary insight to realise that Smith's picture of the Bible, and of the Old Testament in particular, deviated very considerably from that which had long held sway in Scotland.

It was, as his earliest accusers put it, "of a dangerous and unsettling tendency", and whether by direct contradiction or subtle disparagement could be said to represent a threat to "the doctrine of the immediate inspiration, infallible truth, and divine authority of the Holy Scriptures... as set forth in the Scriptures themselves and in the Confession of Faith."[22] Soon vehement attacks (met, needless to say, by equally vehement defences) were being launched against the heretic. The Robertson Smith case was under way.

For four tumultuous years between 1876 and 1880 the accusations – at first very detailed, later much simplified, and finally reduced more or less to a single charge – were debated and voted on in presbytery, synod, and General Assembly, as well as in the press, in learned journals, and in public meetings. Up and down the land, quickly or slowly, men came to a decision about the professor and his cause; and it was generally agreed that in intellectual endowment, if not in discretion, humility and (perhaps) spiritual insight, he stood supreme. "In Old Testament criticism", says Carnegie Simpson, "he was *facile princeps,* but his talents seemed unlimited. In pure theology, he taught his hearers the doctrine of inspiration from the great divines as few had taught it before. In law, he showed a knowledge and an acumen that overwhelmed professional authorities. In sheer dialectic he was irresistible, and many a time left his opponents lying pierced under the fifth rib."[23]

Thanks largely to Smith's pre-eminence (though he had distinguished allies), the Assembly of 1880 decided by a narrow majority of seven votes – 299 to 292 – to terminate proceedings and restore him to the teaching functions from which he had been temporarily suspended. The brethren expressed no opinion, one way or the other, on his critical views, the ultimate decision being left to "future inquiry in the spirit of patience, humility, and brotherly charity". Nevertheless college professors were admonished to remember that "they are set not for the propagating of their own opinions, but for the maintenance of the doctrine and truth committed to the Church", and Smith himself received a moderatorial reprimand for "the unguarded and incomplete statements of his articles, which have occasioned much anxiety in the Church and given offence to many brethren zealous for the honour of the Word of God."[24] A victory for tolerance, if not for liberalism, seemed to have been won. It was, however, more than a little misleading, having been made possible only by divisions within the conservative ranks; and in any case the gains made were soon squandered.

A mere ten days after the crucial debate, there appeared a new *Encyclopaedia Britannica* article by the restored professor. Entitled "Hebrew Language and Literature", it revealed an attitude unchanged in essentials and stated more firmly than ever. Although Smith defended himself with the plea that his article had been in the press long before the recent settlement of his case, many regarded its appearance as a wilful flouting of the Assembly's authority and proof that he was a trouble-maker who must be got rid of. And so the end came. By a decisive vote of 423 to 245 the 1881 Assembly concluded as follows: "That both the tone of the article in itself, and the fact that such an article was prepared and published in the circumstances and after all the previous proceedings in his case, evince on the part of Professor Smith a singular insensibility to his responsibilities as a theological professor and a singular and culpable lack of sympathy with the reasonable anxieties of the Church as to the bearing of critical speculations on the integrity and authority of Scripture: that all this has deepened the conviction already entertained by a large section of the Church that Professor Smith, whatever his gifts and attainments, which the Assembly have no disposition to undervalue, ought no longer to be entrusted with the training of students for the ministry: therefore, the General Assembly, having the responsible duty to discharge of overseeing the teaching in the Divinity Halls, while they are sensible of the importance of guarding the due liberty of professors, and encouraging learned and candid research, feel themselves constrained to declare that they no longer consider it safe or advantageous for the Church that Professor Smith should continue to teach in one of her Colleges."[25] The offender was consequently removed from his chair, though without loss of ministerial status; and the rest of his brief but fruitful career was spent in Edinburgh as co-editor of the *Encyclopaedia Britannica* and in Cambridge as university librarian and professor of Arabic.

Only a few comments on the famous verdict are necessary here. To begin with, it is worth noting that Smith's deposition was powerless to undo his work of educating Scotland in the new views. "He led men's minds back", one commentator tells us, "to the great Reformation doctrine of Scripture which bases its inspiration not on any external things such as its authorship or literary construction, but on the *testimonium Sancti Spiritus,* which criticism can never touch. Scotland began to learn that high and sure doctrine of the Bible, and its teacher was 'the young professor', fighting for his liberty as a teacher at the bar of the Church."[26] Again, the very harsh things said about him – "he is", said one Highland minister, "as empty of reverence and as smart as a weasel"[27] – should not be allowed to obscure the fact that, right on to his death in 1894, Smith professed to be a believer of the evangelical persuasion. At one particularly tense moment during the trial he remarked how, on hearing his interpretation of Deuteronomy made the basis of a serious attack upon his whole attitude to the Word of God, "he felt that he would like to ask the speakers if they had anything higher to say of Scripture than that which he said – that in every part of it God still spoke to us."[28] At another, he assured the Assembly that "he trembled at every word of God, which he took as the absolute rule of his faith and life."[29] And his unalterable position can be summarised in the following phrases, again his own: "If I am asked why I receive Scripture as the Word of God and as the only perfect rule of faith and life, I answer with all the Fathers of the Protestant Church, because the Bible is the only record of the redeeming love of God, because in the Bible alone I find God drawing near to men in Christ Jesus and declaring to us in Him His will for our salvation."[30] Perhaps Smith cannot be called a believer after the old pattern, but there is no doubt that he was a believer: if not a conservative evangelical, then a liberal one.

It is also significant that the Assembly of 1881 contrived to get rid of the heretic without specifying – far less condemning – his heresies. This remarkable omission, which (it has been claimed) secured "critical liberty within the evangelical and orthodox Free Church of Scotland",[31] was almost certainly the achievement of Robert Rainy, who had for some time been distinguishing between "the critical question" and what he called "the unhappy peculiarities of this case".[32] (There was, by the way, no love lost between the Edinburgh principal and the Aberdeen professor. Rainy, in an unusual fit of exasperation, once called Smith "an impossibility";[33] while Smith, some years later, warned a young Cambridge student en route for theology at New College, "don't trust Rainy: he's a Jesuit".[34]) In the words of Rainy's biographer, "There are times when affairs become so critical and complicated that, as a modern statesman puts it who is also a philosopher, the choice is 'between two blunders'. The loss to one of the Church's Colleges of the prince of believing critics was a blunder; but a far greater blunder – an irretrievable disaster with effects injurious not only to but also beyond the Free Church of Scotland – would have been the loss of the man *and* of the principle of toleration of criticism in an evangelical communion.... Principal Rainy,... deliberately and distinctly separated the two interests, and, standing alone, exposed to suspicion and even censure and calumny, won from the conservative majority the preservation of the permanent and vital principle at the cost, the unavoidable cost, of the individual's position as a professor."[35]

Which brings us to the most important point of all. Robertson Smith's deposition did not prevent – may, indeed, have hastened – the ultimate triumph of his approach in the Free Church and its sister Churches of the Presbyterian order in Scotland. On the very morrow of their apparent defeat, the leaders of the pro-Smith party held a largely-attended meeting at which they affirmed their dissent from what had been done and issued a well-signed protest concluding thus: "We... declare that the decision of the Assembly leaves all Free Church ministers and office-bearers free to pursue the critical questions raised by professor Smith, and we pledge ourselves to do our best to protect any man who pursues these studies deliberately."[36] Such action might well have been regarded by the conservatives as a throwing down of the gauntlet, but they made no reply; and the scholars who sympathised with Smith's principles and methods – T. M. Lindsay, J. S. Candlish, and quite a number of others – were allowed to continue unimpeded with their teaching and writing. With every year that passed, indeed, the balance of theological opinion seemed to tip a little further to the liberal side (the enthusiasm of the student's gallery for Smith during the trial in the Assembly Hall had foreshadowed this); and long before the end of the century it was clear that while the conservatives had scored a notable victory in one particular bout their adversaries were on the way to winning a whole succession of return matches.

The most striking of these came in 1890, with the trials for heresy of Professor Marcus Dods of New College and Professor A. B. Bruce of the Glasgow College. Dods (from whose inaugural we quoted in our first chapter) had fallen under suspicion some time earlier for a published sermon on "Revelation and Inspiration". The Assembly, however, had had enough on its hands in 1877–78 with the Robertson Smith case, and the matter was allowed to drop after Dods withdrew the offending pamphlet. But by 1890 he had further alarmed the conservatives by various pronouncements, both oral and written. He had spoken as if the historicity of the Resurrection were a matter of indifference, declared the substitutionary doctrine of the Atonement not to be the only theory which makes Christians, imputed what he called "mistakes and immoralities" to the Old Testament, and so on. Above all, he had caused offence by asserting, in his inaugural lecture at New College, that the doctrine of verbal inspiration (which some believed to be taught in the Confession of Faith) was "a theory of inspiration which has made the Bible an offence to many honest men; which is dishonouring to God, and which has turned inquirers into sceptics by the thousand – a theory which should be branded as heretical in every Christian Church."[37] Nevertheless it was now 1890, not 1875, and in the end the Free Church Assembly decided that there was no ground for a libel (i.e., Dods had not taught anything which belied his ordination vow to uphold the Confession), though it indicated disapproval of some of his statements. Perhaps most interestingly of all, Principal Rainy delivered a speech in which he clearly dissociated himself from the arch-conservatives. To admit inaccuracy in the Bible, he suggested, should not disqualify a man for admission to the ministry of the Free Church, providing he also took it to be everywhere the Word of God. God does not always give us "mathematical lines", and "he rather thought that the primary object of the Bible was to prove itself a sufficient guide to honest inquirers, and not... to enable them with ease to exercise discipline upon dishonest ones."[38]

Professor A. B. Bruce had on the whole an easier passage in this same Assembly. His offence had been committed in a book, published in 1889, whose title was: *The Kingdom of God: Christ's Teaching according to the Synoptic Gospels*. Some of the counts against him need not concern us here – e.g., his strong criticisms of the institutional Church and his rejection of the Calvinist doctrine of election for another which is probably the prevailing one today (election for service, not to privilege) – but others showed him to be in the same camp as Robertson Smith and Marcus Dods. He was *said* to have imputed untrustworthiness to the Gospel writers (the misplacing of incidents, invention of narratives, etc.), and in his own defence he admitted believing that they were not objectively reliable. He was accused of presenting Christ not so much as a divine figure but as a poet, a mystic, even a schemer. In the debate, Bruce defended himself with skill. He pointed out that his book had been written with an apologetic intent: it therefore had to deal with difficulties – though he regretted his infelicities of expression. He reminded the Assembly that the field studied in his book was relatively new, and pleaded for indulgence on that account. Above all, he averred that, though his view of inspiration might differ from the conservatives', he like them was absolutely convinced of the exceptional, divine character of Holy Scripture. Once again, the Free Church's College Committee, while regretting various remarks made by the accused, saw no real case for a heresy charge – and the Assembly agreed with them. And once again Principal Rainy made an important and influential speech, declaring that Bruce must write according to his own principles, not other people's, and that he should be tolerated.[39]

The last of the great heresy cases occurred a dozen years later in 1902, when the professor of Old Testament in the United Free Church's Glasgow College, George Adam Smith, came under attack in the General Assembly. The ground of offence on this occasion was a volume of lectures (originally delivered in the U.S.A.) entitled *Modern Criticism and the Preaching of the Old Testament*. Various alarming views were advanced therein, but from our point of view the most important were the following: that the religion of the Jews down to the eighth century was polytheistic in character, that the early chapters of Genesis were not historical, and owed their origin to Babylonian legend and myth, and that the lives of the patriarchs, as found in Scripture, had their "fanciful" elements.

The College Committee of the Church, to which the charges had been referred, refused, in a carefully balanced report, to indict Professor Smith for heresy. They pointed out that the impugned volume was in intention an apologetic work, defending on critical grounds "the Christian faith in the Old Testament as containing the Word of God". They agreed with the accused that Israel's religion *was* polytheistic before the age of the great prophets. They largely endorsed his interpretation of Hebrew literature and Hebrew history. Most interestingly of all – when one remembers Robertson Smith – they supported his view that the Mosaic legislation of the Pentateuch only assumed its existing form during the Exile in Babylon. And they argued – despite its implications for the literal truth of Deuteronomy – that such a belief was not inconsistent with the divine inspiration and authority of the Bible.

In the end, the Assembly took the College Committee's tolerant view, and carried Rainy's motion that a libel was unnecessary. Professor Smith's views were neither accepted nor rejected, and the critical scholars were warned to be careful in their criticism; but what no doubt remained in most men's minds was Smith's own declaration that "a critical treatment of the facts presented by the Hebrew Scriptures, so far from compelling a thoughtful Christian to give up his faith, furnishes for the main doctrines of our religion what... are stronger grounds than those furnished by the former apologetic of the Church."[40]

In the wake of the scholarly leaders, ordinary ministers gradually appropriated the new theology – appropriated and then proclaimed it. A recent study by W. G. Enright of theology and preaching in nineteenth-century Scotland sees the period between 1853 and 1880 as marked by a transition from the "old" to the "new" evangelical sermon – its characteristics being anti-dogmatism, practicality, and an overriding concern to proclaim the love of God and to induce belief in Jesus Christ. The Robertson Smith case, Enright contends, delivered the *coup-de-grâce* to the old Evangelicalism, and so marked the end of this transition period. There followed the age of the *liberal*-Evangelical sermon preached by men as diverse as John Tulloch, John Caird and Robert Story in the Auld Kirk, and Marcus Dods, Henry Drummond, Walter C. Smith, and Alexander Whyte in the Free. They talked more of love and trust than of intellectual assent, more of religion than theology. They appropriated the Bible in a new way as a book at once human and divine, whose historical setting was of importance. They brought into the centre of the picture a personal experience of the Fatherhood of God and a personal *and* communal realisation of His Kingdom.[41]

E

One of the most impressive aspects of the critical scholarship of the Free Church between 1880 and 1900, and of the United Free Church thereafter was its belief, frequently and fervently asserted, that literary and historical criticism are *not* incompatible with loyalty to the Bible as the inspired Word of God and with a sincere adherence to the historic faith of the Church. We find this, of course, in Robertson Smith, whose very last lecture (at Marischal College in Aberdeen) contained his testimony as a Christian believer. "After contrasting the religion of Israel with all other Semitic religions, he quietly concluded: 'The burden of explaining this contrast does not lie with me. It lies with those who are compelled by false Philosophy of Revelation to see in the Old Testament nothing more than the highest point of the general religious tendency of Semitic religion. That is not the view which that study commends to me.'"[42]

J. S. Candlish, son of the Disruption leader, professor of Systematic Theology in the Free Church College in Glasgow, and one of Scotland's finest theologians, was of the same mind. Writing at the height of the Robertson Smith case, he observed that "We are not in a position to know beforehand in what form God will make Himself known and reveal His Word to us .... To assume that because it is a Divine Book the Bible, or any particular part of it, must be written in any particular way, is to adopt the principle of the most thoroughgoing and dangerous Rationalism. Our only safe method is to learn from the study of *itself* what the Bible actually is, and to judge from the nature of each part and its relation to others what is literal and what is figurative, what is historical and what poetical."[43]

A. B. Bruce agreed. Defending himself before the Assembly, he declared: "Whether we compare the accounts of the origins of things in Genesis with those found elsewhere, or the psalms with the Vedic or Accadian hymns, or the prophets with the highest utterances of poets and sages, or the Gospels with the so-called *Teaching of the Twelve Apostles,* or the Epistles with the ethical doctrine of pagan moralists, the impression ever is – This is a book by itself, the marvellous literature of a very real revelation which God has made to mankind through the Hebrew race. Whatever differences there may be among us as to the exact theological definition of inspiration, or the inferences to be drawn therefrom, or the wisdom and validity of *a priori* inferences on such a subject, a point on which past experience in the history of theology is full of warning, however we may differ on these matters, we are at one on the main question."[44]

And Marcus Dods, also defending himself before the Assembly, reiterated the same message: "As regards the inspiration of Scripture, I hold with the Confession that all the writings of the Old and New Testaments are 'given by inspiration of God to be the rule of faith and life'; but I do not hold that inspiration guarantees Scripture from inaccuracy in all its particular statements; neither do I find that the Confession either expresses or implies any such idea of inspiration. The affirmation of inaccuracy in certain details has assuredly a bearing on one's theory of inspiration; but it does not, on my part, involve the slightest hesitation as to the Divine authority of Scripture, the pervading influence which makes it God's Word, and its fitness, when interpreted, as the Confession itself directs, by a due comparison of its various parts, to be the conclusive rule of faith and life."[45]

Long before 1914, the view taken by Smith, Candlish, Bruce and Dods had triumphed in all the major Presbyterian Churches of Scotland, and the Biblical revolution had run its course.

Notes to Chapter II

1. R. A. Riesen, "'Higher Criticism' in the Free Church Fathers", *Records of the Scottish Church History Society,* vol. XX, pt. 2 (1979), p. 120.
2. ibid., p. 142.
3. J. Strahan, *Andrew Bruce Davidson* (London, 1917), pp. 94–6.
4. ibid., pp. 325–6.
5. ibid., pp. 132–3.
6. ibid., pp. 134–5.
7. ibid., p. 126.
8. ibid., p. 89.
9. J. A. Paterson (ed.), *The Called of God, by the late A. B. Davidson, with Biographical Introduction by A. Taylor Innes* (Edinburgh, 1905), pp. 33–4.
10. A. B. Davidson, review article in *British and Foreign Evangelical Review,* vol. X (1861), pp. 729–30.
11. Strahan, *Davidson,* pp. 197–8.
12. A. B. Davidson, review article in *British and Foreign Evangelical Review,* vol. XXVIII (1879), p. 352.
13. J. S. Black and G. W. Chrystal, *The Life of William Robertson Smith* (London, 1912), p. 339.
14. *The Critical Review,* vol. I (1891), p. 29.
15. Strahan, *Davidson,* pp. 237–8.
16. ibid., pp. 249 and 325–6.
17. ibid., pp. 239–40.
18. Black and Chrystal, *Robertson Smith,* pp. 128–9.
19. ibid., pp. 179–80.
20. ibid., p. 180.
21. Strahan, *Davidson,* p. 252.
22. "The Draft Form of Libel", in Black and Chrystal, *Robertson Smith,* p. 582ff.
23. P. C. Simpson, *The Life of Principal Rainy* (London, 1909), vol. I, p. 334.
24. Phrases quoted are from Dr. Beith's victorious motion, quoted in Black and Chrystal, *Robertson Smith,* pp. 353–4, which also contains a valuable summary of the debate, pp. 349–60. Cf. *Proceedings and Debates of the General Assembly of the Free Church of Scotland, 1880* (Edinburgh, 1880), p. 242.

25. Simpson, *Rainy*, vol. I, p. 388.
26. ibid., pp. 334–5.
27. Black and Chrystal, *Robertson Smith*, p. 401.
28. Simpson, *Rainy*, vol. I, p. 337.
29. ibid.
30. Quoted from "Answer to the Form of Libel" in H. F. Henderson, *The Religious Controversies of Scotland* (Edinburgh, 1905), p. 217.
31. Simpson, *Rainy*, vol. I, p. 398.
32. ibid., pp. 371–2.
33. ibid., p. 400.
34. ibid., p. 396.
35. ibid., pp. 399–400.
36. Black and Chrystal, *Robertson Smith*, p. 450.
37. M. Dods, "Recent Progress in Theology" (Edinburgh, 1889), p. 30.
38. *Proceedings and Debates of the General Assembly of the Free Church of Scotland, 1890* (Edinburgh, 1890), pp. 111–15, esp. p. 115.
39. Useful summary of the issues and the debate in Henderson, *Controversies*, pp. 254–70. Cf. *F. C. Debates, 1890*, pp. 169–73, esp. p. 173.
40. *Proceedings and Debates of the General Assembly of the United Free Church, 1902* (Edinburgh, 1902), pp. 87–118, and College Committee's Special Report, XIA, p. 9. A useful recent study of the relationship between faith and criticism in late-Victorian Scotland is R. A. Riesen, "Faith and Criticism in post-Disruption Scotland, with particular reference to A. B. Davidson, William Robertson Smith, and George Adam Smith" (Edinburgh University Ph.D. thesis, 1981).
41. W. G. Enright, "Preaching and Theology in the nineteenth century: a study of the context and content of the evangelical sermon" (Edinburgh University Ph.D. thesis, 1968).
42. Strahan, *Davidson*, p.251.
43. J. S. Candlish, "The Authority of Scripture independent of Criticism" (Edinburgh, 1877), pp. 17–18.
44. *F. C. Debates, 1890*, p. 174.
45. *F. C. Debates, 1890*, Appendix to College Committee's Special Report, VA, p. 15.

III

The Confessional Revolution

At the outset of the nineteenth century, as we have seen, only the most prescient could have foretold the coming transformation of Scotland's relationship to her inherited confessional standards. By the eighteen-thirties and forties, however, it was altogether otherwise. During those decades of rapid and far-reaching change – social, political and intellectual – attention came to be focused not on the circumference but on the centre of Presbyterianism's traditional faith, and some of the basic doctrines and attitudes of Westminster Calvinism came under serious and sustained attack. Those were the years when Thomas Erskine of Linlathen, from the fringes of Presbyterianism, became known for his constant appeals from the letter to the spirit, from Law to Gospel, from dogmatic formulations to the Lord who transcended them all. They were also the years when Thomas Carlyle, outside the religious camp but still in communication with it, perfected his art of persisting with much of the old phraseology while at the same time conveying the impression that virtually nothing in earth or heaven was exactly as it had been. The fountains of the great deep seemed indeed to be opening up; and the heresy trials of the period only disclosed the magnitude of the revolution that was under way.

To the wisdom of hindsight, Edward Irving – romantic, millennialist, forerunner of modern Pentecostalism – was almost bound to clash with the ecclesiastical authorities of his day. Indeed, it has been plausibly suggested that what united Evangelicals and Moderates against him was not so much his theological idiosyncrasies as his association with the undisciplined enthusiasts of the Gareloch and Regent Square: in other words, the threat which he constituted, at a time of manifold alarms, to the supporters of law and order in the Kirk. However that may be, the overt reason for his prosecution was theological. Irving's stress upon the true, full and real humanity of the Man of Sorrows (he spoke of Christ's assumption of *fallen* human nature at the Incarnation) led him into what many of today's theologians would probably characterise as the incautious statement of a truth rather than a great heresy. But his Christology was clearly at odds with the contemporary understanding of Westminster doctrine, and it was for grave theological error that he was condemned and deposed. For our present purpose, perhaps the chief significance of this star-crossed and erratic genius is to be found in his relative detachment from all dogmatic statements and his declared preference for the Scots as opposed to the Westminster Confession. As he put it, "the Scottish Confession was the banner of the Church, in all her wrestlings and conflicts, the Westminster Confession but as the camp-colours which she hath used during her days of peace; the one for battle, the other for fair appearance and good order."[1] Being the man he was, Irving naturally preferred the document of battle to the document of order – and quite a number of Victorian rebels against Westminster could be grateful for the precedent he set.

An even more considerable figure, John McLeod Campbell, was condemned in 1831 for repudiating (among other things) contemporary Calvinism's imposition of strict limits upon the Gospel offer, and for arguing that Christ had died, not for the elect only, but for all men. In the long run, most Scottish churchmen seem to have come to share his views; and he is now generally regarded as his country's greatest modern theologian and the forerunner of a milder, more loving, more truly evangelical understanding of the faith.

At the time, however, few spoke for him: to diverge from Westminster was to make shipwreck of true religion. Interestingly enough, Campbell had at the outset maintained the compatibility of his new emphases with the teaching of the Standards; but by the close of the trial he perceived otherwise. "After that dreary night in the Assembly," wrote his friend and fellow-sufferer A. J. Scott, "the dawn breaking on us as we returned at length, alike condemned, to our lodgings in the New Town of Edinburgh, I turned round and looked on my companion's face under the pale light, and asked him, Could you sign the Confession now? His answer was, No. The Assembly was right: our doctrine and the Confession are incompatible."[2] For at least a quarter of a century thereafter, no really serious threat was offered to the dominance which Westminster had established over Scottish religious thought.

Three comments may perhaps help towards a verdict upon the case and its implications. According to J. H. Leckie, a perceptive late-Victorian commentator, "The defence of Campbell when on trial was not a strong one. It is worthy of study chiefly as showing the point from which a great man started on his theological pilgrimage, and also as embodying the first determined revolt against the Confessional theology."[3] The arch-rebel, Robert Lee of Greyfriars, remarked that "The courts of the Church" which dealt with Irving and Campbell "have been thought by many ... to have repudiated utterly their Protestant character. They refused to permit the questions at issue to be argued and judged on the ground of Scripture, and insisted that they should be determined simply according to the Confession of Faith. But that Confession itself condemned and renounced the claim of any such authority .... The Church of Scotland followed the example [of Rome, with its emphasis on tradition] which its founders repudiated."[4] But McLeod Campbell himself deserves the last word: "When the Church says to both ministers and people, 'This is my Confession of Faith: if anything in it appear to you inconsistent with the Word of God, I am prepared to go with you to the Word of God to settle the matter', then does the Church speak according to her place. But if instead of this she says, 'This I have fixed to be the meaning of the Word of God and you cannot take any other meaning without being excluded from my communion; and to entitle me so to exclude you I do not need to prove to you that what you hold and teach is contrary to the Scriptures, it is quite enough that it is contrary to my Confession of Faith'; I say, if the Church of Christ use this language she no longer remembers her place as a Church."[5]

Campbell's deposition meant a temporary end to all attempts within the Church of Scotland to construct a broader interpretation of the Atonement, its significance for all men and the way in which its benefits were appropriated by believers. But the insights first given an airing at the trial, and later published to the world in *The Nature of the Atonement* (1856), eventually came to be shared by many of his fellow-countrymen; and in the long run they almost certainly played a vital part in subverting the dominance established over Scottish religious thought by the Westminster Divines.

Scarcely had the tumult over McLeod Campbell died down when controversy of a not dissimilar kind broke out inside the United Secession Church. In 1841 James Morison was expelled by the Synod for a formidable list of erroneous opinions. (He became the founder of the Evangelical Union, which stood for an Arminian theology and a warmly Evangelical piety.) Among the doctrines of scholastic Calvinism with which he found himself in disagreement – if not before his expulsion then soon after – was the teaching that Christ died for the elect only. "If it were not true that Christ died for the heathen", he observed in his tract *The Extent of the Propitiation,* "pray, what gospel is the missionary to preach when he lands on a foreign shore? Is he to tell them that God loved a few men scattered somewhere or other throughout the

world, and that therefore, for aught that he could know, there
may happen to be some of these favoured ones among them,
and for these Christ died?... Men need not go to heathen
lands with the doctrine of a limited atonement in their creed;
or, if they go with it, they must hide it, and preach in a
manner practically contradictory to it."[6] As Drs. Drummond
and Bulloch, who quote this passage, comment later on the
whole Morisonian affair: "There had been a revolt against
Calvinism in what had been its strongest citadel."[7] The echoes
of that revolt were to reverberate through many Presbyterian
strongholds before the century reached its close.

In the immediate aftermath of Morison's trial, two of his
theological teachers within the United Secession Church,
Professor Robert Balmer and Professor John Brown, fell under
suspicion of holding similar views. Although Balmer played
quite an important part at one stage of the debates, he died
before the final judgment was given; and his views were not
sufficiently different from those of his colleague to require
separate treatment here. Brown, however, was a rather more
formidable figure. Revered in the denomination as a pious,
learned and perceptive divine, he was also (in his own quiet
way) something of a fighter, who refused to knuckle under in
face of his accuser's attacks. In the end, his learning and
determination carried the struggle through to a notable victory.
On the central question of the *extent* of the Atonement, Brown
argued that there had always been a kind of duality of
emphasis within the Reformed camp, so that support could be
found there both for the view that Christ died only for the
elect (the "orthodox" position among the Seceders around
1841) and for the view that – at least in some sense – He died
for all. This was true of his own communion: "It is evident
that, during the whole course of its history, the Secession
Church has been anxious to maintain with equal firmness the
doctrine of personal election and personal salvation, and the
doctrine of the unlimited calls and invitations of the gospel;

and that their great object has been to state the doctrine with
respect to the reference of the death of Christ in a manner
which, while agreeable to the word of God, seems best to
harmonise with both these doctrines."[8] And it was true to the
Westminster Divines also. As Brown's biographer tells us,
"After referring to controversies on this subject about the time
of the Westminster Assembly ... [he] quotes the several
passages from the symbols framed by that Assembly, and
contends that they admit the larger interpretation, as well from
their own language as from the unlikelihood that their framers
could have meant to exclude from the ministry 'many of the
best Christians and theologians who adorned that and the
preceding age'."[9]

In the end, Brown's interpretation triumphed, the Synod
resolving "that there exists no ground even for suspicion that
he holds or has ever held any opinion on the points under
review inconsistent with the Word of God, or the subordinate
standards of this Church."[10] Despite this resolution, however,
one cannot help wondering whether the professor and those
who supported him did not somehow tip the theological
balance in a new direction. Brown vehemently contended that
"The doctrine of the general aspect of the death of Christ must
not be given up. That is an essential principle of Christian
truth. The clear exhibition of that truth has been one of the
characteristic glories of the Secession in the whole course of its
history."[11] And John Cairns, his distinguished successor,
agreed, claiming that the decisions of 1845 had "done nothing
to derange its [i.e., Scottish theology's] equilibrium or remove
its landmarks."[12] Yet there seems to be no denying that from
then onwards it was the love of God to all men which
occupied the central place in the teaching and preaching of the
United Secession and (after 1847) the United Presbyterian
Church, and that the old emphasis upon election slipped
further and further into the background.

From our present viewpoint, perhaps the chief thing to

note is what Cairns stressed in his account. "The general results of the controversy", he wrote, "were in a high degree salutary. The gospel was not preached more freely in the pulpits of the Church, for that was not possible. But relief was brought to many minds hampered and disturbed by the apparent inconsistency between a universal offer of salvation and a limited atonement on which to rest it; and an example was afforded of Christian large-heartedness and charity, in giving to the terms of ministerial communion, and to the interpretation of symbolical books, the widest comprehension consistent with truth and sincerity .... Upon the whole it may be affirmed that the controversy, though confined, with the exception of the Scottish Congregationalists, to the United Secession Church, has, by its remote, as well as direct impression, exerted a valuable influence in liberalising the tone of Scottish theology."[13]

It is, nevertheless, important not to exaggerate the changes which had by mid-century taken place in Scotland's relationship either to Westminster Calvinism in general or to the Confession in particular. A few able, far-sighted men like Campbell and Morison had moved to new positions; others like Balmer and Brown had brought certain doctrines into unwonted prominence and relegated others to relative obscurity. But large numbers of people had not been affected, nor had any unambiguously revolutionary pronouncement been made by any Presbyterian Communion – and of course the formation of the Free Church in 1843 brought valuable reinforcement to the conservative ranks. "Our Standards", declared one of its ministers, "are but an echo in human language of the infallible Word."[14] Principal William Cunningham of New College replied to Isaac Taylor's attack on "superannuated logical or deductive theology" by confidently asserting that the work of the sixteenth and seventeenth-century reformers (the men of Westminster undoubtedly included) "in its whole substance and leading features is far too firmly rooted in the Word of God, and has been far too conclusively established, to be ever again seriously endangered."[15] And as late as 1865 Cunningham's successor, Principal Robert Candlish, wrote of the Westminster Assembly that "its doctrinal decisions, on all the questions fairly before it, will stand the test of time, and ultimately command the assent of universal Christendom", and then went on to refer to the Standards as "the only safe anchorage in any and in every storm."[16] All that can be recorded, therefore, are a few premonitory rumblings heralding the earthquake to come – no more; and even those persons who occasionally felt moved to express their disquiet at certain aspects of the reigning theology, or at its imposition upon the Church's ministers and office-bearers, did so in the most hesitant and deferential manner.

In 1850, admittedly, Professor James Buchanan of New College, Edinburgh, conceded that people were becoming increasingly uneasy with all dogmatic or confessional statements. "Some of the questions that are discussed, and many of the technical terms that are necessarily employed in a complete course of divinity," he told a very large and representative gathering of Free Churchmen, "have been described as mere scholastic subtleties – the remnants of a darker age, when the human mind was cramped and fettered by bandages of its own fabrication; and it has been thought that the free theology of modern times may dispense with these artificial aids, and may even grow up to a more robust strength, if left unencumbered by the forms of systematic exposition. The study of Christianity, they say, is one thing as Christianity appears in the living Word of God; it is altogether another thing as Christianity appears in the dead systems of men. Had God intended, it is sometimes added, that his truth should assume the form of a system, the Holy Spirit, who inspired the Scriptures, would have exhibited it in the order of a regular exposition; but he has taken a different method of instructing the minds of men. He has provided for their use a book .... This striking difference between the form in which Christianity is presented in the Scriptures, and that which it has assumed in modern times, has often been insisted on as a legitimate prejudice against the study of systematic theology; and that prejudice has been generally exhibited in the shape of objections against creeds and confessions of faith, while it has occasionally appeared also in the form of opposition to all systematised theology, whether as expounded in the formularies of the church or in the writings of systematic divines."[17] But of course Buchanan had little sympathy for the unease of which he spoke; and it should be remembered that he and traditionalists like him enjoyed a virtual monopoly of all the positions of power and influence in the Scottish Churches. Almost the sole exception one can think of is John Tulloch, who went to teach theology at St. Mary's College, St. Andrews, in 1854 – and quite a few years were to elapse before even he carried much weight in the ecclesiastical world.

Even in the sixties and seventies, the weight of numbers in every Presbyterian communion was still very much on the side of theological conservatism. The Moderator of the Auld Kirk's General Assembly, for example, reminded the fathers and brethren in 1866 that "Our Confession, submitted to the Estates of Parliament, was accepted as the truth of God; and the Church was endowed and established not free at any time to modify, alter, or depart from it, nor to hold the truth of any of its doctrines an open question" – though it is worth noting that this statement provoked seventy ministers, under Tulloch's leadership, to protest that "the old relation of our Church to the Confession cannot continue."[18] Nor should we forget that the "Constitutionalist" opposition to union with the United Presbyterians which almost tore the Free Church assunder between 1863 and 1873 sprang largely from the theological misgivings of James Begg and his reactionary supporters: pietists of a rather old-fashioned kind like Andrew

Bonar and Kenneth Moody Stuart, and ultra-Calvinist warriors of the so-called "Highland Host" like John Kennedy of Dingwall.

On the other hand, the eighteen-sixties also witnessed many indications of a very different mood, less satisfied and much more questioning. What has been described as a "religious upheaval" took place at that time among lay office-bearers of the Church of Scotland who were finding enforced subscription of the confessional formula increasingly hard to bear.[19] Their revolt proved abortive, but it nevertheless revealed the existence of attitudes not unlike those which induced England to accept the laxer terms of the Clerical Subscription Act of 1865. Almost simultaneously, traditional Sabbatarian views took something of a beating at the hands of Norman Macleod in the Auld Kirk and Walter Chalmers Smith in the Free.[20] And a speech made in 1866 by one Free Church Moderator, William Wilson, contained remarks which seem to belie that body's reputation for absolute immobility in doctrinal matters. "We claim", he told his hearers, "no infallibility for [the Confession], or for ourselves who declare out belief in the propositions which it contains .... It is the Word of God which only abideth forever .... It is open to the Church at any time to say, We have obtained clearer light over one or other or all of the propositions contained in this Confession, we must review it; the time has come for us to frame a new bond of union with each other, a new testimony to the world. If this freedom do not belong to us, then indeed we are in bondage to our Confession, and renounce the liberty wherewith Christ has made us free."[21]

The intellectual climate of an exciting decade is perhaps even more strikingly conveyed in the writings of the Edinburgh advocate and lay-theologian, Alexander Taylor Innes. Not content with the publication of what became the standard work on *The Law of Creeds in Scotland*,[22] Innes also produced a thought-provoking essay, "The Theory of the Church and its Creed, with reference to the Law of Scotland", which had some percipient things to say about the various types of confession to be found in history. It contained, furthermore, the following remarks upon the limited effectiveness of any confessional statement whatsoever: "Taking it for granted that all the ministers of the Presbyterian Churches hold *ex animo* all the propositions which the Confession of Faith draws from Scripture, it is at least certain that each of these ministers (who has thought of these propositions at all) differs from every other in the meaning, emphasis, order and relation in which he holds them; and further, that he differs from everyone else in some of the ten thousand minor propositions which are outside the Confession. There is no honest and sane man who will pretend that any proposition in religious truth constructed by others exactly expresses his own view of that religious truth; and though it may be constructed with sufficient care and comprehensiveness to *include* the views of a great number of consentients, it is normally certain that every one of these consentients differs from every other, and from the objective proposition itself, in the exact sense in which he understands it. Confessions are limited, therefore, even when we look to what is attempted to be expressed in them. But this is clearer when we look to what is necessarily left out."[23]

The seventies were no less eventful. There was another flurry of heresy trials – Fergus Ferguson, David Macrae, Robert Wallace, William Knight, and the heresiarch William Robertson Smith; and although most of the accused (Ferguson is a scarcely comprehensible exception) were either condemned by the Churches or driven to withdraw from them, they attracted much publicity and may well have won over a fair number of converts to the newer views. Nor is it without significance that the liberal approach to confessions and confessional subscription was now being advocated not only by young ministers in obscure or distant places, such as Robert Story in Rosneath and Edward Irving in London around 1830, but by men of eminence and influence like John Tulloch at St. Mary's College, St. Andrews, Norman Macleod at the Barony, Glasgow, T. M. Lindsay in the Free Church College, Glasgow, and Alexander Whyte of Free St. George's, Edinburgh.

Scotland, as Principal Fairbairn of Mansfield College, Oxford, observed in the *Contemporary Review* of December, 1872, was drifting further and further away from the theology of the Westminster Divines. "The continuous earnest struggle of Scotch thought to escape from the harsher points of the Confessional theology has been nowhere without result," he wrote. "Years ago the Secession Synod stamped with its approval a double reference theory of the Atonement, which reduced their theology to a modified Calvinism such as the Westminster Divines detested and meant their Confession to condemn. That theory the United Presbyterian Church has never repudiated .... The Free Church, long distinguished by its antagonism to eclectic theologies and double reference theories, has, though duly warned by certain of her own Doctors and Professors, repeatedly declared by great majorities that the modified Calvinism of the sister church was no bar to Union .... Within the Established Church a circle of men of broad and genial culture has been formed, whose beliefs, influenced by the higher criticism ... have not very much in common with the Westminster theology."[24] To complete his history of the change which had taken place in Scottish religious thought, Fairbairn made reference to a recent clash between Professor Crawford of the Auld Kirk and Professor R. S. Candlish of the Free Kirk over certain statements which the latter had made in his public lectures on "The Fatherhood of God". Crawford's position could by no means be described as Calvinist; it was, indeed, "essentially that of men so little Calvinistic as Pearson and Barrow". Candlish, on the other hand, remained "true to the tradition of Beza and Turretin and Rutherford". Yet according to Fairbairn it was Crawford, not Candlish, who appealed more strongly to Scotsmen of the eighteen-sixties. And he found the explanation in a remark which one Free Church member had made concerning the lectures: "I went to the first lecture (by Candlish), but I went to no other; for I felt, sir, that that man was trying to deprive me and my fellow-men of all that was dearest to us in God."[25]

But of course vast changes were by this time well under way in the wider world beyond Scotland; and in the development of its religious thought there is abundant evidence of Continental and English influences. Both Cairns of the United Presbyterian Church and Tulloch of the Church of Scotland were much at home in Germany, and a steady stream of theological students followed them until diverted by the Kaiser's war from Berlin, Halle, Marburg and Tübingen to the Marne, Gallipoli and the Somme. Many used these summer semesters abroad to deepen acquaintance with Biblical criticism of the newer kind, although familiarity with Hegelian philosophy (that other dissolvent of traditional orthodoxies) was perhaps as likely to be picked up from the Caird brothers at Oxford and Glasgow as anywhere else. The impact of English thinking was probably even greater, being mediated through an endless torrent of books, periodicals and newspapers – and in Victorian England the old certainties were steadily giving ground before doubt, infidelity and intellectual unsettlement. As Lord Annan once pointed out in an illuminating essay on "The Strands of Unbelief", a kind of chronology of the mid-century advance of rationalism can be easily constructed: in the forties, Francis Newman's open attack on Christianity and the loss of faith by Froude and Clough; in the fifties, Tennyson's agonisings in *In Memoriam,* George Eliot's essays in *The Westminster Review,* and "Omar Khayyam"; in the sixties, Huxley's debate with Bishop Wilberforce in Oxford Museum, *Essays and Reviews,* and Seeley's *Ecce Homo,* extravagantly denounced by Shaftesbury as "the most pestilential book ever vomited from the jaws of Hell."[26]

We may be sure that many Scots – ministers and divinity students among them – were very much aware of such developments. They felt the force of what might be called the historical argument against belief, inclining to see truth (in Annan's phrase) "no longer as absolute, philosophically static, revealed once for all, but as relative, genetic and evolutionary."[27] They were familiar with Carlyle, and occasionally felt tempted to agree with him that "The name (of God) has become as if obsolete to the most devout of us."[28] They were only too likely to be impressed by the moral counter-attack on Christianity, finding with Francis Newman that the traditional doctrines of the Atonement, Predestination, Redemption by Grace and Eternal Punishment were "horrifying and wicked",[29] and asserting with John Stuart Mill, "I will call no being good who is not what I mean when I apply that epithet to my fellow-creatures."[30] It is hardly surprising, therefore, to learn from the reminiscences of David S. Cairns that "in the seventies and early eighties both the U.P. and Free Churches" (and possibly the Church of Scotland also) "lost quite a number of able theological students who slipped quietly out of the theological halls, finding the traditional *Weltanschauung* too narrow for them."[31]

Is it possible, then, to distinguish some of the more pervasive influences in the new mood which gradually established itself among churchmen during the latter part of the Victorian age – the mood that in due course brought about a sweeping revision and reconstruction of Scottish Presbyterianism's relationship to its inherited Standards? The following would seem to suggest themselves to even a very cursory glance:

(i) *A new sense of history.* "The present is emphatically an age of historical investigation", observed Principal Rainy of New College in his published lectures on *The Bible and Criticism* (1878). "It is distinguished by diligence in the working out of historical facts and their connections. It is distinguished, also, by a very strong tendency to give to all departments of mental labour, and to all kinds of investigation, either an historical form or an historical appreciation."[32] His judgment is borne out by what happened in virtually every branch of theological study during the nineteenth century. Outstanding among Scottish exemplars of the new attitude was John Tulloch of St. Mary's College, St. Andrews, who used it to bring about a radically altered view of the work of the Westminster Divines. "The Confession of Faith", he asserted in 1865, "in its origin and its principles was the manifesto of a great religious party which, after a fierce conflict, gained a temporary ascendancy in England and Scotland." And he continued: "Indeed, the same thing could be said of every Protestant Confession of Faith …. They are one and all historical monuments, marking the tides of religious thought as they have swelled with greater fullness in the course of the Christian centuries; and none of them can be understood aright simply by themselves, or as isolated dogmatic utterances, but only in connection with their time and the genius and character of the men who framed them." The consequences of such a view, he realised, were far-reaching. "The popular ecclesiastical notion of creeds and confessions as in some sense absolute expressions of Christian truth – *credenda* to be accepted very much as we accept the statements of Scripture itself – is a notion in the face of all theological science, which every student deserving the name has long since abandoned. Those creeds and confessions are neither more nor less than the intellectual labours of great and good men assembled for the most part in synods or councils, all of which, as our Confession itself declares, 'may err, and many have erred'. They are *their* best thoughts about Christian truth as they saw it in their time – intrinsically they are nothing more; and any claim of infallibility for them is the worst of all kinds of Popery – that Popery which degrades the

Christian reason while it fails to nourish the Christian imagination."[33]

(ii) *A new moral sensitivity*. John Stuart Mill's famous aphorism on Divine and human goodness has already been noted. He was by no means unique among the Victorians in professing as keen an interest in the standards which men required of God as in the standards which God required of men; and such an interest led almost inevitably to a rigorous critical scrutiny of many traditional doctrines. But it is also interesting to observe a similarly heightened ethical awareness among Christian theologians. Professor Charteris, for example, once avowed that he had "always held the expression of Calvinism in our Confession of Faith to be ruthless and hard"[34] – a remarkable admission from so conservative a thinker. Professor Flint, similarly, registered "dissatisfaction with the Confessional doctrines of election and reprobation as doubtfully supported by the general tenor of Scripture, and in any case handled in the Confession without regard to the proportion of faith and the witness of the moral constitution of man".[35] And David Cairns tells how, as a young student in the eighties, "I *hated* Charles Hodge, with his hard dogmatism; and remember the horror with which ... I read a sermon of Principal Patton of Princeton ... in which he spoke of God as the Great Artist, who for His supreme work and art needed light and shade in His picture of the Cosmos, needed shade as well as light in His vast creative and redemptive work, chiaroscuro of virtue and wickedness; the Cross and the Great White Throne; Heaven and Hell." The men against whom Cairns and many of his contemporaries reacted were, of course, regarded as being among the world's finest champions of Westminster orthodoxy – which perhaps adds significance to his comment that "the unbelief of today" (c. 1950) "or perhaps of yesterday, is in part a reaction against such misrepresentation of Almighty God."[36]

One consequence of this fresh sensitivity is to be found in

a growing disinclination, among even the most cautious of theologians, to follow what Principal Rainy once called "the juridical way" of formulating Christian doctrines, the doctrine of the Atonement in particular. Addressing the World Presbyterian Alliance at Philadelphia in 1880, he drew attention, with thinly-veiled approval, to the contemporary tendency to stress "disciplinary" rather than "vindicative" righteousness (the terms are his). In the old understanding of things, he suggested, "Desert, rendering of what is due upon trial, under law, is made the key to the whole state of nature ... [and] Grace takes character insofar as it appears over against this." Now, however, there had been a retreat from this "juridical way of conceiving ... the divine procedure"; and two reasons were adduced to account for it. One was a heightened awareness of the *educational* character of the Creator's dealings with the human race; the other, what Rainy called a "Maurician" concentration upon the Fatherhood of God – "implying", as he put it, "certain affections always to be ascribed to Him in dealing with His creatures, certain claims which all men have on Him as His children, and can never cease to have."[37] Before the kind of audience which confronted him in Philadelphia – the representatives of Reformed faith and churchmanship from many countries – there was no need for the principal to spell out all the implications of the change he had been describing for the characteristic doctrines of seventeenth-century Puritan scholasticism: Election and Reprobation.

(iii) *A new picture of the natural world.* This picture was, of course, derived from natural science, the geological and biological sciences in particular; and in some crucially important respects it differed from that with which the seventeenth-century divines had been familiar. The fairly recent origins of the earth and of man's appearance on it, the fixity of species, and the uniqueness of man's place in nature: all ceased to be dominating and unchallengeable assumptions, and were gradually replaced by that great constellation of ideas which can be summed up in the one word, Evolution. Still more important, acceptance of the findings of Lyell and Darwin and others meant that many of the fundamental Christian doctrines – of God, of man, of sin and the fall, of providence and of Scripture – came under penetrating scrutiny. Churchmen of all traditions, including those whose roots were in Geneva and Westminster, clearly had a great deal of rethinking to do; but by the closing decades of the century there could be little doubt that the initial reactions of alarm and hostility had in the main given place to either cautious acceptance or whole-hearted enthusiasm.

Of cautious acceptance two instances may be given. During Professor George Adam Smith's heresy trial in 1902, Principal Rainy – looking back on the conflicts of a lifetime – called to mind the "geological difficulties" that had been raised only a generation before concerning the Creation story in the book of Genesis. Such difficulties, he told the U.F. Assembly, had on occasion been denounced as the product of "infidel science". But in due course the matter became (as he put it) "simply a question about the respect due to facts"; and "as soon as men became satisfied that the facts were so, then they acknowledged that the facts were part of what they had to take with them in considering what was intended to be the divine instruction for them."[38] About the same time as this interesting concession was made from one side of the ecclesiastical divide in Scotland, a statement with similar implications came from the other. Professor Robert Flint of Edinburgh (the Auld Kirk's most eminent philosophical theologian) expressed, we are told, his "willingness to review the confessional doctrines of Creation, origin of man, and Fall, in the light of the assured results of science and history."[39] Both Rainy and Flint were famous for their constitutional inability to indulge in either rash speculation or extravagant utterance; and that they could speak as they did is a measure of the rapid intellectual transformation that had taken place in Scotland in less than half a century.

The outstanding exemplar of whole-hearted enthusiasm for the new world-view was Professor Henry Drummond, who taught in the Free Church College at Glasgow from 1878 until his early death in 1897. Such esteem as Drummond still enjoys depends almost entirely upon the skill and grace with which he commended the Faith to student audiences all over the world; but in his own day he was equally well known within church circles as a populariser of evolutionary theory, and his volumes on *Natural Law in the Spiritual World* (1883) and *The Ascent of Man* (1894) were very widely read. The approval of Darwinian views which permeates these writings (and which had no small influence on the attitude of the late-Victorian laity) is particularly evident in an article contributed by Drummond to the *The Expositor* in 1885. There he referred to the "Bible in two forms" which confronted the scientists of his day. "The one is the Bible as it was presented to our forefathers; the other is the Bible of modern theology. The books, the chapters, the verses, and the words are the same in each; yet in form they are two entirely different Bibles. To science the difference is immediately palpable …. The one represents revelation as having been produced on the creative hypothesis, the Divine-fiat hypothesis, the ready-made hypothesis; the other on the slow-growth or evolution theory. It is at once obvious which of them science would prefer – it could no more accept the first than it would accept the ready-made theory of the universe." He then went on to link the changes which had taken place in science with the parallel changes in Biblical interpretation, registering equal satisfaction with both. "Nothing could be more important than to assure science that the same difficulty has for some time been felt, and with equal keenness, by theology. The scientific method in its hand, scientific theology has been laboriously working at a reconstruction of Biblical truth from this very viewpoint of development. And it no more pledges itself today to the interpretations of the Bible of a thousand years ago, than does science to the interpretations of nature in the time of Pythagoras, and the Bible is the same today as a thousand years ago. But the Pythagorean interpretation of nature is not less objectionable to the modern mind than are many ancient interpretations of the Scriptures to the scientific theologian."[40]

(iv) *A new estimate of human nature.* Here again it is Rainy who expresses the change most succinctly. "Their theology", he told the Free Church General Assembly in 1891 during a debate on the highly controversial Declaratory Act, "would be greatly damaged if it were not associated with a full recognition of facts." But in the circumstances of the seventeenth century (when, of course, the Confession had been drawn up) there had been what he called "a sparingness and timidity" in recognising those "elements in human nature which reminded them of its original greatness." And as if to drive his message home to men acquainted with the Westminster doctrine of total depravity, he added that "He did not know any thought that went through the *Pensées* of Pascal more than this – you understand Christianity only if you realise together the greatness and the meanness of man, that it is his grandeur and his fall together that bring out to you what Christianity really means and what it proceeds upon."[41]

(v) *A new tolerance and tentativeness.* The tolerance which was so prominent a trait in late-nineteenth-century religion was very largely, one suspects, a reaction against the embattled controversialism of preceding generations – the kind of attitude to be found in theological iron-clads like William Cunningham of New College. Young Thomas Davidson's humorous denunciation of the intolerance of Thomas Boston (to be found in those charming letters which make up the greater part of James Brown's *The Life of a Scottish Probationer*) is one particularly attractive expression of it.[42] Another is Professor Flint's remark in 1881 that "The Church of Scotland has no right to tolerate sceptical teaching and fundamental heresy, but neither has she a right to repress variety of opinion, or to violate constitutional procedure, or to treat all errors as heresies, or to be over-rigid with any man."[43] The tentativeness which often accompanied this tolerant spirit no doubt had similar roots; but it was perhaps due more to a sensitive awareness of contemporary thought than to a recollection of how the dogmatists of the past had thought and acted. To quote again from Rainy's 1880 address: Current theology asks, "Did not all those theologies overdo the confidence of their interpretations and the sweep of their conclusions? ... Did they not ... trust their sources too simply? Did they not ... interpret [them] too unguardedly?" Its own approach, by contrast, was to "take counsel in various quarters". It carefully considered the thought-processes and methods of the sacred writers, asking how far their utterances were meant to go and what inferences they warranted; it meditated upon the history of theology, tracing the influences under which particular doctrines arose; it consulted philosophy, seeking where possible to make adjustment to its views; and it surveyed the history of religion. In consequence of all this, Rainy observed, current theology was "more calm, more catholic, more considerate, more human ... [It was] the faith dealing with perplexities and feeling its way through niceties and competing considerations rather than uttering the trumpet tones of confidence and enthusiasm." So – embodying the very spirit of which he had been talking – the principal advised his fellow theologians to practice self-criticism: "Suppose it became usual for us to recognise degrees of certainty in our conclusions on different points, and to seek to appreciate these degrees – distinguishing what is fundamental in the faith, and ranks as clear Christian certainty, from what is more or less matter of inference or speculation?"[44] Such counsel would hardly startle any of today's theologians, but in the eighteen-eighties it was fresh as well as eminently relevant.

(vi) *A new preference for the apologetic, as opposed to the dogmatic, spirit*. To quote him yet again, Rainy spoke on one occasion (apparently with approval) of what he called "a modified and retrenched theology, shorn of many of its leaves."[45] By the seventies there was certainly a very marked tendency among theologians, partly (it may be suspected) under the influence of Albrecht Ritschl, to distrust all metaphysical systems – and theological systems also, the Westminster one among them. We have already noticed James Buchanan's early allusion to this development; but Scotland's most persistent advocate of anti-dogmatism was John Tulloch, whose years of university teaching extended from 1854 to 1886. "I must venture to say that the most ominous and saddening signs I can see on the religious horizon", he told his St. Andrews students in 1864, "are not the spirit of inquiry, whether within the Church or without it, but the unreasoning dogmatism with which in many cases this spirit has been met. The spirit of inquiry may be harmful ... but it is not necessarily either injurious or dangerous; while one has only to open any page of the New Testament, or study any century of Christendom from the beginning, to see that a blind and angry dogmatism is no weapon of spiritual warfare, and can never advance the cause of truth." He continued, in words which were not only a kind of condensed *apologia pro vita sua* but a programme for the theologians who were to succeed him in Scotland: "Christianity claims to be an eminently reasonable faith. It is the 'wisdom' no less than the 'power' of God. It is, if it is true at all, the highest truth; and so it is the business of Christian apology, in the face of unbelief, to show evidence of this .... There is no higher task for the Christian reason in every age than to vindicate the eternal basis of Christianity as a truth for the reason no less than for the conscience and the heart, as the highest philosophy no less than the highest expediency. To abdicate this rational ground of defence is to confess the Gospel to be a superstition – to acknowledge a

hopeless schism between reason and conscience, between
philosophy and religion .... No doubt the Church has its
rights of utterance – its power to condemn as well as its duty
to inquire and defend – but none the less true is it that men no
longer heed utterances which are not weighty in argument as
well as in tone, nor bow before a condemnation which is not
reasoned as well as authoritative."[46]

(vii) *A new awareness of other religions and of the problems
posed by them.* Britain's imperial expansion, in which Scotsmen
played so prominent a part, made missionary enterprise both a
possibility and a duty. By the later Victorian period, however,
the intellectual problems raised by that enterprise and its very
limited success were gradually forcing the Churches towards a
rethinking of their whole doctrine of the ways of God to men
– non-Christian men in particular. The Westminster system
was (in A. R. MacEwen's words) "an exclusive one, concerning
itself mainly with the position and the prospects of believers,
and furnishing only a few loopholes from which furtive glances
can be taken at the justice of God's providence and the
breadth of His mercy in dealing with all His children."[47] The
missionary experience of the nineteenth century did more than
anything else to destroy that exclusiveness.

(viii) *A new approach to evangelism (and possibly, in
consequence, a new understanding of the Evangel).* The principal
factor here, it need hardly be said, was the influence of
American revivalism, chiefly in the persons of Moody and
Sankey, who first campaigned in Scotland in 1873–74. These
men laid much emphasis on the convert's decision – which, as
John Kennedy of Dingwall realised, was to undermine the
traditional Calvinist approach.[48] They distinguished between
complicated inessentials and simple essentials (though John
Locke would have been surprised to hear what their essentials
were!). And they offered the Gospel to everyone: an approach
which, according to one nineteenth-century observer, "did
more to relieve Scotland of the old hyper-Calvinist doctrine of

election, and of what the theologians call limited atonement, and to bring home the love of God and the grace of God to all men, than did even the teaching of McLeod Campbell"[49] – or, one might add, the teaching of Thomas Erskine, James Morison and George Macdonald as well.

Against this background of criticism and reassessment, the different Churches took up the task of redefining their relationship to the Confession; and from approximately 1860 on to 1910 (or even 1921) there raged what might be called The Great Confessional Controversy. The United Presbyterians led the way – perhaps because of a long-standing tradition among them of relatively liberal Biblical interpretation, perhaps because their notable zeal for overseas missions had confronted them more insistently than others with the problems raised by the unevangelised heathen, perhaps because at least one chapter of the Confession had long been modified among them on account of its allegedly persecuting and intolerant implications. Things came to a head in the late seventies, by which time two alternatives seemed to offer themselves to the Synod. On the one hand, use of the Confession as a theological test might be abandoned altogether and perhaps a new statement drawn up. On the other hand, the old Standard might be adhered to, while at the same time redefining the Church's attitude to it and allowing ministers and office-bearers some freedom in their interpretation of it. Under the guidance of John Cairns, the revered College principal, the Synod opted for the second alternative.

A special committee having been set up to deal with the problem, it reported in 1878, recommending that candidates for the ministry or the eldership should in future signify their acceptance of the Confession in the light of a newly-drafted Declaratory Statement which took account of (or maybe simply reflected?) some of the changes in attitude examined above. The four opening paragraphs of this declaration dealt with certain peculiarly controversial topics in the original

Confession: "the doctrine of redemption", "the doctrine of the divine decrees", "the doctrine of man's total depravity", and the doctrines concerning the ultimate destiny of the heathen and of children who die in infancy. Each paragraph had the clear purpose of guarding against extreme or erroneous inferences that had sometimes been drawn from the high Calvinism of Westminster, and in particular of balancing (whether permissibly or not is another question) the limitation of effectual grace to the elect with the proclamation of the love of God for all mankind. Two less significant paragraphs followed; but the Statement closed with the celebrated "conscience clause", whose value to troubled minds both then and since can hardly be exaggerated. "In accordance with the practice hitherto observed in this Church" – so ran the vital sentence – "liberty of opinion is allowed on such points in the Standards, not entering into the substance of the faith, as the interpretation of the 'six days' in the Mosaic account of the Creation: the Church guarding against the abuse of this liberty to the injury of its unity and peace."[50]

The committee's recommendations were duly adopted by the Synod, Cairns assuring them that he did not regard the Statement as either contradicting or cancelling Westminster doctrine but simply as "checking and counter-balancing it, giving a counterpoise to what otherwise might be looked upon as too strong and extreme."[51] Whether his judgment was to be relied upon in this matter is one of many questions which the settlement arouses in the mind of latter-day observers.[52] Two others which persistently recur are: did it really try to reconcile the irreconcilable? and, what were "the essential articles" and "the substance of the faith" to which reference was so confidently made? At any rate, from 1879 onwards the Declaratory Act was part of the law of the United Presbyterian Church, and a notable milestone in Scottish history had been quickly and unspectacularly passed. In 1892 the Free Church followed suit in a similarly-worded Declaratory Act[53] (though

Rainy had more difficulties to cope with than Cairns – including the secession of the Free Presbyterians); and in 1910 the Church of Scotland produced an altered form of subscription which required no more than acceptance of the Confession as the Church's Confession, and profession of belief in "the fundamental doctrines of the Christian faith contained therein".[54] As a result, none of the major Presbyterian bodies in Scotland was any longer bound with the former stringency to the utterances of Westminster. The old exclusiveness (and no doubt the old definiteness and consistency) of Reformed theology was at an end, and the confessional revolution had reached its goal.

Notes to Chapter III

1. E. Irving (ed.), *The Confessions of Faith and the Books of Discipline of the Church of Scotland of date anterior to the Westminster Confession* (London, 1831), p. xciii. Cf. also M. Oliphant, *The Life of Edward Irving* (4th edn., London, n.d.), p. 337f.
2. W. Hanna (ed.), *Letters of Thomas Erskine of Linlathen* (4th edn., Edinburgh, 1884), p. 106.
3. J. H. Leckie, *Fergus Ferguson, His Theology and Heresy Trial* (Edinburgh, 1923), p. 18.
4. R. H. Story, *Life and Remains of Robert Lee* (London, 1870), vol. II p. 38.
5. D. Campbell (ed.), *Memorials of John McLeod Campbell* (London, 1877), vol. I p. 85.
6. J. Morison, *The Extent of the Propitiation; or, The Question, for whom did Christ Die? Answered* (London, 1847), p. 156.
7. A. L. Drummond and J. Bulloch, *The Scottish Church, 1688–1843: The Age of the Moderates* (Edinburgh, 1973), p. 219.
8. J. Cairns, *Memoir of John Brown* (Edinburgh, 1860), p. 225.
9. ibid., p. 223.
10. ibid., p. 252.
11. ibid., p. 243.
12. ibid., p. 255.
13. ibid., pp. 254–5.
14. *Proceedings and Debates of the General Assembly of the Free Church of Scotland, 1868* (Edinburgh, 1868), p. 3.
15. A. C. Fraser, *Biographia Philosophica: A Retrospect* (2nd edn., Edinburgh, 1905), p. 161.
16. R. S. Candlish, *The Fatherhood of God* (2nd edn., Edinburgh, 1865), p. 289.
17. *Inauguration of the New College of the Free Church, Edinburgh, November, 1850, with Introductory Lectures on Theology, Philosophy, and Natural Science* (London, 1851), pp. 84–5.
18. A. T. Innes, *Studies in Scottish History, Chiefly Ecclesiastical* (London, 1892), pp. 257–8.
19. W. Wallace, "The Religious Upheaval in Scotland", *The Contemporary Review*, vol. XXX (1877), pp. 240–63.
20. D. Macleod, *Memoir of Norman Macleod* (London, 1876), ch. 18. Cf. J. R. Fleming, *The Church in Scotland, 1843–74* (Edinburgh, 1927), pp. 212–20.
21. *Proceedings and Debates of the General Assembly of the Free Church of Scotland, 1866* (Edinburgh, 1866), pp. 7–8. Cf. A. T. Innes, *The Law of Creeds in Scotland* (Edinburgh, 1902), pp. 244–5 n. 2.

22. 1st edn., 1867.
23. Innes, *Studies*, pp. 241–2.
24. A. M. Fairbairn, "The Westminster Confession of Faith and Scotch Theology", *The Contemporary Review*, vol. XXI (1872), p. 80.
25. ibid., pp. 81–2.
26. N. Annan, "The Strands of Unbelief", *Ideas and Beliefs of the Victorians* (London, 1949), p. 150.
27. ibid., p. 151.
28. J. A. Froude, *Carlyle's Life in London* (London, 1884), vol. II, p. 370, quoted in B. Willey, *Nineteenth Century Studies* (London, 1949), p. 125.
29. The phrase is Annan's. "Strands of Unbelief", p. 153.
30. J. S. Mill, *An Examination of Sir William Hamilton's Philosophy* (3rd edn., London, 1867), p. 124.
31. D. and A. Cairns (eds.), *David Cairns: An Autobiography* (London, 1950), p. 125.
32. R. Rainy, *The Bible and Criticism* (London, 1878), p. 49.
33. M. Oliphant, *A Memoir of the Life of John Tulloch* (3rd edn., Edinburgh, 1889), pp. 222–3.
34. A. Gordon, *The Life of Archibald Hamilton Charteris* (London, 1912), p. 420.
35. W. P. Paterson, "Outline of the History of Dogmatic Theology" (Edinburgh, 1916), p. 20.
36. Cairns, *Cairns*, pp. 87–8.
37. *Reports of Proceedings of the Second General Council of the Presbyterian Alliance* (Philadelphia, 1880), pp. 83–4.
38. P. C. Simpson, *The Life of Principal Rainy* (London, 1909), vol. II, p. 272.
39. Paterson, "Outline", p. 20.
40. H. Drummond, "The Contribution of Science to Christianity", *The Expositor* (3rd Series, vol. I, 1885), pp. 104–5.
41. Simpson, *Rainy*, vol. II, pp. 126–7.
42. J. Brown, *The Life of a Scottish Probationer* (4th edn., Glasgow, 1908), pp. 261–4.
43. D. Macmillan, *The Life of Professor Flint* (London, 1914), p. 379.
44. *Second General Council* (1880), pp. 87–8 and 90.
45. ibid., p. 80.
46. J. Tulloch, "Introductory Lecture delivered at St. Mary's College, St. Andrews, November 21, 1864" (Edinburgh, 1864), p. 10.
47. A. R. MacEwen, *Life and Letters of John Cairns* (4th edn., London, 1898), pp. 662–3.
48. cf. J. Kennedy, "Hyper-Evangelism: 'Another Gospel'', Though a Mighty Power. A Review of the Recent Religious Movement in Scotland" (2nd edn., Edinburgh, 1874).
49. Simpson, *Rainy*, vol. I, p. 408.
50. Convenient text in J. T. Cox and J. B. Longmuir (eds.), *Practice and Procedure in the Church of Scotland* (5th edn., London, 1964), pp. 411–12.
51. MacEwen, *Cairns*, p. 674.
52. cf. I. Hamilton, "Some aspects of the erosion of Westminster Calvinism among Scottish Seceders" (Edinburgh University M.Phil. thesis, 1981).
53. Convenient text in Cox-Longmuir, *Practice and Procedure*, pp. 412–13.
54. ibid., p. 410.

IV

The Liturgical Revolution

An early sign of the impending change in Scottish worship is provided by a work which dates from the closing year of the eighteenth century: Professor Alexander Gerard of Aberdeen's posthumous volume on *The Pastoral Care*. The book contained some sensible – and also prophetic – comments on the conduct of religious services, which may well have had their effect in the succeeding generation. Gerard suggested, for example, that the obvious disadvantages of praying without set forms might be "effectually remedied by a proper directory (such as our own is in some measure) containing either a variety of forms, any of which might be used, or a large collection of materials for prayer out of which a choice may be made". And he also observed that "Because a minister is not obliged to read a liturgy prescribed by authority, it does not therefore follow that he is to pour out such petitions as occur to him, without any method, choice, or premeditation. On the contrary, we ought to be as careful about what we say in prayer, as about what we say in preaching, as solicitous to speak with propriety when we address ourselves to God, as when we address the congregation."[1] In the eighteen-twenties and subsequently, men's minds were further prepared for new developments by that influential triumvirate, Thomas Erskine, John McLeod Campbell, and Edward Irving. Each of them in his own way questioned the traditional Scottish approach to religion and – by implication – the worship that went with it. Together, they had the effect of warning against an over-intellectualised and abstract piety, discrediting a degenerate Puritanism, balancing the doctrine of the Atonement with an equal emphasis upon the Incarnation, and reminding their contemporaries that "the letter killeth, but the Spirit giveth life". Of course, the Calvinistic counter-attack was fierce and (temporarily) successful; and in any case churchmen during the thirties and forties were more often concerned with ecclesiastical politics than with the questions which had troubled Erskine and his friends. Yet the leaven continued to work; and even the Disruption, which at first glance might seem to have pointed in another direction, eventually produced a mood more favourable to liturgical reform than any that had existed in Scotland since the days of Knox.

Three indicators of the new openness in everything pertaining to worship call for special mention. Extending over more than fifty years, they take us from the first decade of the century down to the end of the sixth, by which time the liturgical revival's take-off point had clearly been reached. First, there was the appearance of several useful compilations of worship material. In 1802 came Harry Robertson's *The Scotch Minister's Assistant*; in 1829, George Burns' *Prayers adapted for Public Worship, the Domestic Altar, Sunday Schools, and the Chamber of Sickness and Death, to which are added Prayers for the use of Young Persons, and Graces before and after Meals, with a Conclusion recommendatory of Prayer as a Christian Duty*; in 1843, William Liston's *The Service of the House of God, according to the Practice of the Church of Scotland; intended chiefly to assist the Devotion and direct the Meditations of those who are necessarily detained from Public Worship; and to form a Directory to young Clergymen on their first entering on their official Duties*; and in 1848, Alexander Brunton's *Forms for Public Worship in the Church of Scotland*. Second, some of the most important Reformed service-books were republished, each with a valuable, scholarly introduction: John Cumming's edition of *Knox's Liturgy* in 1840; Thomas Binney's *A Chapter on Liturgies*, itself a reissue of Charles Baird's compendium, *Eutaxia*, in 1856; and Andrew R. Bonar's *Presbyterian Liturgies, with Specimens of Forms of Prayer for Worship as used in the Continental Reformed and American Churches; with the Directory for the Publick Worship of God agreed upon by the Assembly of Divines at Westminster; and Forms of Prayer for ordinary and communion Sabbaths, and for other Services of the Church,* in 1860. Finally, two exceedingly frank assessments of the Church of Scotland (including its worship) were given to the world by a pair of distinguished well-wishers, one an elder and one a minister: the Duke of Argyll's *'Presbytery Examined': An Essay, critical and historical, on the ecclesiastical History of Scotland since the Reformation,* in 1848; and Robert Lee of Greyfriars' *The Reform of the Church of Scotland in Worship, Government and Doctrine: Part I – Worship,* in 1864. The rethinking set in train by works like these produced so fundamental and far-reaching a transformation of Presbyterian worship by 1900 that Gerard and Brunton – and maybe even Bonar – would have required all their scholarship and commonsense to discern any kinship between what had been done in their day and what became the norm just two or three generations later.

One of the most potent impulses towards change was provided by a sudden revival of the influence and popularity of Scottish Episcopalianism. This revival, which took place in the years just before and just after the Disruption, provoked the Church of Scotland not only to alarm but also to self-criticism, particularly in liturgical matters. The Duke of ˙Argyll, for example, argued in his *'Presbytery Examined'* that it was aesthetic considerations which were attracting proselytes to the Episcopal Church, and pleaded for improvements in Presbyterian worship to redress the balance. Some sixteen years later, Lee of Greyfriars made the same point in his reform manifesto. Completely rejecting the notion that people were attracted by either the preaching or the organisation of Episcopalianism, he declared: "There remain but two motives to account for those separations: the influence of fashion ... and the character of the worship, especially the manner of praying and the general want of solemnity, decorum and refinement in the [Presbyterian] services. This latter is, undoubtedly, the reason generally assigned: 'We go to the Episcopal chapel because we like *the worship there* better than that in the Kirk' .... I believe it is the chief reason."[2] And one of Lee's correspondents went even further along the same lines. "You have", he agreed, "truly pointed out the cause of the secessions to the English Church. But the Scots never can be Episcopalians, and never would be, were their own worship made *worship* and not mere preachings and irreverent discords of atrocious noises, considered 'singing from the heart' .... But if we had the Praise and the Prayer – the *worship* – right, little fault could be found, even with poor sermons."[3] Incidentally, the most recent historians of the Church in Victorian Scotland, Drs. Bulloch and Drummond, tell us that "Episcopalian worship had a strong attraction for Presbyterians in the first half of the century", but that "in the second half the attraction declined, and then disappeared".[4] Perhaps Lee and his friend were right!

But of course the Episcopalian advance was only one of many influences which brought about this remarkable reappraisal within the Kirk. As far as the ecclesiastical parties were concerned, the Evangelicals' intense awareness of the great issues at stake whenever a congregation gathered for worship undoubtedly contributed something. So did the old Moderates' sense of what was decent and fitting, or lamentable and ludicrous, in religious observances. Closer contacts with England, the Continent, the Colonies, and North America (due in large measure to improvements in transport), introduced Scotsmen to liturgical traditions other than their own – the

Catholic Apostolic, for example, or the Anglo-Catholic – and frequently precipitated comparisons not always to the advantage of the homeland. A growing volume of research into the history of the Reformed Churches (one aspect of that fascination with the past which had given rise, a generation earlier, to the novels of Sir Walter and the biographical writings of Thomas M'Crie and the genesis of various historical clubs) led, as we have seen, to several scholarly republications. An awakening sensitivity, in what was supremely the Age of Reform, to the demands and aspirations of ordinary people found expression in the call for a less cerebral, more affective worship, and for fuller congregational participation in it. The waning of scholastic Calvinism, and the influence of the Romantics' stress upon "the purity of the heart's affections", pointed in the same direction. Improving educational standards made the pew somewhat more critical of the pulpit than previously, while a realisation of the missionary function of worship in an age of doubt and intellectual perplexity deepened the concern for appealing and effective services. Not least important, increasing material prosperity prompted a revolution in taste among the prosperous bourgeoisie of Scotland which was reflected in Lee's avowal – at a famous "breakfast at Slaney's" in 1866 – that "Many things may have been tolerable or even necessary in a different state of society or in older times, which are not necessary now – which are not proper now – which are now an obstruction instead of a help."[5]

By the eighteen-fifties, then, a whole host of developments had prepared men, both intellectually and emotionally, for sweeping changes. But it was hardly to be expected that the transition to a new order would take place without any kind of trouble: the old was too deeply entrenched, and had too many devoted protagonists, for that. Right on to the end of the century, therefore, the Church was racked by a succession of conflicts as one innovator after another – Marshall Lang,

Robert Lee, James Cooper, and John Macleod in particular –
challenged existing practices in the name of good taste, the
best Reformed traditions, and Catholic truth, and brought
down upon himself the ire of his congregation, or of the
ecclesiastical courts, or of both. The immediate results of most
of these *causes célèbres* generally looked like a victory for the
status quo; but hindsight shows it to have been quite otherwise,
and the innovators might well have affirmed, with their
contemporary Arthur Clough, that

> ...while the tired waves, vainly breaking,
> Seem here no painful inch to gain,
> Far back, through creeks and inlets making,
> Comes silent, flooding in, the main.

The most celebrated case was, undoubtedly, that of the
minister of Greyfriars, which dragged its slow length along
from 1857 right through to 1867. The renovation of his church
after a fire gave Lee his chance – and he took it with both
hands. Coloured windows were introduced, along with a
harmonium (later, an organ); the congregation were
encouraged to stand for praise and kneel for prayer and make
their responses according to forms printed for them in a
service-book. All this in the church where the National
Covenant had been signed! Uproar followed, and Lee was
formally accused of introducing illegal "innovations in the
worship of God". Ordered by presbytery and synod to
discontinue his obnoxious practices and "conform in future to
the order and form of public worship as established in the
Directory of Public Worship, confirmed by Acts of Parliament
and Assembly, and presently practised in the Church", he
appealed to the General Assembly. There, the only censure
sustained was that which had dealt with the reading of prayers
from a book, and in consequence the way seemed open for
reasonable, gradual advance. But this was by no means the
end, partly because of various defects in Lee's character, partly

because of the bigotry, prejudice, spitefulness and adamantine conservatism of his opponents. Lee – contentious, stubborn, scornful of opposition and eager to provoke the timid or the reactionary – made many mistakes. Four years after accepting the Assembly's prohibition of a printed liturgy, he began to use his book again, and compounded the offence by introducing a pipe-organ. At one moment we find him declaring that his action was in agreement with the *Directory,* which did not explicitly forbid read prayers; at another, opining that ministers were in any case not legally bound by the *Directory*. He suggested that there was no liturgical uniformity in Scotland for him to break, although the findings of an Assembly inquiry indicated otherwise. He utterly failed to see the difference between reading prayers from a carefully-prepared manuscript and using a printed book which lacked official sanction. He overlooked the discretionary character of Knox's Liturgy, ignored the inconvenient fact that the whole tenor of the Directory was against set forms, and showed unnecessary and exaggerated scorn for the authority of use and wont – the practice of worship as it had obtained in the Kirk ever since 1690. Between them, he and his antagonists inflicted a good deal of needless injury upon the Church, though the ultimate outcome of their squabbling was no doubt beneficent. From his point of view, the brightest moment may have come in 1864, when the Assembly seemed to suggest that innovations would be permitted so long as kirk sessions agreed to them and no congregational dispeace ensued; the darkest a year later, when the so-called Pirie Act transferred the power of regulating public worship to presbyteries and thus obliged would-be reformers to convert not only their congregations but their ministerial colleagues as well. In the end, two things completely altered a very threatening situation. One was a decline in the willingness of presbyteries to interfere in matters of worship unless a congregation were seriously divided; the other was the sudden, incapacitating and ultimately fatal illness of the central figure. Shocked and at the same time relieved at Lee's removal from the scene, the Assembly of 1866 postponed consideration of his case, and the Assembly of 1867 took it no further. Henceforth, the operation of the Pirie Act worked more in favour of change than against it.[6] Toleration had triumphed – really through inaction; and for the remainder of the century the refashioning of Scottish worship was free to proceed with ever-quickening pace.

Changes, it has been pointed out, came in at two levels. "Firstly, the General Assembly, acting mainly through specially appointed committees, slowly and cautiously authorised changes in the Church's public worship. Secondly, and chiefly, the revival was promoted through the work of individual ministers, and the activities of newly-formed societies. In the long run, the work done at this secondary level, and without the official encouragement of the Church, greatly influenced the attitude and policy of the General Assembly."[7] To begin with the unofficial influences, pride of place must be given to the Church Service Society, that monument to the enthusiasm of men like R. H. Story, Cameron Lees, John Tulloch, George Sprott and Robert Lee himself. Founded at the very height of the Greyfriars case, in 1865, and made possible by the existence of a growing body of opinion favourable to liturgical reform, the Society carefully disavowed any intention of imposing a fixed liturgy upon the Church. Its chief aim, as stated in the constitution, was "the study of the liturgies – ancient and modern – of the Christian Church, with a view to the preparation and publication of forms of prayer for public worship and services for the administration of the sacraments, the celebration of marriage, the burial of the dead, etc." But the founders also desired to build up a kind of treasury of prayers on which the ordinary minister might draw: "a great magazine of prayers", as they called it, "to which every minister might have access."[8]

Even in the first half-century of its existence the Society

made remarkable strides towards the fulfilment of both these
aims, recruiting into membership more than one-third of the
clergy of the Church of Scotland, many eminent and scholarly
men among them. Its greatest single achievement came early,
for *Euchologion, or a Book of Common Order* appeared only
two years after the original meeting in the manse at Eastwood.
Produced under the supervision of Sprott, Story, and Tulloch,
it contained forms for Baptism, the Lord's Supper, Marriage
and Burial, tables of Psalms and Lessons, and a selection of
prayers for public worship; but according to its sponsors it was
not intended to supersede extemporary prayer. Rather was its
purpose to give ministers "models or aids to devotion" which
might gradually enrich and dignify the worship of the
sanctuary. Judging by the frequency with which it was reissued
over a period of more than fifty years, the book obviously met
a need. And although liturgical scholars have criticised certain
aspects of it, most of them would agree with W. D. Maxwell
that it made "a distinctive and brilliant contribution to the
renascence of Scottish worship".[9] The successive editions of
Euchologion, however, represent only a small part of the
Church Service Society's work. It also reprinted a number of
liturgical classics – including Knox's Liturgy and the Directory
of Public Worship – and enriched them with fine historical
introductions and notes; built up a collection of books on
worship for presentation to the General Assembly's own
library; provided, through its annual meeting, a platform for
scholars and a rallying-place for enthusiasts; and helped, by its
orders of service for special occasions, to introduce
imagination and variety into the worship of the parishes. All in
all, it did much to promote the cause of order, reverence, and
– a favourite word with its supporters – dignity in the
sanctuary.

Of course, many changes made in Scottish worship
between 1850 and 1900 had little or no connection with the
work of the Church Service Society, while some of its activities

were misguided and others notably ineffective. As Dr. Robertson has pointed out in his valuable but regrettably unpublished study: "A group of liturgical scholars, like the leaders of the Church Service Society, in preparing orders of service which were not to be submitted to the Assembly for official sanction, which did not need to be such as could, or would, be put into immediate use in the average parish church, exposed themselves to the danger of composing services which were not likely to be typical of the public worship of the Church. The Society engaged in some wishful thinking. The orders of service which they published sometimes expressed what in their view these services should be, rather than put into a fair form the type of service which was to be found throughout the Church. The fundamental assumption that only Laud's folly and Puritan influence prevented the Kirk from inheriting a liturgical service underlay all the Society's work. But the mass of the people, and the majority of the clergy, long used to a simple, free, and direct type of service, in all probability did not share their view .... Men like Professor Flint and Dr. Archibald Scott stood for a more careful preparation of *non*-liturgical prayer. Perhaps this was the main stream."[10] That is wise comment; yet when all reservations have been made there is still little doubt that without the Society's labours the entire devotional life of Scotland would be not only very different from what it actually is today but also manifestly poorer.

A smaller but also influential enterprise was the foundation of the Aberdeen Ecclesiological Society in 1886 and of the Glasgow one in 1893. (They came together in 1903 as the Scottish Ecclesiological Society.) Concerned with the principles of Christian worship – particularly in their implications for the architecture, decoration, and furnishing of church buildings – they sought, consciously or unconsciously, to do for Scotland what the Camden Society had done for England. Their appreciation of the rôle of form, colour and symbolism in public worship, their recruitment of distinguished architects like Macgregor Chalmers for the building of new churches or the renovation of old ones, and their eagerness to enlist skilled craftsmen in stone and wood and glass, in metal-work and embroidery, for the adornment of the sanctuary, gradually helped to create a new sensitivity in all such matters, and freed Presbyterian Scotland from some of the worst consequences of an undiscriminating Puritanism. They made their mistakes, needless to say. What may be appropriate for Anglican or Roman Catholic worship is by no means always suitable for the services of a Church which claims to stand in the Reformed tradition; and there was something comic – if not worse – in the Societies' enthusiasm for deep chancels, choir-stalls, prayer desks, eagle lecterns, small side pulpits, ornate stone communion-tables, and even a new church that had been planned after the pattern of a thirteenth-century monastery. Yet while admitting all this – and remembering that devoted worshippers are the fairest of all "church furnishings", and the distinction between the beauty of holiness and the holiness of beauty an important one – most Scottish churchmen would be happy to acknowledge the value of what these pioneers sought to do and to give them credit for the transformation which they brought about.[11]

Alongside the work of the Societies must be set what was achieved, both within their own parishes and beyond, by individual ministers sympathetic to the renascence. While some of them were relatively obscure, others were conspicuous and even controversial figures; and three at least cannot go unmentioned. First, John MacLeod (minister at Duns from 1862 to 1875, and at Govan from 1875 until his death in 1898), with his indebtedness to the ritual of the Catholic Apostolic Church; his zealous observance of the great Christian festivals; his reintroduction of symbols on font and communion-table; his phenomenal church-building achievements; his diligent pastoral oversight and fervent preaching; his belief – above all else – that new life would come to the Church only if the weekly, dominically-ordained celebration of the Eucharist were restored.[12] Second, James Cooper (minister at Broughty Ferry from 1873 to 1881, and East of St. Nicholas, Aberdeen, from 1881 to 1898; professor of Ecclesiastical History in the University of Glasgow from 1898 to 1922): conductor of retreats; pioneer in the observance of Christmas Day and Holy Week; advocate of more frequent communion; restorer of weddings in church and private communion of the sick and regular daily services; respecter of both Catholic tradition and ancient Reformed usages; inspirer of several generations of students with his compelling vision of the Church – One, Holy, Catholic and Apostolic.[13] Third, James Cameron Lees (minister of Paisley Abbey, and of St. Giles', Edinburgh, from 1877 to 1909): the son of a Stornoway minister, and so another in the long line of Highlanders who have periodically helped to revive the Church. He could probably have made an impression anywhere, but it was in the historic shrine at the heart of Scotland's capital that he really came into his own. The building had recently been restored and unified, and with nearly all its ancient grandeur recovered could again provide a worthy setting for the most solemn and representative services of both the city and the nation. Cameron Lees entered upon his task with zest and sensitivity, and under his command the worship soon came to match the surroundings. 1883 saw the introduction of a service-book, compiled by the minister, which was to continue in use for forty years; 1884 the institution of daily prayers. Thanks largely to Cameron Lees' notable tact and discretion, practices which under Lee or Macleod or Cooper could have provoked fierce resentment and accusations of disloyalty to the Reformed tradition encountered little or no criticism: they were, indeed, welcomed by vast congregations of citizens and visitors as being not only appropriate to the setting but also well calculated both to edify and inspire.[14] What St. Giles' does today is not, of course, what the rest of Presbyterian Scotland will necessarily do, or even wish to do, tomorrow; but under Cameron Lees the worship of the High Kirk of Edinburgh clearly exerted an ever-increasing influence upon liturgical thought and practice throughout the country, and even those ministers who were least impressed could hardly afford to disregard it. In Cameron Lees, the liturgical revolution had become respectable; and the long campaign, begun in Greyfriars half a century before, could claim to have reached its goal at last.

Meanwhile, in the wake of individuals and societies, the official Church began to move – cautiously and slowly, because peace and unity must be preserved and no violence done to the guiding principles laid down by the first Reformers and the Westminster Divines. Some of the chief landmarks deserve notice. In 1856, the General Assembly enjoined all ministers to observe the recommendations of the Directory on the reading of Holy Scripture at each diet of public worship – an order which greatly encouraged those who felt that the sermon did not require supplementation by the lecture, and desired the full range of Biblical material to have its place, unannotated, in the services.[15] In 1859, after ten years' work, an Assembly Committee under Professor Crawford published *Prayers for Social and Family Worship,* a manual of devotion for church members in the remoter parts of Scotland, as well as in India and the Colonies, who might be cut off from the normal services of worship and thus obliged to conduct their own. Four years later, the book received Assembly recognition: the prejudice against read prayers (in the home, at least) was gradually being overcome.[16] Change came very slowly, however, and the Aids to Devotion Committee frequently complained of the general indifference to its work. The General Assembly, tacitly accepting what it felt unable to prevent and timidly encouraging where encouragement was scarcely needed, seemed content to lead its rather disordered regiments from behind – and the same was true of the supreme courts of the other Presbyterian denominations. Not until after the outbreak of the First World War did a full printed order of service (to be used on the first Sunday of the New Year) appear with Assembly approval; and it was as late as 1923 before *Prayers for Divine Service* was issued, for voluntary use, by its authority.

In praise, rather more progress (if that is the right word) could be reported – probably because a start had been made earlier. Improvements in church music can be traced as far back as the seventeen-fifties, and during the second half of the eighteenth century the gradual adoption of the paraphrases had breached the principle of using nothing but psalms in the worship of the sanctuary. That forward-looking body, the Relief Church, produced a hymn-book in 1794, and its daughter the United Presbyterian Church did the same in 1851. In 1870 the Auld Kirk authorised the *Scottish Hymnal* for optional use in church services. During the sixties, moreover, the use of pipe-organs had been successfully pioneered by Marshall Lang in Anderston, Glasgow, and by Robert Lee in Greyfriars, Edinburgh; and soon congregations were vying with each other to install them. This development, as its opponents had suspected, rapidly altered the whole scene so far as church praise was concerned, and spelt the demise of much more than the precentor. The Presbyterian Churches of Scotland had set their feet on the road which led to the production in 1898 of the *Church Hymnary* – a much more comprehensive and discriminating collection than any they had previously used – and of the *Metrical Psalter* a year later. If the Hymnary proclaimed the desire of Scottish churchmen to re-enter their Catholic heritage, the Psalter bore witness to their continuing pride in the Reformed tradition. Together, they may be regarded as a vivid expression of the ideals of the liturgical revolution, and proof of the solid achievements which stood to its credit at the close of the Victorian age.

There is a postscript to the story, however. Understandably, men of very diverse aims and opinions collaborated in the movement we have just examined: theological liberals of the stamp of Lee, Tulloch, Story and Caird; scholars bent on a recovery of what they considered best in the Reformed tradition, among whom George Sprott and Thomas Leishman were outstanding; "high church" men like William Milligan, John Macleod and James Cooper. In the closing decades of the nineteenth century these various groups began to draw somewhat apart from each other, and in 1892 the Scottish Church Society came into existence to further the views of the "Catholic" party among them.

What, then, were the motivating forces which impelled Professor William Milligan of Aberdeen and those who associated with him to act as they did? Obviously important was the feeling that aesthetic considerations had exercised too great an influence in some of the earlier "reforms" – even, on oocasion, to the extent of endangering theological orthodoxy. Also to be detected among the Society's leaders was a reaction against the extremer manifestations of theological liberalism and the literary and historical criticism of the Bible. Two further considerations, each related to events of the seventies and eighties, played their part in bringing the new Society into being. One was, quite simply, disquiet at certain aspects of the Moody-and-Sankey phenomenon; the other was the Disestablishment campaign which placed the Church of Scotland in constant jeopardy for the best part of a generation. (The ultimate loyalty of Milligan, Leishman, Cooper and the others was, of course, to the Church Catholic, not to the Church by Law Established; but the longer that agitation continued the more tempted they were to equate the two, denouncing the enemies of the state connection as sectarians and schismatics and praising its friends for their loyalty both to Evangelical Truth and Catholic Order.) So was born the Scottish Church Society, its stated aim being "to defend and advance Catholic Doctrine as set forth in the Ancient Creeds and embodied in the Standards of the Church of Scotland; and generally to assert Scriptural principles in all matters relating to Church Order and Policy, Christian Work, and Spiritual Life, throughout Scotland".[17]

A close scrutiny of the Society's constitution, as well as the utterances of its leaders, reveals three main areas of concern: the Church, the Ministry, and the Sacraments. First, the Church. Paragraph IV, subsection 1, calls for "The consistent affirmation of the divine basis, supernatural life, and heavenly calling of the Church", while subsections 2 and 21 advocate "The fostering of a due sense of the historic continuity of the Church from the first" and "The deepening of a penitential sense of the sin and peril of schism."[18] According to Scottish Church Society principles, the Church is not a merely natural phenomenon – a convenient meeting-place, as it were, for Christians in search of the best way to formulate their beliefs and order their actions. It has been brought into existence by God Himself through His gifts of Word, Ministry and Sacraments (all of them anterior to it), and is therefore a divine institution of Christ's own appointing. It is the "extension of the Incarnation" in human history, Christ's Body upon earth, in which men are supernaturally incorporated by Baptism and supernaturally nourished by Communion; the agent of His prophetic, priestly and kingly activity in the world. Outside it there is no salvation; separation from it – schism – is a deadly sin; and to seek the full recovery of its visible unity is a supremely important obligation upon Christians everywhere. The Christian, said H. J. Wotherspoon in 1895, "discerns the *Lord's* body; the Church which he sees is the representative to him in time and place of that. And as he sees, so he endeavours to order himself in relation to it."[19] With much – perhaps most – of this the majority of Scottish Presbyterians were doubtless in agreement. Yet when it was first enunciated they could not avoid a sneaking suspicion that somehow or other it blurred the old and tenaciously-held distinction between the visible and the invisible Church, demanding of men a more unquestioning loyalty to the existing institution and its ministers than they had any call to give. That suspicion probably did as much as anything to prevent the Society's ideals from reaping the harvest in Scottish opinion which might have been predicted for them in its early, confident springtime.

Second, the Ministry. Among the Society's aims its constitution mentions "The fostering of a due sense of the historic continuity of the Church from the first" and "The maintaining of the necessity of a valid Ordination to the Holy Ministry, and the celebration in a befitting manner of the rite of Ordination."[20] A doctrinal continuity with apostolic times was, of course, laid claim to by virtually every Scottish Presbyterian, in the nineteenth as in earlier centuries. But the men of the Scottish Church Society, like the Westminster Divines and a fair number of Scots thereafter, went a good deal further. In consequence of their ordination by presbyters, the apostles' designated successors in the Christian ministry, they also believed themselves to enjoy "a *lineal* succession from Christ" – and attached very considerable importance to it. "Our ministry", one of them quoted, approvingly, from a seventeenth-century authority, "is derived to us from Christ and His apostles by succession of a ministry contained in the Church for 1600 years."[21] No doubt there was something here which merited at least the respectful consideration of Presbyterians anxious to magnify their office in controversy with rival understandings of the ministry, Roman Catholic, Anglican or Independent. But it also betokened an unhealthy preoccupation with what was, to say the least, a questionable doctrine of the ministry and ministerial succession; smacked not a little of sacerdotalism; led to some slightly ridiculous *rencontres* with Anglicanism; and obscured the fact that in the Reformed Churches the *really* important succession is not of persons but of doctrine, and that it is the divine call (of which the people's call is a part), not the imposition of hands by the presbytery, which they regard as the only sure guarantee of grace.

Third, the Sacraments. Three key phrases in the Society's policy statement indicate its last main area of concern. Subsection 4 is entitled, "The assertion of the efficacy of the Sacraments"; subsection 5, "The promotion of the religious education and pastoral care of the young, on the basis of Holy Baptism"; and subsection 6, "The restoration of the Holy Communion to its right place in relation to the worship of the Church and to the spiritual life of the baptised."[22] It will be remembered how Knox and his colleagues in 1560 fiercely repudiated the slanderous suggestion that they held the sacraments to be "nothing else but naked and bare signs", declaring *per contra* their belief that "the faithful, in the right use of the Lord's Table, do so eat the body and drink the blood of the Lord Jesus, that He remaineth in them and they in Him".[23] To this "high" doctrine, which the Church of Scotland has never consciously repudiated (though Zwinglianism has at times made inroads in practice), the leaders of the new Society sought to recall their brethren; and at first sight there seemed to be nothing at all novel in what they had to say. Yet, as so often happens when reformers invite men to return to the old paths, the balance was altered in various subtle ways. It is doubtful whether classical Presbyterianism ever taught Baptismal Regeneration – but John Macleod certainly did. It is equally doubtful whether Presbyterians of an earlier day would have agreed with Cromarty Smith and others in their urgent stress upon *anamnesis* as the central aspect of the communion service. Their teaching on the eucharistic sacrifice, though impressive, cannot be acquitted of the charge of idiosyncrasy. And neither the first reformers nor any generation of their successors has been prepared to say without equivocation, as some of them did, that "[Communion] is not merely part of the worship, but it is the distinctive Christian worship which the Lord ordained. He did not ordain less than this, and He did not ordain more than this .... Weekly celebration is thus in accordance with the mind of the Lord."[24]

Despite all its eloquence and industry, therefore, the Scottish Church Society never quite persuaded more than a small minority of ministers to accept its sacramental teachings in full. Baptismal regeneration is still not orthodox doctrine; weekly Communion remains a rarity; Macleod's closely-argued teaching on the eucharistic sacrifice continues to be little known and little understood; receptionist views of Communion remain predominant; and the sermon still holds the central place in most Church of Scotland services. This is not, however, to say that the sacramental ideals of the Society were totally unrealised. As a result of its efforts, the tide of opinion undoubtedly began to flow in a new direction; the language used about both Baptism and the Lord's Supper, as well as the attitude generally adopted towards them within the Church of Scotland, approximated more and more closely to what Anglicans had long been familiar with; and the "Catholic" aspect of the Kirk came increasingly to the fore.

Looking back on the work of the Scottish Church Society in its most active period – the years since 1929 have been ones of relative quiescence – one is tempted to join Bishop Hensley Henson in his typically mordant description of it as "a small, unrepresentative group ... a small coterie of enthusiasts ... insignificant in number ... lukewarm Presbyterians".[25] But this would not be altogether fair or accurate. The Society failed, admittedly, in its attempts to have Scottish Episcopalianism included in the negotiations which led up to the 1929 Union of the Churches, to secure an official ban on the use of individual communion cups, and to incorporate the Nicene Creed in the ordination formula signed by all ministers of the Kirk (to mention a few of its favourite themes). Perhaps it also failed in its grand design of persuading Presbyterian Scotland to regard Catholic tradition and Scriptural principles as being in all points perfectly compatible with each other. Yet much was achieved. As Dr. Robertson contends, with almost the minimum of partisanship, "The Society exercised an influence out of all proportion to the size of its membership. In particular, it safeguarded the doctrine of the Ministry and the rite of Ordination; it stood for a full Biblical theology in a day of doubt and criticism; it engendered an ecumenical outlook within the Church of Scotland; it kept the vision of the Church Catholic before a Presbyterianism which was sometimes in danger of falling into a provincial and sectarian outlook; it gradually reminded the Church of the supreme importance of sacramental worship, and it was chiefly responsible for the Church's coming to view public worship primarily as an offering made to God."[26] Over and above all that, it helped to counter the liberalism of men like Tulloch and Caird, to strengthen the traditionally conservative position of Scotland on doctrinal matters, and to pave the way for that Biblicistic and Church-centred reaction in theology which is associated with the Barthian movement of the nineteen-twenties and thirties. There are not many ecclesiastical pressure groups of which as much could be said.

Notes to Chapter IV

1. A Gerard, *The Pastoral Care* (London, 1799), pp. 369–71.
2. R. Lee, *The Reform of the Church of Scotland in Worship, Government, and Doctrine. Pt. I Worship* (Edinburgh, 1866), p. 53.
3. R. H. Story, *Life and Remains of Robert Lee* (Edinburgh, 1870), vol. II, p. 57.
4. A. L. Drummond and J. Bulloch, *The Church in Victorian Scotland, 1843–1874* (Edinburgh, 1975), p. 213.
5. Story, *Lee*, vol. II, p. 287.
6. There is a detailed account in Story, *Lee*, vol. I, ch. 11 and vol. II, esp. chs. 2, 4, and 6–9. Cf. A. K. Robertson, "The Revival of Church Worship in the Church of Scotland. From Dr. Robert Lee (1804–1867) to Dr. H. J. Wotherspoon (1850–1930)" (Edinburgh University Ph.D. thesis, 1956), pp. 126–78.
7. Robertson, "Revival of Worship", p. 198.
8. J. Kerr, *The Renascence of Worship: The Origins, Aims, and Achievements of the Church Service Society* (Edinburgh, 1909), pp. 72 (for Constitution of Society) and 81.
9. ibid., pp. 74–83 (for Society's "Statement on Public Prayer") and 84–7 (for its note on "Proper Use of Euchologion"). Cf. W. D. Maxwell, *A History of Worship in the Church of Scotland* (London, 1955), p. 177.
10. Robertson, "Revival of Worship", pp. 234–5.
11. ibid., pp. 237–44, for a valuable brief account.
12. ibid., pp. 190–94.
13. ibid., pp. 195–7. H. J. Wotherspoon, *James Cooper* (London, 1926), esp. chs. 4–5.
14. Robertson, "Revival of Worship", pp. 185–9. N. Maclean, *Life of J. Cameron Lees* (Glasgow, 1922).
15. Maxwell, *History*, p. 175.
16. J. M. Barkley, "The renascence of public worship in Scotland", in D. Baker (ed.), *Renaissance and Renewal in Christian History* (Oxford, 1977), p. 341.
17. "Constitution of the Scottish Church Society", para III, in *Scottish Church Society Conferences: Second Series*, vol. II (Edinburgh, 1895), appendix.
18. ibid., para IV, 1, 2 and 21.

19. H. J. Wotherspoon, "The Revival of Churchmanship in Scotland", *S.C.S. Conferences: Second Series,* vol. II pp. 77–89.
20. "Constitution of the S.C.S.", para. IV, 2 and 3.
21. *Scottish Church Society Conferences: First Series* (Edinburgh, 1894), pp. 163 and 177.
22. "Constitution of the S.C.S.", para. IV, 4, 5 and 6.
23. G. D. Henderson (ed.), *The Scots Confession 1560* (Edinburgh, 1960), p. 75.
24. Robertson, "Revival of Worship", p. 334.
25. Quoted in Robertson, "Revival of Worship", p. 370.
26. ibid., p. 427.

V

The Social Revolution

By the end of the eighteen-thirties, Scotland had ceased to be an integrated, Christian community in any meaningful sense. Under the hammer-blows of industrialisation, the population explosion, and the growth of large towns, the old alliance of sacred and secular had broken down; and the mounting sectarianism of the Voluntary and the Ten Years' Conflicts, together with the influx of Catholic immigrants from Ireland after the famine, only intensified and speeded up the process. The time-honoured unities and sanctities would soon be no more. Gone were the days when all classes had assembled in tolerably harmonious unity within the walls of the parish kirk: the decay of Christian fellowship was manifest in the increasing alienation of the "lower orders" from every kind of religious faith and practice. With a few exceptions, the clergy were now religious specialists, detached by their single-minded Evangelical enthusiasm from the ideal of omnicompetence so dear to their Moderate predecessors. The faith had ceased to be the dominating, unifying force in the life of the people; and in the eyes of many religion was little more than a matter of personal predilection, a solace or a challenge to the individual rather than a rallying-point for all. Christian virtues might well provide an excellent foundation for success in business (and certainly were unlikely to put serious obstacles in its way), but they were now a private rather than a community concern. As has often been pointed out, Christian living had come to be seen as almost a part-time occupation, little related to the world of commerce and industry; and with the compartmentalisation of faith and ethics alike the old order had fallen apart.

Not surprisingly, this disintegration was accompanied by a fading of the belief – prominent in the first Book of Discipline, with its Calvinist overtones, but traceable much earlier than Knox – that the whole life of society should be shaped and guided by Christian standards. Various influences were responsible for the change, which began to be evident soon after the Revolution Settlement. Church leaders' critical faculties may have been blunted by the very fruitfulness of that alliance between Church and State which was refashioned in 1690 and, despite Jacobites, Episcopalians and Presbyterian Dissenters, flourished throughout the eighteenth century. The interests of the landowning and governing classes quite possibly carried too much weight with clergymen who were often either relatives or dependants of a local laird or a distant lord. A theology which numbered the laws of economics, as described by Adam Smith and Thomas Malthus, among the laws of nature (which were also the laws of God), could easily find itself exalting civil obedience as almost the supreme Christian duty. After all, had not St. Paul described the powers that be as ordained of God, adding the comment that "Whosoever therefore resisteth the power, resisteth the ordinance of God: and they that resist shall receive to themselves damnation"? At any rate, most Scottish churchmen at the outset of the nineteenth century not only accepted the existing order, political, social and economic, as having been divinely decreed, but felt bound actively to defend it with every weapon at their command. As for the disadvantaged, they were required to remember that no virtues are more praiseworthy than submission to one's superiors, patient endurance, and gratitude for mercies received.

By the time of Chalmers and Brewster the implications of these developments were becoming only too obvious. Concern for the unfortunate was no doubt as lively as ever, and philanthropic acts by individual Christians may even have been on the increase; but criticism of the system which had produced distress of such intensity and on so vast a scale was almost entirely absent. If Christian standards were applied to social and economic conditions, it was generally in peripheral rather than central matters. Indeed, it almost seems as if churchmen felt obliged to cultivate a kind of disdain for all things material, focusing as much of their attention as possible on things spiritual, which alone ultimately mattered. "We leave to others the politics and passions of this world",[1] said Chalmers in one of his most famous utterances; and during his last great crusade in Edinburgh's slumland he proudly assured the Countess of Effingham that he had "raised no fund and recommended no method for providing for the temporal wants of the inhabitants of the West Port – convinced that if this formed any ostensible part of our proceedings it would vitiate and distemper our whole system, and raise an insuperable barrier in the way of achieving a pure Christian and moral good among the families of our district".[2] Although such an attitude could be accompanied by great liberality and genuine compassion, it could also lead, with distressing frequency, to a strange blend of private piety and public callousness.

Furthermore, because a distinctively Christian approach to commerce, industry and the problems of community life was lacking, all tended to be given over to the mercies of contemporary economic theory. Like practically everyone else, churchmen believed that men pursuing their own self-interest would be led by an "invisible hand" to promote the general welfare; wages also, being determined by the immutable natural law of supply and demand, could not be altered either by government regulation or workers' protest. "With the dynamic power of the Gospel shackled by cast-iron economic dogmas," writes a modern commentator, "any effective Christian criticism of the existing economic order was virtually impossible. By 1830, with both its ultimate goals and the means required for their achievement left unquestioned by the Church, 'laissez-faire' capitalism was free to pursue its own natural course unhindered. So industry and commerce, subject only to autonomous economic laws, grew up largely motivated by self-interest with little social or moral concern."[3] What was already a potentially disastrous situation was made even worse by the fact that the outstanding preacher of the day, Thomas Chalmers, not only shared the prevailing view but – himself an enthusiastic writer on economic subjects – propagated it with all the energy and eloquence at his command. No wonder, therefore, that modern historians have tended to give him an almost uniformly bad press. "James Begg was once described by Rainy as the evil genius of the Free Church," observe Drummond and Bulloch, "but if any man can be called the evil genius, not merely of the Free Church but of all the Presbyterian Churches of Victorian Scotland, it might well be the much venerated Thomas Chalmers, so earnest and well meaning .... If the age would have listened to any prophetic voice, it would have been his, but Chalmers had so accepted the economics of Adam Smith that he gave something like a divine sanction to the consequences of uninhibited free enterprise. Here, of course, he was not alone, but unfortunately his influence was as great as his prestige was high. Victorian Scotland followed his lead."[4]

It is not difficult to discern some of the more important consequences of the Church's fateful capitulation to contemporary economic theory, and its abandonment of any distinctively Christian critique of the social order. Especially prominent (to twentieth-century eyes) was the almost total neglect of what we have learnt to call "the environmental factor" in social distress. A contributor 'to *The Witness* newspaper in 1841 probably spoke for most of his generation when he declared: "irreligion is the cause of this miserable state of things, and ... religion is the only cure."[5] In other words, early-Victorian Christians had fallen into the habit of reducing exceedingly complex political, social and economic problems to a simple matter of personal religion and personal morality; and the result was a tragic narrowing of vision. "Being insufficiently alive", says Donald Smith, "to the radical nature of the changes taking place in the whole fabric of social life, whereby a simple, agrarian, paternalistic society was being rapidly transformed into a complex, competitive, industrial one, the Church merely stressed with renewed emphasis in these decades the traditional moral virtues and values which were largely meaningless in the industrial context. She simply tried to moralise all the new social and economic relations by treating such transactions as a case of personal conduct, involving personal responsibility."[6]

Noticeable also was a trust in voluntary effort, and a reluctance to permit state intervention in industrial and commercial affairs. Such a trust was due partly to economic individualism, partly to the personal emphasis of contemporary theology. Best exemplified in Chalmers' rejection of anything save ecclesiastically-managed charity, it was widely shared. "Compulsory assessments ought to be regarded in the light of a moral evil," declared an article in *The Witness* for 1841. "The necessity for having recourse to them ought always to be deplored, and the time when they shall be general cannot be looked forward to without the utmost alarm. Let the means of religious instruction and moral training be multiplied in the land. Let the moral and religious condition of the population be thus elevated and the evil will be corrected at the source."[7] Even contrary evidence had little power to shake the views of those who were thus minded. The failure of Chalmers' West Port venture in the eighteen-forties had plainly demonstrated what Stewart Brown calls the "incapacity of voluntary effort"[8] to solve the problems of urban life; but it took another generation to desert the assumptions on which that venture had been based. Only in such matters as the provision of church buildings and the payment of ministers' stipends, the education of children and the elimination of moral offences like Sabbath-breaking and intemperance, did the survival of the old Establishment ideal encourage recourse to the Government for financial and legislative support. Otherwise, all was left to the free-lance effort of interested individuals.

Another distinguishable mark of early-Victorian churchmanship was a distrust of political democracy, and a consequent reluctance to favour the extension of the franchise. Among Tories especially – and in the opening decades of the century most ministers of the Church of Scotland (whatever might be true of Dissenters) belonged to that party – the advent of Reform in 1830–32 caused great unease. "It is truly lamentable", observed that mouthpiece of vital Evangelicalism, *The Edinburgh Christian Instructor,* "to see men excited even to ferocity on the subject of a reform in Parliament, while they are totally insensible to the glaring defects of their own character, and to their own urgent need of reform themselves. Of all the miserable objects and scenes that earth presents, there can be few more miserable than that of a man discussing the question of parliamentary reform with all the eagerness of an enthusiastic partisan, utterly unmindful the while of the squalid wretchedness of his wife and children, who are in want of the necessities of life while he goes to swell a reforming or anti-reforming mob."[9] Nor was the rising leader of the Evangelicals any more friendly. "At the first passing of the Reform Bill through the House of Commons", his son-in-law and biographer tells us, "there was a popular demand for an illumination in Edinburgh. Dr. Chalmers did not illuminate, and in common with many others had the windows of his house in Forres Street broken by the mob."[10] One suspects that he and others like him felt as the Duke of Wellington did when he wrote: "The revolution is made, that is to say that power is transferred from one class of society, the gentlemen of England, to another class of society, the shop-keepers, being dissenters from the Church, many of them Socinian, others atheists."[11] Moreover, even those churchmen and Dissenters who were supporters of the Act tended to look upon it as marking the extreme limit of concessions to the disfranchised, and valued it because it would *strengthen,* not destroy, the existing order.

The underlying unity of Whig and Tory churchmen in this matter was plainly shown by their common attitude to the Chartist demand for universal suffrage in the years after 1832. Young Norman Macleod, recently settled in the Ayrshire weaving parish of Loudoun, replied to a Chartist parishioner's query about his views on the "seven points" with this unequivocal assertion: "In my opinion, your principles would drive the country into revolution, and create in the long run national bankruptcy."[12] And only a few months later, in the summer of 1839, the even more youthful John Cairns, future leader of the United Presbyterians, wrote to his father from Edinburgh: "Next week there is to be what the Chartists call a 'glorious demonstration', i.e. a meeting of the simple-minded workingmen of this city to gaze at and applaud the selfish gang of English democrats who, under the lure of universal suffrage, are seeking to establish a community of property and to revolutionise the existing state of society. The people of Scotland appear as yet to have too much sense and education to go into so pernicious a scheme, which has been eagerly adopted by multitudes of ignorant and half-blackguard English working-people. In Edinburgh, at all events, as the late election showed, the party is as small in numbers as it is contemptible in point of respectability and talent, and its whole secret lies in frequent meetings and blustering placards couched in a style as pompous and magniloquent as if they meant, by giving everyone a vote, to alter the nature of human life, and free the whole kingdom in all time to come from 'all the ills that flesh is heir to.' I am truly sorry to see a well-meaning people deceived by their ridiculous promises, and the more so that they bring a scandal on the cause of true reform."[13] One suspects that for Cairns, as for Macleod and Chalmers and many lesser folk within the Churches, "true reform" consisted in a change of personal life-style rather than any movement of political emancipation.

Along with this distrust of political democracy went a not dissimilar view of economic democracy, which was regarded at best with scepticism and at worst with downright hostility. Here once again Chalmers is fairly typical. While holding the repeal of the anticombination laws to have been justified, he nevertheless considered the unions to be (in Laurance Saunders' phrase) "as intolerant and monopolistic as any of the old mercantile corporations".[14] As for strikes, his animus against them is clearly revealed in the remark that "employers will never be on so secure and kindly a footing with their workmen as when the latter have been taught by sad experience precisely to estimate how much they have to fear from any scheme of hostility against the interest of the former and how much it is they owe for admission and continuance in their service".[15] He expressed gratification at "the power which masters have of replacing those who have struck by other hands"; indicated that ringleaders should certainly be dismissed and their followers admitted "on less favourable terms than before"; and even suggested how an employer might recover damages from his striking employees.[16] All over Scotland, Chalmers' fellow-ministers were in agreement with him: their contributions to the First and Second Statistical Accounts reveal, we are told, that strikes are anathema to most of them, while "unions which are struggling both to organise themselves and to create a bargaining power are regarded as subversive of all authority".[17] In the light of all the evidence now available, it is hard not to endorse Donald Smith's depressing summary of how things stood, and his equally depressing summary of the consequences. "Churchmen", he writes, "taught the industrial workers to shun methods of combination as a means of bettering their social and economic condition. This they taught at the very time when the exploited workers' most crying need was, in fact, just such an instrument of power .... Not surprisingly, the democratically-inspired but politically and economically disinherited industrial worker, having been denied the sympathy much less the support of the Church – a Church which, unfaithful to her own Reformed social heritage, no longer championed the cause of the poor, the underprivileged, and the oppressed – turned increasingly to other agencies for support and leadership. Not a few came in this period to regard the Church as an arch-enemy hindering the social and economic advance of the workers."[18]

During the middle years of the century – in ecclesiastical terms, roughly from the Disruption in 1843 to the abolition of patronage in 1874 – there was no very perceptible alteration in the attitudes thus described. Churchmen, it is clear, still accepted the existing order with almost unquestioning complacency, still taught submission as the prime virtue of the disadvantaged. The greater part of Scotland's poverty and misery was still ascribed to human failings, moral and spiritual, and the rôle of the environment minimised or ignored. The assumptions and assertions of the classical economists were still endorsed, eagerly or with resignation. While the United Presbyterians were of a somewhat more liberal mind, there was continuing hostility within the Church of Scotland and the Free Church to popular democracy, and a marked lack of enthusiasm for the extension of the franchise in 1867. Trade Unions were still viewed with aversion and dislike. At the same time, however, changes were beginning to make their appearance, as may be gathered from a brief scrutiny of two prominent ministers of the period – one very much a middle-of-the-road man, the other a stormy petrel in almost everything and a radical in social matters.

William Garden Blaikie, the moderate, was minister of Pilrig Free Church, on the road between Edinburgh and Leith, from 1844 to 1868. He was professor of Pastoral Theology at New College from 1868 to 1897. He attained high eminence not only within the Free Church (of which he became Moderator in 1892) but throughout the Presbyterian world (becoming President of the Presbyterian Alliance in his moderatorial year). He was also a prolific writer, and much of what he wrote, especially in his earlier years, is redolent of the old order: paternalistic, otherworldly, wary of working-class assertiveness, eager to preach submission, careful to preserve the existing state of affairs in all its essentials. Viewing society as static and hierarchically organised, he remarked in *Better Days for Working People* that "all cannot be ladies and gentlemen; all cannot attain to a refined and easy mode of life; many must continue to be hard workers – hewers of wood and drawers of water".[19] He never failed to recommend personal virtue as the best way of improving society, and laid particular stress on temperance and education. "Working people", he wrote in "Six Lectures addressed to the Working Classes", "are sometimes apt to envy capitalists, and to speak very bitterly against them, as if they sinfully monopolised the comforts of life. But in what way have capitalists obtained their capital? Very generally by the plan now described. Industry, patience, self-denial, abstinence from expensive habits and indulgences, delay in entering on the matrimonial state, and other such means, have enabled them to accumulate a capital which has grown by degrees to gigantic dimensions. We know of several cases in point. The way is open for others to go and do likewise."[20] His description in *Better Days* of the ideal working man, with its pietistic overtones, might have been borrowed from his own most honoured teacher, Thomas Chalmers: "His days are usefully and creditably spent from the dawn of manhood to the close of active life; habits of patience, diligence and sturdy perseverance grow with his growth and strengthen with his strength; a thoughtful and affectionate regard for the welfare of his family secures peace and prosperity at home; a course of economy and forethought protects him from the disasters that overwhelm the careless and improvident; the consolations of Christianity mitigate his sorrows and brighten his blessings; no turbulence or lawlessness is associated with his career; his life, simple though it be, is rich with domestic joys and inward tranquillity; and when his sun goes down it leaves a glory behind, and the certainty that it will rise again and shine in a brighter firmament."[21] Of strikes (which he dealt with at length in his "Six Lectures") Blaikie had little good to say. They were permissible but not expedient, "and although it may be true that they have raised the rate of wages ... this might have been accomplished otherwise, while undoubtedly they have been productive of very serious moral evils".[22] As for any good which might derive from working-class involvement in political affairs, his expectations here were small indeed. "Experience shows", he wrote, "that if they can possibly keep aloof from such questions it is better to do so."[23]

At the same time, signs of a more liberal perspective are not entirely absent from Blaikie's writings – and his actions. There were limits to his satisfaction with things as they were. "When I came to Edinburgh", he tells us in his memoirs, "and became familiar with the life of the working classes, I could not but feel its conditions were unsatisfactory in some respects .... I always thought that their earnings should be more than they were, and even than they are at the present day. For undoubtedly, though labour is not the only source of wealth, and of the comforts which wealth brings, it is one of the principal sources, and it seems to me unnatural that the class that expend so much physical labour should have the least comfortable life."[24] He was prepared to question, if not to reject, the economic dogmas of the day. "What is a fair day's wage?", he asked in *Better Days,* and observed that "Political

Economy has *its* ready answer …. Wages, we are told, must depend on the law of supply and demand." But after commenting that "As a general principle, this is doubtless correct," he went on to say: "It is still a question whether the law of supply and demand is a purely self-regulating one, whether it can be trusted to adjust itself, or whether it may not require at times a little artificial pressure – the kind of pressure which is supplied by combinations and strikes – to determine what the relation of demand to supply is at the time, what is the highest sum that employers can give, and the lowest that workmen will accept?"[25] He was alert to the pressing problem of material conditions, remarking in his early "Six Lectures" (1849) that "Houses scarcely fit for the brute creation are all that many of them [the working classes] have for shelter; and it is only within the last few years that attention has been turned to the necessity of so providing for the healthfulness of districts where they cluster, as to prevent their being mowed down in scores and hundreds by the ravages of disease."[26] He was less furiously opposed to Chartism than many of his contemporaries. "That they [the working classes] ought to have the suffrage", he tells us in his autobiography, "seemed to me perfectly true" – though he adds the qualification, "but that it would bring all that was hoped for from it, I greatly doubted."[27] Though deeply critical of most forms of industrial action, he was (like his mentor Chalmers, and probably for the same *laissez-faire* reasons) a believer in the legitimacy of "combinations" and a supporter of men's right to strike when dissatisfied with pay or conditions.[28]

Still more important, Blaikie's active concern for better working-class housing set him apart from most of his fellows. Like his nearby colleague, the Reverend William Mackenzie of North Leith Free Church, he believed that one-roomed houses (which were then exceedingly common) made it impossible to fulfil the dominical command, "When thou prayest, enter into

thy closet and shut the door." Along with some business and
professional friends he therefore brought about the founding of
an Association whose object was to erect a number of
"improved dwellings" for artisans, each with its own front
door, a plot of garden ground, and "the various conveniences
of a self-contained house". The first row of these, near Leith
Walk, was completed in 1849, the fourth and last in 1862 –
62 houses in all, with an average rent of £7 to £10; and
valuable recognition came when Lord Ashley visited the
scheme in 1850 and suggested the title, promptly adopted, of
Pilrig *Model* Dwellings. Although the properties were disposed
of by the Association in the eighteen-nineties, the idea had
caught on from the beginning; and various similar enterprises
stemmed from it, notable among them being the Edinburgh
Co-operative Building Company of 1861.[29] Despite all its
limitations, both in conception and in execution, Blaikie's work
for improved housing may be looked on as one of the earliest
signs among Victorian churchmen of a determined will to
better the material circumstances of the working classes in
Scotland. In its small way it quite probably marked the turning
of the tide which had been on the ebb for several generations.

If the coming revolution in social attitudes can be dimly
descried in Blaikie's ministry, it is clearly discernible in that
of his contemporary, James Begg – a man whose reputation
for contentiousness has unfortunately obscured his other (and
more creditable) claims to fame. A disciple of Stevenson
McGill at Glasgow University and Chalmers at Edinburgh,
Begg made his first on-the-spot encounter with gross economic
deprivation during his period as assistant minister at North
Leith from 1829 to 1830. It is perhaps noteworthy that one of
the four parishes to which he ministered between then and the
Disruption was in Paisley, simultaneously the scene of Patrick
Brewster's labours. Only in 1835, however, with his
presentation to Liberton, near Edinburgh, did he begin to
manifest a lively interest in social questions; and the full

flowering of his concern had to wait until, after his adherence to the Free Church, he took charge of its Newington congregation in 1843.

As early as 1841, Begg helped to form the Edinburgh Association for Improving the Lodging Houses of the Working Classes, which opened its first establishment in the West Port some three years later and followed that up with two others before the end of the decade.[30] In 1846, he became a founder-member of the Scottish Patriotic Society, set up to alleviate social distress by "improving dwellings, increasing sanitary regulations, and establishing local funds for assisting industrial workers under temporary difficulty".[31] In 1849, he secured the free opening of the East Meadows as a bleaching green and recreation area for the poor of the capital – and thereby won a battle which he had been waging with the great Lord Cockburn on "How to Promote and Preserve the True Beauty of Edinburgh".[32] During the late forties, and subsequently, he conducted a vigorous campaign (his journalistic and pamphleteering gifts were considerable) on behalf of the Early Closing and Saturday Half Holiday movements.[33] In 1850, he not only gave his support to the National Education Association of Scotland's campaign for a truly national, non-sectarian educational system: he also provided the newly-constituted Scottish Social Reform Association with an impressive eight-point charter, which included better dwellings for the poor, public wash-houses and bleaching greens, reform of the land laws, and greater parliamentary justice for Scotland among its demands.[34] During the years immediately thereafter, he conducted an energetic campaign for extension of the Scottish franchise to include 40/- freeholders, contributing a pamphlet entitled "Scotland's Demand for Electoral Justice".[35] He called for the spread of small-holdings and the abolition of the antiquated laws of entail and primogeniture; agitated against the evils of the "feeing markets" which were traditional in country districts; and by his support for rural housing improvements succeeded in alienating such distinguished landlords as Lord Dalhousie and Lord Kinnaird.[36] On several occasions from 1857 onwards he lectured to the influential Social Science Association.[37] In the early sixties, he was one of those who secured the appointment of the first Officer of Health for the city of Edinburgh – Dr. Littlejohn, whose 1865 Report was a landmark in the sanitary improvement of the capital.[38] In the late sixties, he was much involved in the work of the newly-founded Association for Improving the Condition of the Poor, and in June 1869 the *Daily Review* observed that "Dr. Begg's evidence before the Poor-Law Committee [of the House of Commons] is certainly the most valuable – we had almost said the only valuable – evidence which the Committee has yet got."[39]

Chief among the objects of Begg's wide-ranging social concern was the housing of the underprivileged in both town and country. As early as 1849, after investigating the condition of the wynds and closes off Edinburgh's High Street, he wrote a series of letters to *The Witness* in which he drew attention to the overcrowding, lack of sanitary provision, disease, drunkenness and extreme poverty to be found there – a state of affairs so distressing (by his way of it) that the very pigs on his glebe, "luxuriating in clean straw and breathing the pure air of heaven", were "gentlemen in comparison" with those who had to endure it.[40] In 1861, following upon some twenty years of propaganda in favour of home ownership by the working classes, he helped to form the Edinburgh Co-operative Building Association and laid the foundation-stone of its first house at Stockbridge. (By 1865, some 200 houses had been built, accommodating over 1,000 people; by 1872, the number had passed 900.)[41] A recent student of Begg's work has claimed that he was more responsible than anyone else for the insertion of a column on housing in the 1861 Census form;[42] and certainly the facts elicited thereby provoked him to one of his most telling indictments. "There are thus in Scotland", he told readers of his *Happy Homes for Working Men and How to Get Them* (1866), "no fewer than 7,964 houses – if they can be called houses – without windows! and 226,723 houses of only *one apartment*; proving that nearly one million of the people of Scotland – or *nearly one-third of the entire population – are living in houses* – places improperly so called – in which neither the comforts nor decencies of life can be secured, and which are thus totally unfit for human habitations. This one fact, were there no other, affords a sufficient explanation of almost any amount of moral and social evil which may be found to prevail .... The dreadful and extensive nature of the evil with which we have to grapple in Scotland is thus beyond all doubt. The only question which really exists is, how to remedy it."[43]

Not the least of Begg's achievements was his success (admittedly only partial) in awakening his own denomination to the problems of a new society. One sign of this was the setting-up of the Free Church's Committee on Social Evils in 1859. It lasted a mere two years, but its brief reports nevertheless indicated a slightly more open mind. Another sign was the creation in 1860 of the Free Church's Committee on the State of Religion and Morals. Despite its somewhat restricted understanding of morals, this committee's activities signal the onset of the age of reports, digests and statistics; and in the seventies it began to include social as well as strictly religious matters among its concerns. Still more significant was the Committee on Working-Class Housing, established by the Free Church at Begg's instigation in 1858. The criticisms made of this body by modern historians are many. It seems to have been more exercised about the dangers of the so-called "bothy system" in country districts than about the vastly greater distress of the urban slums. Perhaps it opposed some social evils more because they put obstacles in the way of evangelisation than simply because they were evils. It was strongly averse (the Chalmers legacy!) from any form of state intervention – and so while enabling the better-off to help themselves left the really destitute in much the same plight as before. And in any case the General Assembly discharged it in 1867 on the surprising grounds that "public attention was thoroughly alive on the subject". Clearly, over-enthusiastic claims should not be made for it, though there may be little exaggeration in describing it as the precursor of a more sensitive social awareness in all the Presbyterian Churches of Scotland.[44]

As for Begg himself, no exceptional discernment is required to see him as Patrick Brewster's true-born successor, the Elisha to his Elijah. With him, the heirs of the Scottish Reformation began – slowly and hesitantly – to adopt something of the old prophetic attitude to society. His services to Church and community (as we have seen) were many. But there can be little doubt that the greatest consisted in reminding his fellow-Christians of the intimate connection between sacred and secular, spiritual and material, and of the dangers threatening any body of men who dared to separate them. In the preface to his pamphlet on "Pauperism and the Poor Laws", published as early as 1849, he remarked how "Various opinions have prevailed in regard to the true origin of such evils [i.e. pauperism and crime], some tracing them exclusively to moral, and others to physical causes." He then continued: "The truth is, that they spring from both, which plainly act and react on each other. Moral degradation leads to physical, and physical again plunges its unhappy victims into deeper moral debasement, and both causes working together soon destroy the very foundations of the social fabric." In the same preface he also declared that "He must be a hard-hearted minister who does not sympathise with the temporal sufferings and difficulties of his people at such a time as this ... and he a very ignorant minister who knows not that it is his duty to 'do good to all men as he has opportunity', and that in the very temporal prosperity of his people the absence of many obstacles in the way of his work, and their ability to aid in advancing the cause of God, are essentially involved. The statesmanlike Presbyterians of the past, Knox and George Buchanan, Henderson, Rutherford, and Carstares, Chalmers with his civic economy, and Duncan with his Savings' banks, all knew this, although it may be a mystery to some of our smaller men."[45] In 1853 he made a similar statement, drawing from it what was to him the obvious conclusion. "The earlier class of Protestant ministers, including the reformers, were sensitively alive to the connection between things temporal and spiritual", he wrote to *The Witness*. "But we have passed through a cold period since, and a mawkish notion of spirituality has led many of our modern ministers to stand aloof from all such movements, and allow the people to be gradually enslaved. This, again, is naturally breaking out in a contempt for religion itself, and a profanation of the day of rest. Nothing could tend more to sweeten the breath of society, and protect the day of God, than for every minister at present to throw his influence into the movement in favour of the Saturday half-holiday and all similar movements on the part of the working classes."[46] Until other and less happy crusades engaged his energies, Begg's ministry was dominated by these convictions.

The story of the revival of prophetic social criticism within the Scottish Churches may, broadly speaking, be divided into three main phases. The first, which lasted from the eighteen-fifties through to the end of the eighteen-seventies, had as its principal feature an increasing awareness of the gravity of the problems confronting Church and State alike – though it provided little evidence of agreement concerning the methods whereby these problems might be tackled. The second, which spanned the eighteen-eighties and nineties, saw a continuance of analysis and diagnosis; but now there seems to have been a good deal more clarity about what should be done, and evidence of fresh, almost revolutionary attitudes is not hard to find. The third, that tumultuous period which extended from around the beginning of the twentieth century to the outbreak (or even the close) of the First World War, revealed that while older ways of thinking still persisted they were indubitably in retreat: both Churches and individual Christians had abandoned the positions once so passionately defended by Chalmers and his entire generation, and the approach which we have associated with the names of Brewster and – in lesser or greater degree – Blaikie and Begg was clearly and dramatically in the ascendant. This three-phased development now falls to be examined.

While the eighteen-thirties and forties had been largely preoccupied with the exultations and agonies of the conflicts between Voluntaries and Establishment men, Intrusionists and Non-Intrusionists, Assembly and Court of Session, Free Church and Church of Scotland, the ensuing decades presented churchmen with more down-to-earth – and perhaps more recalcitrant – problems. Sometimes in the background, but oftener brought painfully to the fore by personal experience or the eloquent reports of men like Begg or Thomas Guthrie, were the fearsome conditions prevalent throughout the cities and larger towns of Scotland. Sexual immorality, intemperance, ignorance, destitution and criminality, all distressingly resistant to the efforts of a host of missionaries and philanthropists and all on a scale which numbed the imagination and inhibited action, seemed (if anything) to increase rather than diminish with each successive decade. "This, Sir, is a wonderful place", wrote Chalmers of Glasgow in 1815, and went on to express his desire "to establish it as a doctrine that the life of a town minister should be what the life of a country minister might be, that is, a life of intellectual leisure, with the *otium* of literary pursuits, and his entire time disposable to the purposes to which the Apostles gave themselves wholly, that is, the ministry of the word and prayer."[47] Thirty years later, the wonders of the city were perhaps harder to seek, and an effective ministry even more difficult to exercise. Only the blind could continue in complacency, and one senses a kind of desperation behind the steady flood of analyses and reports. Was there perhaps no answer to the condition-of-Scotland question?

But the gravity and persistence of social distress was not the only troublesome aspect of the mid-Victorian scene. There was, for one thing, the gradual overrunning by secular influence and state control of various provinces once securely within the Church's empire. Whatever else might be said about the Poor Law Amendment Act of 1845 (and it would be hard to balance advantages and disadvantages), there is no denying that it took exclusive responsibility for the care of the poor out of Church hands – thus ending a system which went back at least to the Reformation. Nor were developments in education any less disturbing. Donald Withrington has recently recalled how "debates in parliament on a new education bill in 1869 – 71 made it increasingly plain that there might well no longer be any formal provision for, and no safeguard for, the teaching of religion and no statutory connection with the Established or any other church"; and he goes on to remark that "only a last-minute amendment introduced a clause into the 1872 Education Act which made any positive reference to religious instruction – that it might be taught, under restrictions, according to 'use and wont'". Of course, it has also to be remembered (as the same writer puts it) that "for all the forebodings of these years, the school boards were to give religion a securer place and the churches a more effective influence under a state system than either had enjoyed in the schools for decades".[48] But Drummond and Bulloch point us to a thought-provoking comment made by A. E. Taylor in his Gifford Lectures, *The Faith of a Moralist*. "It may quite well be", he wrote, "that the future philosophical students of history will yet find the most significant and disquieting of all the social changes of the 'Victorian age' to be the combination of universal state-enforced primary education with the transference of the work of the teacher to the hands of laymen under no effective ecclesiastical or theological control. The effect of this successful laicisation of education has inevitably been to raise the immediate practical question whether moral conduct, the direction of life, does not form a self-contained domain, and ethics a wholly autonomous science, neither requiring support or completion from religion, nor affording rational grounds for religious convictions of any kind. The gravity of this practical issue can hardly be exaggerated."[49] Moreover, no sooner had the education issue been settled than the repeal of patronage helped to touch off the formidable Disestablishment campaign which kept the Auld Kirk in a constant state of apprehension almost to the end of the century.

Still more worrying was that "indifference" to religion, manifested above all in non-attendance at church, which had been worrying ministers and concerned laymen ever since the onset of the industrial revolution. Their instinctive reaction had been either to provide new sanctuaries for unchurched or under-churched areas (as in the Church Accommodation campaigns of Chalmers in the eighteen-thirties or Robertson in the eighteen-forties and fifties) or to conduct "missions" to needy districts like Fountainbridge in Edinburgh or the Wynds in Glasgow. Neither proved really effective, despite the generosity and sacrificial devotion which went into them. One Free Church leader, Robert Buchanan, admitted in 1851 that "all the ministers and churches that have been added during the last thirty years would not have more than sufficed to overtake the religious destitution which existed in the city of Glasgow twenty years ago" – though he still put his faith in the old remedies. "I know of nothing that will do", he continued, "but the scheme which Knox devised at the Reformation, and which Chalmers laboured to restore in our own day. Churches and schools upon the parochial or territorial system will, by God's blessing, give us back a humanised and christianised population in the outfields of our city, and nothing else will."[50] By the eighteen-seventies, however, it had become incontrovertibly clear that to rectify the maldistribution of churches and the underprovision of "sittings" within them was not to solve the problem. A fundamentally new approach seemed to be required; and at long last signs began to appear of a change of mind and heart within the mainstream Churches.

This change showed itself in various ways. For one thing, Scottish Christians could no longer be accused of regarding purely social issues as beneath their consideration or patient of simplistic solutions. "It is certainly the case", says Withrington in the article already quoted, "that the eighteen-sixties saw the publication of more direct and public comment on social problems than before: churchmen responded to pleas to speak out more plainly and clearly against sexual promiscuity, especially in the upper and middle classes; church-going manufacturers were instructed that their Christian purpose should extend to the weekday factory as much as to Sabbath attendance on ordinances; there was more concern for prevention of crime and redemption of criminals, especially young offenders, than for their punishment alone; there was questioning yet again of the principles behind a poor relief which appeared to cost more and more; there was a greater readiness to listen to complaints that the churches were too often run by the upper and middle classes *for* the upper and middle classes."[51] At the same time, the mounting anxiety, the thirst for reliable facts about the situation, and the willingness to undertake a thoroughgoing reappraisal of long-accepted tactics and strategy, all combined to produce a perfect flood of enquiries and surveys. Beginning perhaps with the comments elicited by the Religious Census returns in 1851, these reached a climax in the numerous questionnaires sent out from 1870 onwards by the Church of Scotland's newly-founded Life and Work Committee – as well as in the debates which that committee's annual reports precipitated at Assembly level and elsewhere.

It is possible that churchmen were becoming better-informed than ever before. They were also, apparently, growing less doctrinaire, more ready to consider practical, down-to-earth remedies for improving the situation: the revitalising of kirk sessions, for example, and the greater involvement of ordinary members in congregational life. Above all, they displayed a more open-minded and humble spirit. Was the cause of Scotland's ills (they began to ask themselves) not to be found, at least in part, within the walls of the Churches – in their class structure, their class bias, their insensitivity to the moral issues raised by uncontrolled *laissez-faire* capitalism, and so on? "Are the churches", asked the author of a treatise on *The Ecclesiastical and Religious Statistics of Scotland,* published in 1874, "capable of dealing successfully with the great moral and social and religious evils which now threaten to sap the foundations of society? ... Are the churches in Scotland mere conservative institutions existing for themselves and for the salvation of individual souls, or do they exist for the salvation of society and for the sweetening and sanctifying of all relations: between man and man as well as between man and God?"[52]

This analytical, self-questioning mood continued and even intensified during the last two decades of the century – at least partly because of dramatic changes in the world outside the Churches. Britain was a much tenser, more conflict-ridden society in late-Victorian times than it had been during the so-called "age of equilibrium" between the collapse of Chartism in 1848 and the advent of Gladstone's first ministry in 1868. Economic growth was slowing down, both absolutely and in comparison with our overseas rivals. The problem of urban poverty seemed no nearer solution, and class animosities were if anything more bitter. Working-class expectations of better days may still have been very great, but repeated disappointments had produced a certain disillusion, which was only magnified by the onset of mass democracy, the spread of literacy after the Education Acts of 1870 and 1872, and the rise of a cheap press. The unions became more militant. Socialist theories exercised a stronger appeal among both workers and middle-class intellectuals than at any time since the days of Robert Owen. The possibility of a working-class party was about to be realised: in 1888 the Scottish Labour Party came into existence, and in 1892 Keir Hardie entered Parliament. Everywhere there were signs of a growing awareness of the influence of the environment upon the individual, a growing openness to state intervention on behalf of the poor, the sick, the old and all the disadvantaged in society. Rejected by Alfred Marshall and many others, the classical economics was on its way out, yielding to an appreciation of the fact that the interests of the individual and of society as a whole did not necessarily coincide, and that the State might often be required to impose limits upon the exercise of irresponsible freedom. Against such a background, the Church's change of mind and heart can be readily understood.

In some respects, indeed, there was greater cause for unease than ever before. The misery and despair of those at the bottom of the social heap were such that Robert Howie – hinting darkly at a London or Glasgow Commune on Parisian lines – could warn the Free Church Assembly in 1871 of "a population growing up with tendencies that might ... give trouble to them as patriots as well as Christian men".[53] It was also beginning to be realised that men who were now able to read for themselves, in literature of their own choosing, were unlikely to listen with traditional respect to the pronouncements of their elders and betters, the clergy included. Church-going and church membership were being adversely affected by the tendency of those who had risen in the social scale to take with them the attitudes and practices of their previous class rather than adopt (as formerly) the attitudes and practices of the class above them. The birth rate of the more steady and prosperous families, from which all the Presbyterian Churches in Scotland drew a high proportion of their members, was apparently declining faster than the birth-rate of the poorer classes who had lapsed into paganism in the early stages of the Industrial Revolution: a fact with ominous implications for the future. Nor did the enquiries of the Church of Scotland's Life and Work Committee add much brightness to the picture. "Out of 706 parishes in a population of 1,354,084 which replied by 1874", report Drummond and Bulloch, "the Church of Scotland had 679,488 members and adherents, but only 174,371 had actually been present at communion in the year .... Total neglect of Christian ordinances was exceedingly rare in the country districts, but standards of membership were low. Large numbers in the city had no contact with the Church. Many nominal members were seldom at Church and it was observed that ministers were more concerned with them than with the lapsed masses. In some instances baptism was celebrated only as a mark of social respectability .... Standards of giving were very low, and not always because of poverty. Rural morals were 'lamentable'."[54] Most alarming of all, things seemed on the whole to be getting worse rather than better. "They are departing," Marshall Lang of the Barony told the Synod of Glasgow and Ayr in 1887, "men in thousands and tens of thousands .... The drift is representative of different attitudes of mind – the hostility of some types of socialism, the infidelity championed by Bradlaugh, the stolid indifference of practical if not theoretic agnosticism, the brutalized feeling of the drunkard, the hopelessness of the unfortunate. But at one point all these attitudes meet: people decline to enter within the gates of any ecclesiastical society. In Scotland we are all asking, what is to be done?"[55]

At the same time, most Church leaders were now not only

aware of the gravity of the situation but prepared to abandon time-honoured prejudices in order to cope with it. The outstanding instances of this preparedness probably come from the Auld Kirk's Glasgow presbytery, where men like Marshall Lang and Donald Macleod brought about a whole series of reports and debates on bad housing and its religious implications. The Church, declared the 1888 report on *Non-Church-going and the Housing of the Poor,* must undertake the task of creating a new and healthier attitude on such matters: "It has to teach that it has more to do for these so-called 'lapsed masses' than to assault them with armies of district visitors and to shower upon them tracts and good advices, while we are leaving them to swelter in dens and under conditions where Christian life is difficult, if not impossible, to realise."[56] As Donald Withrington has commented, "We are here a long way from the 1860's", in which the prevailing view had been that "If the lower orders occupied an unfairly weak position in the battle, their depressed state was not of their own making but the way out of it most certainly was; the churches' task was to stand by and to shout encouragement to them". Now, by contrast, Lang and Macleod and David Watson and others believed that "environmental factors and not personal sinfulness lay behind immoral, irreligious, unsocial behaviour of all kinds, and the churches must remove or help to remove the environmental problems before evangelisation had any hope of success."[57]

Parallel developments of equal importance were taking place in the theological realm. Not all would agree with Donald Smith's dictum that Westminster Calvinism had been, during the greater part of its existence, "a natural and loyal ally of economic individualism and 'laissez faire', and a most effective sanctifier of the social and economic *status quo".*[58] But there can be little doubt that the decline of the old theology was accompanied by the rise of a more humane, less deterministic world-view, and a preference for "practical

Christianity" rather than theological rectitude. An outstanding example of this was William Denny the Glasgow shipbuilder. Having rejected the Calvinism of his youth with the exclamation, "Rather atheism than belief in such a God", Denny contrasted Christ's teaching "that selfishness is death" with the older economists' teaching "that selfishness is salvation". He also declared that the newer outlook was destined to produce "changes which will be as evident in the form of society as in the individuals composing it."[59]

Of the various influences which helped in the making of the emergent Liberal Theology, two would seem to have had special significance for the change in social attitudes. The first was a rediscovery of the Hebrew prophets and their distinctive emphasis on communal as well as individual righteousness. Several Old Testament scholars might be mentioned in this connection, but outstanding was George Adam Smith, successively minister of Queen's Cross church, Aberdeen, professor in the Glasgow College of the Free Church, and – from 1909 until his retirement in the nineteen-thirties – principal of the University of Aberdeen. In his Lyman Beecher Lectures at Yale in 1899 (published under the title *Modern Criticism and the Preaching of the Old Testament*), Smith repeated what he had long been saying about "the civic preaching of the prophets". He then continued: "To go into detail ... would amount to an exposition of the larger part of the books of Amos, Hosea, Isaiah, Micah and Jeremiah. Let these four general statements suffice. *First,* the careers of the Prophets were contemporary with the development of Hebrew society from an agricultural to a commercial condition, and with the rise of the City. The social evils, therefore, with which the Prophets deal, are those still urgent among ourselves. *Second,* the Prophets, while inculcating, from God's treatment of the nation, tenderness and pity in the nation's treatment of their poor and enslaved, dwell with still greater emphasis upon the need of justice and equity. We enjoy a legal freedom and justice far beyond those of the Oriental society which the Prophets addressed; but no man can deny the frequent want of honour and equity among us in such social relations as are outside of the laws. *Third,* the Prophets, when enforcing religious observances and institutions, do so most frequently for social ends, or with regard to the interests of the poorer classes of the community. And fourth, there is the emancipation of the individual from a *merely* national religion .... There could not be preaching more relevant to the conditions and temptations of our own life."[60]

The second ingredient in the Liberal Theology of the eighteen-eighties and eighteen-nineties was a concentration upon the so-called "historical Jesus" and His teaching about the Kingdom of God. Here again many Scottish scholars were involved, but none more prominently than A. B. Bruce, professor of Apologetics and New Testament Exegesis in the Glasgow College of the Free Church from 1875 until his death in 1899. Bruce's concern with the message of the Kingdom is evident throughout his writings, but one particularly striking example occurs in a Sunday evening lecture which he delivered in both Dundee and Aberdeen during 1885. After remarking that "The term *kingdom* conveys the idea that Christianity is a social thing", Bruce went on to indicate the improvements which would follow if the standard of the Kingdom of God were applied to modern society. "We should", he declared, "no longer see human beings treated as if after all a man were not so valuable as a sheep, an ox or a horse; half-starved in a wealthy land, housed like swine, regarded simply as labour-drudges, their life of no consequence, seeing when they die their places can easily be supplied from an over-stocked labour market. Thank God there are many among us of all ranks and occupations to whom such a state of things appears intolerable, and who will not rest until remedies or amelioration have been found. Let the doctrine of the Kingdom only have time to work, and eventually it will leaven the whole lump."[61]

The important thing about the use of Biblical insights in the cause of social reform is, of course, that whereas ecclesiastical conservatives might shrug off the comments of politicians and sociologists they found it more difficult to ignore views professedly based on what all good Presbyterians acknowledged to be the Church's ultimate authority – its "supreme rule of faith and life". It was only a matter of time, therefore, before the views of scholars like Smith and Bruce were being echoed in sermons delivered up and down the land, and social criticism of a quite radical and far-reaching kind became almost commonplace within the Churches of Scotland.

Of the large Presbyterian denominations, it was the smallest – the United Presbyterian Church – which proved most responsive to the new mood. Although no very remarkable pronouncements emanated from its supreme governing body, the Synod, Donald Smith's thoroughgoing investigation of the periodical literature of the time has revealed just how advanced *The United Presbyterian Magazine,* its official publication, could be. "Editorially", he reports, "this journal continued its earlier support for progressive extension of the franchise in the direction of full democracy. It was a strong supporter of the Reform Bill of 1884 and of Chamberlain's Liberal Radicalism against the less advanced Liberals ... it criticised the proposals of the 1884 Bill for not giving the vote to women householders ... of all the Scottish ecclesiastical publications, it was the only one which condemned and opposed Britain's participation in the Boer War .... When the tragic City of Glasgow Bank failure took place in 1878, it denounced – to a much greater extent than the other Church journals – the dishonesty and fraud of the directors, many of whom were prominent Church members, and raised some searching questions about the ethical validity of many business practices."[62] Smith also notes that (judging by the radical character of many articles contributed by U.P. ministers and laymen to this and other religious periodicals of the time) "a remarkable change had taken place in the social attitudes and outlook of large numbers of U.P. churchmen in the closing years of the last century".[63]

Perhaps the most impressive exemplar of the change was Scott Matheson, who ministered in Alloa, Liverpool, Claremont church, Glasgow, and Dumbarton between 1862 and 1909, and published two substantial volumes, *The Gospel and Modern Substitutes* in 1890 and *The Church and Social Problems* in 1893. The second in particular is a remarkable piece of work, revealing the author to be very widely read in the economic and sociological literature of the time, as well as a sensitive and percipient thinker. For the Church to interest itself in social matters, argued Matheson, would accord with the needs of the time, put it in line with emergent democracy, uphold the best traditions of its history, restore the lost function of prophecy, bring out the ethical emphases of the Gospel and the teaching of the Kingdom, and counteract the commercialism of the age. At the outset of his comprehensive survey of such diverse subjects as land reform, hours and wages, housing, sweating, child rescue, the place and influence of women, and the co-operative movement he set a passionate statement on "The Duty of the Church in relation to Social Problems" which may be taken as typical of the committed radicalism to be found within the U.P. Church at the end of the nineteenth century. "It is a complaint among the people", he wrote, "that the Church has fallen out of step with them, and that the primary question is not a non-churchgoing community but a non-going Church – a Church too much at its ease in Zion, talking a theology they cannot understand, and neglecting a philanthropy they can well appreciate but do not behold. It is not necessary to exaggerate the gulf between the Church and the working classes; they form the élite of many a Christian congregation; but on the whole they have got to think that the Church is on the side of the strong against the weak, of the capitalist against the labourer, of the rich

against the poor; and they resent being put off with promises
of justice and happiness in another world .... The Church is to
see God's will done on earth as it is in heaven, and part of
that will is to grapple with social wrongs, abolish poverty, and
join in all lawful efforts to obtain for labour its due reward,
and for the toilers a larger degree of amenity in their lot."[64]

The spirit of change so manifestly at work among the
United Presbyterians was perhaps less obvious in the Free
Church. Its General Assembly, being deeply involved in
theological controversy throughout the eighties and nineties,
did not (with a few exceptions) give considered attention to
social issues, and the tone of its official journal, *The Free
Church Magazine,* was set by a strongly conservative editor.
Quite radical views were nevertheless frequently expressed at
regional or synodical conferences organised by its Home
Mission and Life and Work Committees; socially-concerned
congregations developed the practice of discussing
contemporary problems at Sunday evening meetings; and of
course some of the most advanced thinking of the time on
social matters was being engaged in by scholars like Bruce,
Smith and Dods. If one were to look for a representative
spokesman of progressive attitudes within the denomination,
an obvious choice would be the Reverend George Reith of
College church, Glasgow (father of the first Director-General
of the B.B.C.). Reith was no extremist. He took care to agree
with those who asserted that improvement of outward
circumstances could neither produce nor take the place of "the
New Birth, without which a man cannot enter the Kingdom of
God", that widespread material comfort would not necessarily
carry with it man's highest spiritual and moral welfare, that
the Church should be "jealous of her independence of all class
prejudice and party spirit", and that "The essence of the Social
Problem is the soul."[65] At the same time, he could be as
critical as Matheson of the existing order, and his article on
"The Church and Social Problems" is an interesting specimen

of the kind of teaching given from a West End pulpit in Glasgow at the close of the century.

"I take it for granted", Reith declared, "that no one cares to defend the existing social or economic order, in view of the anomalies that spring from it, or at least are bound up with it. When, following our Lord's advice, we judge it by its fruits, it is condemned." He went on: "Not because a state of things exists, and is accepted as inevitable even by good men; not because the law of the land throws its shield over it; not because the entire social organisation is involved in it, and interference might mean serious dislocation, amounting to a revolution or something akin to it, is it therefore to be approved.... Surely it is not God's intention that the few should be at the top of the tree of life, sitting secure, and that the many should be struggling to get, or keep, a mere foothold on its lowest branches; that men – I do not say of different nationalities, but men of the same race – should be hopelessly divided into castes estranged in sympathies, and in a relation of mutual suspicion and distrust, deepening into positive hostility." The large amount of Christian philanthropy evident in areas of need was not, he believed, to be depreciated. Yet "such Christian and philanthropic workers appear to me to be simply physicians and nurses treating the wounded on the field of battle. They are doing noble work. But what we want is: no wounded, and no battle to inflict wounds." And towards the close of his analysis he included an assertion whose significance is all the greater for coming from a minister of the Church most noted in nineteenth-century Scotland for its devotion to the Evangelical faith: "We are all praying for a spiritual revival: please God it may come. Perhaps the Lord sees that our need for an ethical revival, for a social order rebuilt on the foundation of righteousness, and with the mercy that characterised Himself, is – I shall not say greater – equally great."[66]

The Auld Kirk of the period resembled its sister Churches

in providing very little evidence, either in official publications or in Assembly debates, of a changed outlook on social problems; but, again like them, it could point to a number of leading ministers with progressive views and to a marked alteration in the general climate of opinion. Conservative Evangelicalism of the kind so strongly represented in the Free Church had never carried comparable weight in the post-Disruption Establishment, and during the last decades of the century it was overshadowed by both the Broad and High Church schools – neither of which was likely (though for very different reasons) to favour the older brand of pietistic individualism. Among Broad Churchmen none was more eminent or influential than Principal Caird of Glasgow University. His famous sermon on "Corporate Immortality", contributed to the highly contentious *Scotch Sermons* of 1880, made short work of the other-worldliness favoured by a certain kind of Evangelical, and pointed quite explicitly towards social involvement. "The supreme aim of Christian endeavour", Caird asserted, "is not to look away to an inconceivable heaven beyond the skies, and to spend our life preparing for it, but it is to realise that latent heaven, those possibilities of spiritual good, that undeveloped kingdom of righteousness and love and truth, which human nature and human society contain.... If heaven is for the pure and holy, if that which makes men good is that which best qualifies for heaven, what better discipline in goodness can we conceive for a spirit, what more calculated to elicit and develop its highest affections and energies, than to live and labour for our brother's welfare?"[67]

Profound theological differences separated Caird and his disciples from the High Church school of men like Marshall Lang, John Macleod and Wallace Williamson. Yet it is interesting to see how close the latter's understanding of the Church as a corporate, organic entity brought them to the former's stance on social matters. Their most copious writer in this area was probably Lang, who despite his exceedingly cautious and measured language could on occasion say things which would have astonished the previous generation. His moderatorial address of 1893, for example, touched at considerable length on the plight of the masses, affirmed that "There is a relation between character and wages – well-to do-ness and well-doing-ness. And by placing wages on a surer footing the union has blessed society in general", and declared that working-class agitation – "an effort by the people for the people to realise better distribution of wealth and more equitable adjustments in condition" – was both just and praiseworthy.[68] Even his somewhat non-committal Baird Lectures of 1901 were quite clear about the demise of *laissez-faire* economics and the consequences which flowed from it. "The State", he observed, "is not now viewed merely as a constable, with the two commands, 'Keep moving', and 'Hands off from one another.' It is looked upon as the instrument by which, through legislation confirming action by individuals or public bodies, and in certain cases initiating action, the good of the community may be furthered, healthier and wealthier life may be secured, and society may be enabled to make increase to 'the edifying of itself in love.' And if in recent years it has more and more acknowledged an ethical character and responsibility, is not this only the carrying out, in the changed circumstances of the day, of a traditional ideal of government?"[69] When one who was both an ex-Moderator of the General Assembly and a university principal (as well as the father of a future Archbishop of Canterbury) could express such views, it was obvious that fresh winds were blowing in Scotland's religious Establishment.

Three particularly striking instances of the late-Victorian revolution in social attitudes have yet to be noticed. One was a dramatic weakening of the traditional animosity against Socialism in any shape or form. A sentence or two from *The Scottish Christian Herald* (quoted by Donald Smith in one of the most valuable sections of his study) vividly conveys the

mingled fear and hatred with which the men of Chalmers'
generation regarded this many-headed threat to all that they
held most dear. "The rapid progress of the abominable
doctrines of Socialism in both ends of the island", declared the
writer, "calls for interference of the civil authorities, to defend
the community from opinions subversive at once of religion,
morality, and social order." And he went on to assert that
"The system is, in its very nature, essentially atheistical and
blasphemous; and its practical effect has been – to reduce its
votaries below the level of the brutes."[70] That was in 1840. By
the eighteen-eighties and nineties such views are seldom
encountered. The learned Robert Flint, it is true, was
consistently hostile, largely because he identified British
Socialism with the revolutionary Marxist version which
prevailed on the Continent. But even Flint considered Socialist
thinking to be worthy of careful, scholarly exposition and
consideration, while many other Christian writers of the period
were prepared to acknowledge the validity of some at least of
its insights and to let themselves be influenced by it to a
greater or lesser degree. According to A. B. Bruce, it was not
necessarily atheistic. According to Donald Macleod, it was a
useful corrective of undue individualism.[71] According to Scott
Matheson, "Christianity and socialism need not be spoken of
as rivals; they are compatible, and should not be made parties
in a quarrel. The fact is" – here he echoes J. M. Ludlow's
aphorism from the eighteen-forties – "that Socialism needs to
be Christianised, and that Christianity needs to be
socialised."[72] Most interesting of all, in John Glasse of Old
Greyfriars, Edinburgh, the Church of Scotland possessed a
minister who took his stand quite unequivocally in the
Socialist camp. Glasse was a member of the Scottish Land and
Labour League and of the Socialist League which superseded
it; first president, in 1907, of the newly-established Edinburgh
branch of the Fabian Society; author of numerous books and
pamphlets on his favourite subject; friend of Keir Hardie and

other Labour leaders; "a central figure", as Donald Smith describes him, "in virtually all the socialist movements which were formed in Edinburgh in the last two decades of the nineteenth century and the early years of the twentieth century".[73] This extraordinary man was, of course, by no means typical of Christian social thinking in his time. But the very fact that someone who spoke and wrote as he did could occupy a prominent and influential place among the ministers of Scotland's capital is an indication of the change that had been effected since the days of Begg and – still more – of Chalmers.

Another important pointer is to be found in the sympathy which many late-Victorian Scottish churchmen showed to Trade Union activity. Scarcely had persons of conservative mind recovered from the shock of Cardinal Manning's intervention in the London dock strike of 1889 than the leading Free Church minister, Robert Rainy, gave positive encouragement to the workers involved in the protracted railway strike of 1890–91. The old-fashioned view on such matters had been stated by Rainy's opposite number in the United Presbyterian Church, John Cairns, when he declared, at a public meeting crowded with railway workers, that "He lamented the present social disruption and agitation.... He sympathised with the Railway Companies in all their just interests.... As a Christian minister he believed it to be his duty to do justice to both sides.... He sympathised with the men so far as they claimed justice; but he sympathised with the shareholders... – with poor widows and persons of limited income.... Yes, he sympathised with all suffering in this crisis, and he wished that God would lead those who had any influence to wield it justly and in obedience to conscience."[74] Rainy, however, went much further than simply recommending, with his U.P. colleague, that both sides in the dispute accept arbitration – though even that was a step in the workers' direction. He agreed to preside over a public meeting in Edinburgh which the strikers had organised, and made what his biographer calls "a bold speech". Declaring that the hours which the railwaymen were expected to work were quite indefensible, he appealed to the shareholders to "think not only of cheapness and speed and returns" but "of the men who worked". Some days later, at a public rally attended by over ten thousand people, he again spoke in similar terms, strongly criticising the directors of the N.B. Railway Company (whom he blamed for the strike) and moving a motion which called for a ten-hour day. Carnegie Simpson notes how some were dismayed that a minister should espouse the cause of men who had violated the law by breaking their contracts; but he adds his own view that "Dr. Rainy's action shows... his real sympathy for labour – a sympathy which was far deeper in his heart than the opportunities of his too crowded ecclesiastical career gave opportunity for expression."[75] No public utterance by the great principal was ever precipitate or ill-considered: the whole episode can therefore be regarded as both a revelation and a portent.

Of possibly even greater significance in the story of changing social attitudes was the support given by the Free Church, both centrally and locally, to the agitation carried on during the eighteen-eighties against the Highland land laws – an agitation which eventually resulted in the Crofters' Holdings Act of 1886. As early as the eighteen-forties, Hugh Miller and James Begg strongly criticised the great Highland landlords for forcibly evicting their tenants in the latest phase of the Clearances. They do not, however, seem to have realised that what was required was a fundamental reform of the land laws, and it is arguable that their animus against the great landowners was powerfully influenced by the latter's refusal of building sites to Free Church congregations after the Disruption. In any case, the unrest to which they gave expression was less evident in the immediately succeeding decades. With the eighteen-eighties, however, really violent trouble broke out once again in the far North-West; and this time the Free Church had ample opportunity to demonstrate its new hesitancy concerning the traditional bias in favour of property and position and the traditional adulation of submissiveness and endurance on the part of the disadvantaged. With one or two notable exceptions, the Church of Scotland maintained its age-old support for the landlord class and said little or nothing in its courts against a fresh wave of evictions; but things were very different within the Free Church. The so-called "Highland Association" was formed to press for the reforms recommended by the Royal Commission of 1883. In the General Assembly of 1884 the trend of thought was dramatically indicated by Dr. Ross Taylor of Kelvinside's assertion that "there is no absolute right of private property in land". Even the famous Skye riots were not denounced: instead, the Commission of Assembly resolved to memorialise the Government on "the gravity of existing evils" and the need for redress at the earliest possible moment. (Incidentally, the language then used seems almost to echo that of Patrick Brewster half a century earlier. After speaking of "the great evils which have in all times arisen from the prolonged irritation of social evils, acknowledged but not remedied", the Commission observed that "the mere enforcement of obedience to laws, when these do not secure justice, is the smallest part of the duty of any government.") When the first Crofters' Act came before Parliament that same year, Rainy was among those who called for a more liberal measure; and when that was introduced the Assembly of 1886 petitioned in favour of its speedy enactment. Nor did the Church's interest in Highland affairs end there, for the Assembly of 1888 – meeting in Inverness – exhorted the Government to introduce further legislation which would enable the crofters to acquire more land by either the enlargement of existing holdings or the creation of new ones.[76]

It is possible, of course, to argue that the Free Church's concern for the Highlands was hardly disinterested: that just as criticism of anti-social practices had once been directed chiefly against landlords guilty of withholding building sites from the seceders of 1843, so in the eighteen-eighties, when theological disagreements threatened the Free Church with Highland schism, it was found expedient to express sympathy with the social radicalism of the area. It is certainly true that the support given to the crofters seldom erred on the side of incaution, and that the Highland Land League (formerly the Highland Land Law Reform Association), which had connections with the Scottish Parliamentary Labour Party, was not looked on with much favour. James Hunter, indeed, has gone so far as to assert that by the last decades of the century the Free Church had "lost its initial identification with the forces of anti-landlordism", and that its ministers now "had no wish to change the social status quo". "The 1880s", he declares, "therefore witnessed a partial reversal in the earlier rôles of the Free and Established Churches. It was the ministers of the latter body – many of whom had practically no congregation – who had least to lose by joining with the H.L.L.R.A. And the clerics who took the most part in its activities were, therefore, Church of Scotland ministers led by the young and fervently radical Donald MacCallum who was minister at Waternish at the height of the troubles in Skye."[77] At the same time, there is no denying the sympathy with crofters' grievances which was voiced by the General Assembly of the Free Church during the years of unrest and agitation, or the support which it gave to governmental intervention of a kind that would have astonished the previous generation of Scotsmen.

Between 1900 and 1914 the new spirit at work within the Churches became even more evident. Particularly noteworthy were the formation in 1901 of the Scottish Christian Social Union, and the emergence in 1912 of the first permanent

General Assembly committee on social problems. Though interdenominational in composition and appeal, the C.S.U. (modelled, apparently, on the slightly older English body of the same name) owed its origin to an Auld Kirk minister, David Watson of St. Clement's parish, Glasgow. There was nothing revolutionary about Watson – like Professor Flint before him, he could speak very harshly of Socialism – nor, for that matter, about the C.S.U. Yet by its forums and study groups on slum housing, child welfare, sweated labour and unemployment, as well as by its willingness to ask questions and suggest answers on community problems, it stirred the social conscience of the Churches and gave evidence to the world of their deepening social concern. One of Watson's many publications, *Social Problems and the Church's Duty* (1908), had on its title-page the following quotation from F. G. Peabody, the American Social Gospeller: "The only test of the Christian religion which the modern world will regard as adequate is its applicability to the solution of the Social Question."[78] And in the closing pages of the same work he expressed himself in terms which would have seemed alarmingly radical to the preceding generation but were common enough among the members and supporters of the C.S.U. "More and more it is clear", he declared, "that social conditions need to be redeemed as well as men and women.... The Church should lead in social reform and social betterment. It is not enough... 'to mitigate the results of bad social conditions and to save the victims. She must attack the bad social conditions themselves'.... She prays daily for the coming of the kingdom and that the Divine Will may be done on earth, and it is hers to remove everything which hinders the fulfilment of that prayer. The Church must see that child-life is guarded, that youth is trained, that the people are decently housed and the poor humanely cared for, that labour is fairly remunerated, and that our industrial system is thoroughly Christianised.... Finally, let her remember that in proportion to the depth of her spirituality will be her social effectiveness."[79]

It was in 1908 that the General Assembly of the United Free Church instructed its Church Life and Work Committee "to take into consideration in what way or ways the Church may best show her sympathy with, and lend assistance to, the various movements that aim at the betterment of society; and in particular to consider the advisability of establishing a 'Department of Church and Labour', similar to that which has proved so effective in the interpretation of the Church to working-men and of working-men to the Church in the experience of the American Presbyterian Church".[80] In 1909, a first step was taken towards the goal indicated with the creation of a modestly-named Special (that is, temporary) Committee on Social Problems.[81] After a heated debate in the Assembly of 1911, approval was given to the new body's own interpretation of its rôle and functions. Moreover, the dropping of the word "Special" virtually converted it into Scotland's first standing Church committee on social questions, though its term of existence was to begin with limited to four experimental years.[82] The work of "interpretation" referred to in 1908 could now be embarked upon; and the years before the war witnessed an impressive burgeoning of Church-sponsored conferences, public meetings, and consultations with employers, labour leaders, and representatives of Government, as well as careful and informative enquiries into housing conditions, unemployment, child welfare, and allied matters. A great deal of criticism was, of course, directed against all these activities, particularly by a group of Assembly elders who saw in them a sinister capitulation to Socialist ideas and an unwarranted meddling with secular politics. "There is", wrote the Revd. George M. Reith in words with which such critics would have agreed whole-heartedly, "but one social problem before the Church *qua* Church, however many there may be for the politician and the publicist – namely, how to bring the gospel to bear on the conscience of the individual, and thereby reach the social conscience. That process is too slow for the impatient, too unspectacular for those who would work in the limelight. Hindrances to the gospel must be removed by direct action before the gospel can make its way in society. But the Parable of the Leaven is still in the New Testament; the gospel itself is the divinely forged instrument for the removal of hindrances, and ministers who were faithfully doing the work of the gospel in their respective spheres rather resented being told – as they were frequently told – that they were... 'standing aloof' or 'lagging behind', merely because they had little faith in current nostrums."[83]

Though Reith was editor of the Assembly's *Proceedings and Debates* throughout the period presently under review, he seems in this regard to have been out of touch with the majority opinion in his denomination. More representative, apparently, was the attitude expressed in two documents to which general approval was given by the Assembly of 1909. A pastoral letter designed for circulation throughout the Church included this summons to social involvement: "The General Assembly, realising the responsibility of the Church to her great Head for the social as well as the religious welfare of society, feel bound to call upon the members of the Church seriously to weigh the special obligations which rest upon them in relation to the existing condition of things. The faithful prosecution of the Church's mission requires of her a serious and constant regard to the conditions under which the people live and labour; and that, through all opportunities open to her, she use her influence to advance their interests, to put an end to underpayment and sweating in business, to promote adequate housing, to encourage temperance in living, to preserve sacred the Day of Rest, and generally to secure such social conditions as shall conduce to the common well-being, and give reasonable opportunity to all to cultivate and enjoy those things that make for the highest interests and ends of life."[84] (It has been said, incidentally, that this was "the first occasion on which any Protestant Church has addressed its members on social questions".)[85] And a statement on "The Social Teaching of our Lord", prepared by a working group of the Church Life and Work Committee in 1908–9, concluded with the following questions and answers: "What is the Bearing of Christ's Teaching on the Present Social Order? – Christ's teaching contains within it a criticism of the present social system in several respects.... 1. The elements in the present economic system which make the life Christ calls men to live hardly possible – such as unduly low wages, sweating of labour, and oppressive conditions of work. Whatever these are due to, they are contrary in their effects to the mind and the life of the Master. 2. Extreme inequalities of wealth and poverty. So far as these are favoured and fostered by the present system, it can hardly be said to reflect the mind of Christ. 3. So far again as modern conditions foster the alienation of industrial and other classes from one another, the whole spirit of Christ's words is against these conditions. It is plain from the facts adduced earlier in what ways the mind of Jesus condemns all oppressive, unjust, and alienating conditions of life and labour, and favours the more equal distribution of happiness and opportunity. What is the Bearing of Christ's Teaching on the Church's Relation to the Social Problem? – 1. One of the pressing needs is a revival in the mind and conscience of the Christian Church of Christ's great social ideal. The Church's partial neglect of this has had serious results in throwing the leadership of masses of the poor into other hands. Christ's words and example show that the Church *has* a real concern in the physical and social welfare of the people, in conditions of labour, in wages, in social righteousness. 2. Therefore the Church, in its Courts, should examine the facts, and should witness fearlessly against the social evils already mentioned, in such a way as to force them on the general conscience. 3. The Church should lead the way in the exhibition of practical brotherhood, and should supply personal service to the needs of the poor and outcast, in the spirit and methods of Christ's own life. It can carry culture, faith, love, down to the loveless, the ignorant and the lapsed. *'The Son of Man came to seek and to save the lost.'"*[86]

Towards the close of his study of "The Failure and Recovery of Social Criticism in the Scottish Church, 1830 – 1950", Donald Smith remarks that "This period preceding the first World War is of great importance in that it witnessed in the Scottish Church the first significant break from traditional nineteenth-century Christian social concern based on an acceptance of the existing order, and which expressed itself in charitable and reclamation work, and a new Christian social concern based on a suspicion or rejection of the existing order, and which expressed itself in social criticism and in more dynamic and radical forms of social action."[87] Certainly, as one looks back from pre-war Scotland to the Scotland of just a century earlier – the Scotland of Chalmers and Brewster – it is hard to deny that Brewster's call for JUSTICE was at last being heard and acted upon, and that a veritable revolution had taken place in the Churches' attitude to social questions.

Notes to Chapter V

1. W. Hanna, *Memoirs of the Life and Writings of Chalmers,* vol. IV (Edinburgh, 1852), p. 425.
2. S. J. Brown, "The Disruption and Urban Poverty: Thomas Chalmers and the West Port Operation in Edinburgh, 1844–47", *Records of the Scottish Church History Society,* vol. XX pt. I (1978), p. 74.
3. D. C. Smith, "The Failure and Recovery of Social Criticism in the Scottish Church, 1830–1950" (Edinburgh University Ph.D. thesis, 1963), p. 108.
4. A. L. Drummond and J. Bulloch, *The Church in Late Victorian Scotland 1874–1900* (Edinburgh, 1978), p. 128.
5. Smith, "Failure and Recovery", p. 112.
6. ibid., p. 109.
7. D. H. Bishop, "Church and Society: A Study of the Social Work and Thought of James Begg, D.D. (1808–1883), A. H. Charteris, D.D., LL.D. (1835–1908), and David Watson (1859–1943)" (Edinburgh University Ph.D. thesis, 1953), p.9 n.4.
8. Brown, "Disruption and Poverty", p. 76.
9. Smith, "Failure and Recovery", p. 91.
10. W. Hanna, *Memoirs of the Life and Writings of Thomas Chalmers,* vol. III (Edinburgh, 1851), p. 313 n.
11. G. I. T. Machin, *Politics and the Churches in Great Britain 1832 to 1868* (Oxford, 1977), p. 26.
12. D. Macleod, *Memoir of Norman Macleod* (London, 1876), vol. I, p. 119.
13. A. R. MacEwen, *Life and Letters of John Cairns* (London, 1895), pp. 85–6.
14. L. J. Saunders, *Scottish Democracy 1815–1840. The Social and Intellectual Background* (Edinburgh, 1950), p. 219.
15. ibid., p. 220.
16. ibid., p. 220.
17. Smith, "Failure and Recovery", p. 184 n. 2.
18. ibid., p. 186.
19. W. G. Blaikie, *Better Days for Working People* (new edn., London, 1881), p. 64.
20. W. G. Blaikie, "Six Lectures addressed to the Working Classes on the Improvement of their Temporal Condition" (Edinburgh, 1849), p. 32.
21. W. G. Blaikie, *Better Days,* p. 153.

22. W. G. Blaikie, *An Autobiography: "Recollections of a Busy Life"* (London, 1901), p. 152.
23. W. G. Blaikie, "Six Lectures", p. 32.
24. W. G. Blaikie, *An Autobiography*, pp. 148, 151.
25. W. G. Blaikie, *Better Days*, pp. 63–4.
26. W. G. Blaikie, "Six Lectures", p. 8.
27. W. G. Blaikie, *An Autobiography*, p. 150.
28. ibid., p. 152.
29. ibid., pp. 156–9.
30. Bishop, "Church and Society", p. 59.
31. ibid., p. 32.
32. J. Begg, "How to Promote and Preserve the True Beauty of Edinburgh, being a few hints to the Hon. Lord Cockburn" (Edinburgh, 1849). Bishop, "Church and Society", pp. 33–5.
33. Bishop, ibid., pp. 64–7.
34. ibid., pp. 35–7 and 62. cf. T. Smith, *Memoirs of James Begg* (Edinburgh, 1888), vol. II, p. 144.
35. J. Begg, "Scotland's Demand for Electoral Justice, or, The Forty Shilling Freehold Question Explained" (Edinburgh, 1857). Bishop, "Church and Society", pp. 67–9.
36. Bishop, ibid., pp. 69–86.
37. Smith, *Begg*, vol. II, pp. 240, 263, 361. Bishop, "Church and Society", p. 103.
38. Bishop, ibid., pp. 41–2.
39. ibid., pp. 42–3.
40. Smith, *Begg*, p. 131.
41. Bishop, "Church and Society", pp. 34–5.
42. ibid., p. 50.
43. J. Begg, *Happy Homes for Working Men and How to Get Them* (2nd edn., Edinburgh, 1873), pp. 65–8.
44. Smith, "Failure and Recovery", pp. 292–6.
45. J. Begg, "Pauperism and the Poor Laws" (Edinburgh, 1849), pp. iii–iv.
46. Bishop, "Church and Society", p. 66 n.1.
47. W. Hanna, *Memoirs of the Life and Writings of Thomas Chalmers*, vol. II (1850), p. 21 (but cf. p. 19).
48. D. Withrington, "The Churches in Scotland, c.1870–c.1900: Towards a New Social Conscience?", *Records of the Scottish Church History Society*, vol. XIX pt. 3 (1977), p. 156.
49. Drummond and Bulloch, *Late Victorian Scotland*, pp. 134–5.
50. N. L. Walker, *Chapters from the History of the Free Church of Scotland* (Edinburgh, 1895), pp. 83–4.
51. Withrington, "Churches in Scotland", p. 159.
52. ibid., p. 158.
53. *Proceedings of the General Assembly of the Free Church of Scotland, 1871* (Edinburgh, 1871) pp. 248–9. Drummond and Bulloch, *Late Victorian Scotland*, p. 192.
54. Drummond and Bulloch, ibid., pp. 167–8.
55. Withrington, "Churches in Scotland", p. 163.
56. ibid., p. 164.
57. ibid., pp. 164–5.

58. Smith, "Failure and Recovery", p. 307.
59. Drummond and Bulloch, *Late Victorian Scotland*, pp. 186–9.
60. G. A. Smith, *Modern Criticism and the Preaching of the Old Testament* (2nd edn., London, 1901), pp. 272–3.
61. Smith, "Failure and Recovery", pp. 327–8.
62. ibid., pp. 316–7.
63. ibid., p. 322.
64. A. S. Matheson, *The Church and Social Problems* (Edinburgh, 1893), pp. 13–14, and ch. I, *passim*.
65. W. M. Clow, *Dr. George Reith: A Scottish Ministry* (London, 1928), pp. 265–7.
66. ibid., pp. 267–71 and 293.
67. Smith, "Failure and Recovery", p. 339.
68. ibid., p. 344.
69. J. M. Lang, *The Church and its Social Mission (The Baird Lecture for 1901)* (Edinburgh, 1902), pp. 219–20.
70. Smith, "Failure and Recovery", p. 356.
71. ibid., pp. 366–9 for refs.
72. A. S. Matheson, *The Gospel and Modern Substitutes* (Edinburgh, 1890), p. 184.
73. Smith, "Failure and Recovery", p. 369.
74. MacEwen, *Cairns*, p. 766.
75. P. C. Simpson, *The Life of Principal Rainy* (popular edn., London, n.d.), pp. 106–8.
76. Smith, "Failure and Recovery", pp. 383–97, *passim*.
77. J Hunter, *The Making of the Crofting Community* (Edinburgh, 1976), p. 155.
78. D. Watson, *Social Problems and the Church's Duty* (London, 1908), p. iii.
79. ibid., pp. 199–201.
80. *Reports of the General Assembly of the United Free Church of Scotland, 1909* (Edinburgh, 1909), XVIII, pp. 3–4.
81. ibid., pp. 10–11.
82. *Reports of the General Assembly of the United Free Church of Scotland, 1911* (Edinburgh, 1911), XXXII, *passim*.
83. G. M. Reith, *Reminiscences of the United Free Church General Assembly (1900–1929)* (Edinburgh, 1933), pp. 235–6.
84. *Proceedings and Debates of the General Assembly of the United Free Church of Scotland, 1909* (Edinburgh, 1909), pp. 379–80.
85. Smith, "Failure and Recovery", p. 425.
86. *U.F.C. Reports, 1909* (Edinburgh, 1909), XVIII, Appendix I p. 16.
87. Smith, "Failure and Recovery", pp. 435–6.

VI

The Revolution in Life-Style

Along with the late-Victorian revolution in social attitudes went an equally far-reaching change in the tone and temper of Scottish piety – a change which could almost be described in the one word, "De-Puritanisation". Something of its scope and significance may be conveyed by a brief glance at three representative ministers, one from each of the great Presbyterian denominations of the period: Norman Macleod, Thomas Davidson and Alexander Whyte.

It is perhaps hardly surprising that Norman Macleod (1812–72) should have contributed more than almost anyone else to the altered life-style of church folk in the latter half of the nineteenth century, for his character and experience were marked from first to last by a notable blend of the conventional and the unconventional. His family was a phenomenally clerical one – it has given six Moderators to the General Assembly of the Church of Scotland, and Norman's grandfather, father, uncle John and brother Donald were all ministers – but the religion which it practised never quite matched the stereotyped patterns of the age. It always seemed to be shot through with the poetry and the passion of the Celtic temperament, and in Norman's case was accompanied by a good deal of animal high spirits as well. His parents may have been tolerably strict in their management of the home, but he was eager to defend them against any accusation of narrow-mindedness or killjoy-ism. "The liberty they gave us", he wrote many years later, "was as wise as the restraints they imposed. Their home was happy – intensely happy. Christianity was a thing to be taken for granted, not forced with scowl and frown. I never heard my father speak of Calvinism, Arminianism, Presbyterianism or Episcopacy, or exaggerate doctrinal differences in my life. I had to study all these questions after I left home. I thank God for his free, loving, sympathising and honest heart."[1]

After completing his Arts course at Glasgow in 1831, Norman went to Edinburgh for the study of Divinity. There he came under the spell of Thomas Chalmers, an encounter which possibly helped to ensure that he would always be more of an Evangelical than a Moderate. Yet like Chalmers himself he wore his Evangelicalism with a difference; and his tendency to deviate from the norm was confirmed – even before the antics of the non-Intrusionist leaders disillusioned him – by certain experiences of his later years as a divinity student. Having become tutor to the son of a Yorkshire gentleman, he toured central Europe in his charge's company during much of 1834 and 1835. The young men's stay in the famous little town of Weimar was particularly enjoyable, and seems to have formed a kind of turning-point in Norman's life. "He may have often given too great a rein to that 'liberty' which was so congenial to his natural temperament", brother Donald tells us in the Victorian biography, "but it is marvellous that the reaction was not greater in one who, brought up in a strict school, was suddenly thrown into the vortex of fashionable life. He was passionately fond of music, sang well to the guitar, sketched cleverly, was as keen a waltzer as any attaché in Weimar, and threw himself with a vivid sense of enjoyment into the gaieties of the little capital. His father and mother frequently warned him against going too far in all this; and he often reproached himself for what he deemed his want of self-restraint when in society. Nevertheless, the experience he gained in Weimar became of immense practical importance to him.... When he and Preston returned to Moreby, Norman had become in many ways a new man. His views were widened, his opinions matured, his human sympathies vastly enriched, and while all that was of the essence of his early faith had become doubly precious, he had gained increased catholicity of sentiment, along with knowledge of the world."[2] From then onwards, Macleod's life was set in its distinctively un-Puritanical mould.

In 1838 he was inducted to his first parish, Loudoun in Ayrshire. There he gained first-hand experience of the devastating impact of industrialism on the ancient pieties of rural Scotland, and began a battle with secularism which was to occupy him for the rest of his days. Two elements in his response call for special notice. The first was his rejection of what might be termed "the Westminster approach" to current religious problems. "The tendency of ultra-Calvinism", he remarked, "(if not its necessary result) is to fill the mind with dark views of the Divine character; to represent Him as grudging to make men happy; as exacting from Christ stripe for stripe that the sinner deserved. Hence a Calvinist fanatic has the same scowling, dark, unloving soul as a Franciscan or Dominican fanatic who whips himself daily to please Deity. They won't enjoy life; they won't laugh without atoning for the sin by a groan; they won't indulge in much hope or joy; they more easily and readily entertain doctrines which go to prove how many may be damned than how many may be saved; because all this seems to suit their views of God's character and to be more agreeable to Him than a cheerful, loving bearing."[3] Such a mind was, of course, anathema to Macleod.

The second noteworthy aspect of his approach was a broadminded and humane interpretation of the ministerial task. Soon after being inducted to the Barony parish of Glasgow (1851), he summarised his views as follows: "The common idea at present is that the whole function of the

Church is to teach and preach the Gospel, while it is left to other organisations, infidel ones they may be, to meet all the other varied wants of our suffering people. And what is this but virtually to say to them, the Church of Christ has nothing to do as a society with your bodies, only with your souls, and that, too, but in the way of teaching? Let infidels, then, give you better houses or better clothing, and seek to gratify your tastes and improve your social state: – with all this, and a thousand other things needful for you as men, we have nothing to do.... Whereas the Christian congregation or society ought not to consider as foreign to itself any one thing which its loving Head Jesus Christ gives to bless and dignify men, and desires man to use and enjoy. We must not separate ourselves from any important interest of our brethren of mankind, calling the one class of blessings spiritual, and accepting these as the special trust of the Christian Church, and calling another class temporal, and recognising them as a trust for society given to the unbelievers. In so doing we give Satan the advantage over us. Let congregations take cognisance of the whole man and his various earthly relationships, let them seek to enrich him with all Christ gave him, let them endeavour to meet all his wants as an active, social, intellectual, sentient, as well as spiritual being, so that men shall know through the ministrations of the Body, the Church, how its living Head gives them all things richly to enjoy!"[4]

Macleod acted upon these convictions, and by the time of his death few Scottish ministers were better-known or more popular than he – and that despite the markedly pro-establishment, anti-Socialist, anti-Chartist opinions which he often expressed. His ministries at Loudoun, Dalkeith and the Barony showed how an entire congregation could be made an agent of mission to its parish (the Chalmers pattern), and how many aspects of urban life might be worked upon and elevated by Christian influences. He also did a great deal to raise and liberalise the standards of taste in religious journalism, particularly by the editorship of *Good Words*. "I believe", he once wrote, "it is the fushionless, unreal, untruthful, 'pious' story-telling, which some of our tract societies alone patronise, that has produced the story-telling without piety, but with more truth and more trash, which is devoured by the working classes."[5] Above all, he contributed materially to the liberalisation of the traditional Scottish Sabbath.

For some decades before the show-down of the eighteen-sixties, Sabbath observance in Scotland had been under attack. Its defenders were vigilant and influential, however, and only a kind of capitulation from within the Sabbatarian citadel brought about a crumbling of the old structure. Appropriately enough – for the revolution in transport was an integral part of the wider social revolution – the decisive battle took place over Sunday travel. In January 1865, the North British Railway introduced a regularly scheduled service of Sunday goods trains between Edinburgh and Glasgow. Loud protests failed to bring about its withdrawal; and then in the early autumn, after a merger of the North British and the Glasgow and Edinburgh companies, regular Sunday services for passengers were also instituted. The general assumption was that the Kirk would oppose such measures – and Glasgow Presbytery did issue a pastoral letter calling upon dutiful members to "sanctify the Sabbath" and resist all encroachments upon it. Norman had other ideas, however, and on 16th November 1865 he delivered a $3\frac{1}{2}$-hour speech in presbytery criticising what he called the Pharisaic behaviour of his fellow-Christians. As he saw the matter, they were behaving like Jews not Christians, and stressing the Old Testament trappings of the Lord's Day rather than its distinctively New Testament features. "Where", he asked, "is His [Christ's] authority for keeping the Sabbath law of the fourth commandment after His resurrection?... It has died out with the old economy. The Passover has gone, even without formal abrogation, and we have the Lord's Supper; circumcision has died out, and we have baptism; the Sabbath has died out, and we have the Lord's Day."[6]

Very revealingly, Macleod was not condemned by any church court. The presbytery of Glasgow confined itself to admonition, and the General Assembly of 1866 refused to censure him. In 1869 he was chosen as Moderator. Why such leniency? Various explanations suggest themselves. He had distinguished allies: Tulloch, Lee and Milligan in the Auld Kirk, Eadie of the U.P.s, and Marcus Dods and Walter C. Smith (who narrowly escaped a heresy trial on the same subject) in the Free Church. Also, a great many ordinary church members seem to have felt relief that someone of eminence should have arrived, by way of theological reasoning, at conclusions which they had already tacitly reached by instinct or self-interest. Above all, a multiplicity of social and intellectual changes had made it virtually impossible – outside the Highland area – to maintain the ordering of life previously epitomised in the rigid and sometimes legalistic observance of the Sabbath. For an outstanding religious leader like Macleod of the Barony to sound the trumpet of defiance was enough to bring the walls of Jericho tumbling down. The episode was a turning-point in Scottish religious life, however, and Macleod knew it. As he commented after his triumph in the 1866 Assembly, "The politics of one party were to represent the past only, to lie at anchor as if the voyage in history was reached, to accept the findings of the Westminster Assembly as perfect and incapable of improvement. The politics of the Church...are, sail on, not back, to hold by the past but to grow out of it; and as a living organic whole to develop all that is good in it into a stronger, expansive, and more fruitful tree."[7]

Of the drift away from the old standards Macleod was a prominent exemplar. A much more inconspicuous one was Thomas Davidson, a probationer of the United Presbyterian Church who never received a call from a congregation and died of tuberculosis in 1870 at the age of thirty-one. The life of this shepherd's son from the Jedburgh area was in the main obscure and uneventful; though he seems to have been an able and popular student while at Edinburgh, and travelled quite widely thereafter to fulfil preaching engagements both north and south of the Border and in Ireland. Yet his vivacity and charm, his skill as a versifier (in 1860, Thackeray accepted a poem of his for *The Cornhill*), and the blend of wit and pathos which marked his extensive correspondence were affectionately remembered by his fellow-students. One of them – Dr. James Brown of Paisley – produced in the eighteen-nineties a memoir of Davidson which revealed him to be no unworthy champion of a milder and more benign faith and life-style. A letter written by him in 1869 may therefore be quoted as an amusing illustration of the change which was coming over Scottish piety during the middle years of Victoria's reign. It deals with the subject of traditional Calvinist orthodoxy and, in particular, with one of its minor classics, Thomas Boston's *Fourfold State* (1720). The most relevant passage runs as follows:

"To show you how placable, how mild, how sweet milk-tempered and altogether loving and charitable I am become, I will relate a little anecdote. Give ear! Once upon a time, in my hot youth, and that is long ago, I had occasion to be rejected by the Edinburgh Presbytery. Well, I have forgiven the whole Court; there isn't a living soul of them but I can think of him without the least inclination to swear. But what I was going to tell you was this. The Rev. — God bless him, the old Drumclogger! – asked me what kind of books I read? for he had a feeling – good soul that he is – that my views were a little dishevelled. I felt a little backward about confessing to certain Ballad-books and other kinds of the literature of levity, and I said that 'it would be hard to tell!' Upon which — advised me to read Boston's *Fourfold State*. Now some days after this I went down Leith Walk, and upon an old book stall at which I halted for a minute, what should catch my eye but a copy of Boston's *Fourfold State*. I grinned at him and denounced the Rev. — in my mind, and was just going to pass on when I felt inspired by what I considered the most ingenious method of gratifying my spleen that could possibly occur to any mortal. 'Buy thee', quoth I to the *Fourfold State*; 'yes, thou shalt be bought with a vengeance! Thou shalt be so effectually bought that thou shalt be withdrawn from circulation. I will bury thee beneath all the rubbish I possess, and there thou shalt slumber unread till "cockle-shells be silver bells" – thou old nighmare!' So I bought him for a shilling, and buried him with much care and deliberation at the bottom of a box of the most forsaken and desolate literature I possessed; and after that had wonderful ease of mind for many years."

The story does not end there, however. With the passage of time, Davidson felt able not merely to run away from the old order but to face up to it, to refute it, and even to pass charitable and humorous judgement upon it. He goes on: "Now, some time ago (it was before I caught my last dose of cold), I had occasion to turn this sepulchral box upside down, and there, in his quiet grave, I ushered in a resurrection morning upon Boston's *Fourfold State*. The whole story of my 'superfluity of naughtiness' rushed upon my mind with such irresistibly ludicrous force that it put me in a roar of laughter; I plucked the old mummy out of his corner, and, just to convince myself that I felt amiably towards the Rev. —, that, in fact, I entertained a kind of laughing kindliness towards him, I said to myself, 'I will read this book'. And I *did* read it. Now, if I were writing a tract, I should feel that I had come to that point where the crisis ought to come on, and I should therefore state that I was greatly benefited by the *Fourfold State*; in fact, I should hint that I had been converted by the *Fourfold State*. But, O Thomas, great is truth; and behold the truth is, I think Boston's *Fourfold State* a very poor book; I mean poor as a theological book to recommend any latter-day student of divinity to read. In some other points of view the phenomenon is not devoid of a curious interest. There are indications here and there that the old shepherd of Ettrick must have been rather a kindly soul; and yet he can utter repeatedly, and without very much perceptible shuddering, the terrific imagination that 'God will hold up the wicked in hell-fire with one hand, and torment them with the other.' This is apt to bring a cold sweat over the reader of these times.... But to do Mr. Boston justice, I suppose his idea was one of the theological commonplaces of his time. But I will not let him off for this one: 'The righteous shall then (that is in the world to come) rule over the wicked; and', he adds, 'they shall rule them with a rod of iron.' Now, if any human being can feel satisfaction at this prospect of his duties as a saint, he must be in a bad way. But I suppose the human heart five or six generations ago would be very much the same as it is now. Probably Boston was as free from enjoying that prospect of getting possession of a rod of iron as any of us; perhaps he merely had a dim and confused idea that it was the proper thing to be capable of rising towards attainment of such a state of feeling, while he was as far from it in reality, as he supposed the wicked themselves to be. But this is a digression, and in a direction where there is very little to be got. The *Fourfold State* is, I believe, already consigned to dark oblivion; it is dead and gone – dead as the proverbial door-nail, or my best sermon; and perhaps when I entombed it at the bottom of my rubbish-box I was merely the typical sexton of Fate, performing an act of burial that had long been due. In the meantime, just to prove to myself that I am at peace with all men against whom I ever had any ground of quarrel, I have set the old anatomy upon a bookshelf in respectable company; and whenever I look at it I say to myself, 'The Rev. — is a nice man, and so are all his co-presbyters – all nice men; and, good heavens, what an amiable creature am I!'"[8]

Whereas those who knew them well tended to think of

Thomas Davidson with affection and of Norman Macleod with admiration, it was with something bordering on reverence that they thought of Alexander Whyte. There seems to have been at least a touch of spiritual genius about this illegitimate son of a Kirriemuir handloom weaver who from 1870 until his retirement in 1917 was minister of St. George's Free (later, United Free) Church in Edinburgh: the man of whom J. M. Barrie once said that "To know him was to know what the Covenanters were like in their best hours".[9] The genius was evident in his work both as a pastor and a teacher, but it was as a preacher that he excelled, earning a reputation almost unequalled in the English-speaking world. In the opening sermon of his ministry at Free St. George's he spoke of consecrating himself to "the instant pursuit of the one work of saving myself and them that hear me", and added an explanation of what that would mean: "To interest the young in the Church, and in good men, and in good books, and in good works.... To teach you all how to read and use your Bibles wisely and with profit – to read with understanding, and to read often, the deepest parts of them. To press continually the sovereign and uncompromising place of prayer in the Christian life, and in a word to set Christ in His fullness, in His Person, and work, and rule – continually before you."[10]

Meticulously prepared, with an almost finicking attention to style and presentation, the sermons delivered in pursuit of this ideal displayed a deep insight into human nature, a high dramatic talent, well controlled, a fine command of literary allusions, and an imagination notable for its freshness and range. Whyte was averse from social comment of the usual kind, eschewed philosophical speculation and concentrated upon the inward, the personal and the ethical; but there were few parts of Scripture, few significant spiritual themes, which his preaching did not illuminate. There has been nothing quite like it since. He was at his best (so it was said) when seeking to plumb the depths of human sinfulness or scale the heights of divine grace; and for sermons of comparable vividness, psychological penetration and sense of the numinous one would probably have to go back behind Chalmers, back even beyond Whitefield and Ebenezer Erskine, to that most mystical and rapturous of Puritan divines, Samuel Rutherford. When at last, in the grimmest days of the First World War, he ceased to occupy the pulpit of Free St. George's, there were many in Scotland who felt as Oxford did in the eighteen-forties on losing John Henry Newman (one of Whyte's own heroes): "It was as when, to one kneeling by night in the silence of some vast cathedral, the great bell tolling solemnly overhead has suddenly gone still."

For the historian, however, the most arresting thing about Alexander Whyte is the distinctive blend of old and new in his religious attitudes. In quite a number of ways his Evangelicalism was hardly to be distinguished from that of the preceding generation. Throughout his life, for example, he played an enthusiastic part in evangelistic campaigns of the sort familiar to Scotland since the days of Whitefield. His ministerial career really began during the 1859 awakening in the North-East. Then a university student of twenty-three (the interval since schooldays had been spent as a herd-boy, a shoemaker's apprentice and a teacher), he often attended the revivalists' services in the Aberdeen area; and years later he liked to tell how that same summer he "first opened his mouth in preaching the Gospel" in a little Perthshire schoolroom. The later stages of the movement found him serving as a missionary assistant near Huntly, where he worked alongside such leaders as Duncan Matheson, James Turner, Reginald Radcliffe and Brownlow North, and preached frequently in the open air to shepherds and farm servants. To the very close of his ministry he remembered, and was influenced by, the experience. "A Revival", he told a commemoration meeting fifty years later, "quickens dead men, touches men's imaginations, and sets loose their hearts.... There is a Divine mystery about Revivals. God's sovereignty is in them." With such convictions, Whyte naturally gave his whole-hearted support to the Moody and Sankey campaign of 1874, and found time – though just entering upon the sole pastorship of Free St. George's – to assist Henry Drummond in his popular Sunday evening addresses to young men. In the mid-eighties, again, he supported the meetings which Drummond and others held for students. And at the very end of his life he "entered with great zest" into the campaign carried on by the Americans Chapman and Alexander in the early months of 1914. His regular attendance at their gatherings linked the enterprise with that of Moody and Sankey exactly forty years before; and when asked how he could spare time and strength to be present so often he made the revealing reply, "I simply can't stay away."[11]

Whyte's affinity with "the old-time religion" was equally evident in his theological attachments. Marcus Dods (a lifelong friend) described him as "a very high Calvinist" in his youth – and the picture is only slightly modified by G. F. Barbour's comment that "of the doctrines grouped under the title of Calvinism he instinctively dwelt on those with the most direct bearing on life and conduct. He had less to say about Election than about the inability of the human will to raise and redeem itself, and the need for, and sufficiency of, the divine work of Grace in the heart of man." He lectured to his famous Sunday evening "classes" on both the Shorter Catechism and the Westminster Confession, and made a habit of presenting young ministers with copies of that compendium of rigorous Calvinism, Charles Hodge's *Systematic Theology*. We are also told that it was because Robertson Smith interested himself chiefly in the reinterpretation of the Bible, and not in any restatement of dogma which would have undermined Presbyterianism's doctrinal Standards, that Whyte like others felt able to take his stand unhesitatingly at the professor's side. Even in his later years he could seize the Free Church Crisis of

1900–5 as an opportunity to reaffirm those central doctrines of the Calvinist faith which had never ceased to claim his allegiance. "Predestination", he declared, "is not for the platform. Predestination is not for the pulpit, except on very special and very exalted occasions. At the same time, I will take it upon me to say that both the sovereign predestination and the sovereign election of Almighty God are far too little preached in these slight and surface days of ours."[12]

This willingness to be numbered among the Calvinists was accompanied, not surprisingly, by an ardent admiration for the great names of Puritanism. First among these, it seems, stood the Independent divine Thomas Goodwin. "As a young minister", Whyte once testified, "I carried about a volume of Goodwin with me wherever I went. I read him in railway carriages and in steamboats. I read him at home and abroad. I read him on my holidays among the Scottish Grampians and among the Swiss Alps. I carried his volumes about with me till they fell out of their original cloth binding, and till I got my book-binder to put them into his best morocco. I have read no other so much and so often." During the eighteen-sixties, moreover, he spent much of his time in preparing the index columns for an edition of Goodwin's works, and his biographer assures us that "Its preparation brought both the style and matter of the great Puritan's thinking into the very fibre of his apt and devoted pupil's mind." But there were many other seventeenth-century theologians to whom Whyte turned his attention. Richard Baxter, Robert Blair, John Bunyan, George Fox, Thomas Halyburton, John Livingston and Samuel Rutherford all received treatment in his class lectures; and he published notable studies of *Bunyan Characters* and of *Samuel Rutherford and some of his Correspondents*. One might almost suggest that what Tractarian scholarship had sought to do, a generation earlier, for Anglican devotion was now attempted – single-handed, but not without success – for its Puritan counterpart by this industrious late-Victorian Scot.[13]

Yet while Puritan-minded Evangelicals could find much in Alexander Whyte that was praiseworthy, other things about him were only too likely to disturb or alienate them. One of these must certainly have been his attitude to scholarly study of the Bible, which seems to have clarified itself before he was out of his twenties. At New College, he was among the students who signed a memorial in favour of A. B. Davidson's promotion from tutor to full professor. During the same period, he also became acquainted with those budding stalwarts of liberal theology, Marcus Dods, Sutherland Black and Taylor Innes, whose friendship he retained throughout his life. It was, therefore, no surprise to those who really knew him when, at the induction of Marcus Dods to the Chair of New Testament in New College, Whyte declared that "The historical, exegetical and theological problems connected with New Testament study in our day are not the ephemeral heresies of restless and irreverent minds; they are the providential result of that great awakening of serious thought, and of scholarly and devout inquiry, which began at the Reformation and has been in steady progress in the best schools of Christendom ever since."[14] But perhaps the most striking proof of Whyte's alignment on the liberal side was provided during the Robertson Smith case. It may be true (as Smith's biographers contend) that Whyte "never publicly committed himself to any of the views of the critical school" – although he is said to have used Matthew Arnold's controversial study of Isaiah and even averred in 1881 that he had found Smith's teaching "most reassuring to his own faith".[15] He was, however, deeply devoted to the principle that inquiry should be free and that the authority of Scripture should find a more secure basis than the old, rigid theory of verbal inspiration. And it was this concern which led him, at a moment of crisis in Free Church history, to oppose Principal Rainy himself on the treatment to be meted out to the heretic from Aberdeen.

Before Smith's condemnation in 1881, Whyte pleaded with

the Assembly for further discussion and a more open-minded approach. "Speaking broadly", he maintained, "we have on the one side in this great controversy the conservative caution and sensitive reverence of the Church, and on the other the keen, restless, insatiable spirit of modern critical inquiry.... Principal Rainy's motion articulates this caution, the solicitude, the anxiety – may I not fairly say the timidity, the mistrust, the panic that is natural to one state of mind...whereas the other motion claims that the devout sentiment and solicitude that is in the Church shall not persecute out of it the faithful and diligent student, or be a barrier in his way in seeking out the whole truth attainable concerning the past ways of God with His Church, and the work of the Spirit of God in the production, preservation, and transmission of the Word of God." His peroration, therefore, boldly summoned the commissioners to courage and Christian tolerance. "You cannot", he told them, "arrest the movement of mind in Christendom of which these inculpated writings are an outcome. Had this movement of the theological mind been confined to Professor Smith and a handful of German or Germanised scholars like himself, you might have ignored it or arrested its progress in your Church. But the movement is not of them; they are rather of it. They are its children, and they cannot but be its servants. Fathers and brethren, the mind of the world does not stand still. And the theological mind will stand still at its peril. No man who knows, or cares to know, anything of my personal sympathies and intellectual and religious leanings will accuse me of disloyalty to the Calvinistic, Puritan, and Presbyterian polity, or neglect of the noble body of literature we inherit from our fathers. But I find no disparity, no difficulty, in carrying much of the best of our past with me in going out to meet and hail the new theological methods. Of all bodies of men on the earth the Church of Christ should be the most catholic-minded, the most hopeful, the most courageous, the most generous, sure that every movement of the human mind is ordered and over-ruled for her ultimate establishment, extension, and enriching. The Church of Christ of all institutions on the earth should be bold to bear all things, hope all things, endure all things. And her divine wisdom is shown in times of trial like this when she has to meet foes, as they seem to her, and seek as long and lovingly as may be to reduce them to friends."[16] Whyte was defeated, of course; but his speech on that occasion remains one of the finest defences ever offered in Scotland on behalf of the liberal cause.

Another aspect of the ministry at Free St. George's which must have caused some mystification among the conventionally devout was its breadth of literary interests. This was (to say the least) unusual, especially in a man of Whyte's upbringing and theological allegiance. An address which he once delivered to the students of New College recalled, most revealingly, the enthusiasms of his early years. "It was a great time", he told his youthful audience, "when I was attending the university and New College. The works of Dickens and Thackeray were then appearing in monthly parts. The Brontë family were at their best. George Eliot was writing in *Blackwood*. Carlyle was at the height of his influence and renown. Ruskin, Macaulay, Tennyson and Browning were in everybody's hands. And I read them all as I had time and opportunity."[17] Later in life, he gave ample evidence of his admiration for Milton, Scott, Wordsworth, Shelley and Matthew Arnold, quoted Shakespeare with dramatic effect, read and reread his beloved *Divine Comedy* – and even, on one occasion, mentioned that he had begun to tackle Rabelais.[18] Saturday evenings at the manse were devoted to such diverse weeklies as *The Spectator, The Saturday Review* (later replaced by *The Nation*), *The Athenaeum, The Academy* and *The New Statesman*.[19] Nor is evidence lacking of an interest in the natural sciences. He seems to have taken *Nature* regularly, and there is a story of his presenting the *Life and Letters* of Darwin to a friend.[20]

But it was in theology that he ranged most widely. At the age of thirty or so he filled the pages of his diary with the titles of books he wished to read or consult, and they included not only Chalmers and Jonathan Edwards (as might have been expected) but patristic writers on the Trinity from Tertullian to Ambrose, the Bampton Lectures of Pusey and Mozley, and Manning's *The Temporal Mission of the Holy Spirit*.[21] While a young minister in Glasgow he took part in reading *The Dream of Gerontius* aloud at his senior colleague's fireside, and his high esteem for Newman's sermons dated from the same period.[22] The lecture-classes of his maturer years devoted attention not only to the representative figures of Protestantism but also to St. Teresa (the published version of this appreciation was recommended to Friedrich von Hügel by Dom Cuthbert Butler of Downside), Sir Thomas Browne, Bishop Lancelot Andrewes and Cardinal Newman.[23] The author of the *Apologia*, in particular, cast a lifelong spell upon him: he paid a visit of homage to the Oratory in 1876, and the two men engaged in a desultory correspondence thereafter.[24] Would-be translator of the pastoral letters of a twentieth-century Roman Catholic abbé and panegyrist of Mr. Gladstone, Whyte also praised the writings of Lord Acton, paid a friendly visit to the agnostic John Morley, and corresponded amicably with the sceptical Leslie Stephen.[25] He was indeed possessed of unusually catholic sympathies.

Notwithstanding his intense loyalty to the Free and later the United Free Church, this catholicity of taste and spirit formed an essential part of Whyte's whole outlook, and he saw no inconsistency in it. "The true Catholic", he remarked in his *Thirteen Appreciations,* "as his name implies, is the well-read, the open-minded, the hospitable-hearted, the spiritually-exercised Evangelical", for "he belongs to all sects, and all sects, belong to him."[26] At one time a supporter of the campaign for Disestablishment, he later gladly took part in preliminary conversations about the reunion of the two large

Presbyterian Churches in Scotland.[27] He welcomed the pioneering World Missionary Conference – "Edinburgh, 1910" – to his city, shared in its planning and rejoiced at its success.[28] He even earned the odd distinction, for a Presbyterian, of having his books described as "beautiful – wonderful" by the Vatican's Cardinal Secretary of State, and of being himself acclaimed as "a rare man".[29] And his genuinely ecumenical understanding of things found expression in the following phrases from a sermon which he preached on Whit Sunday, 1906: "The first step to a real union of Christendom will be taken when we come to admit and to realise that the Greek Church was the original mother of us all; that the Latin Church was her first child; and that through both those Churches we ourselves have our religious existence; through them we have the universal foundation of our Creeds and Confessions and Catechisms; our public worship also; our Christian character and our Christian civilisation; and everything indeed that is essential to our salvation.... When we have humbled ourselves to admit that some other Churches have things of no small moment to teach us and to share with us, and things it will greatly enrich us to receive and to assimilate; when we are of a Christian mind enough to admit and even to welcome thoughts and views and feelings like these – then the day of a reconstructed Christendom will have begun to dawn, at least for ourselves."[30]

It would be absurd to claim Macleod or Davidson or Whyte as typical of late-Victorian Scottish Presbyterianism. Yet they were trail-blazers of a new attitude, and in the less strait-jacketed, less censorious, more broadminded way of life for which they stood we can see a fresh ideal emerging and gaining ground among the Christians of Scotland. It may have lacked some of the majesty and the consistency of the Puritanism which preceded it, but it had its own strength and attractiveness. It helped to carry at least some Christian graces and convictions into an age of increasing secularity, disorder and despair.

Notes to Chapter VI

1. D. Macleod, *Memoir of Norman Macleod* (London, 1876), vol. I, p. 7.
2. ibid., pp. 47–9.
3. ibid., pp. 148–9.
4. ibid., vol. II, pp. 7–8.
5. ibid., pp. 109–10.
6. Quoted in R. D. Brackenridge, "The 'Sabbath War' of 1865–66: The Shaking of the Foundations", *Records of the Scottish Church History Society*, vol. XVI – pt. I (1966), p. 28.
7. Macleod, *Macleod*, vol. II, p. 202.
8. J. Brown, *The Life of a Scottish Probationer: Being a Memoir of Thomas Davidson with his Poems and Extracts from his Letters* (4th edn., Glasgow, 1908), pp. 148–9.
9. Quoted in G. F. Barbour, *The Life of Alexander Whyte* (5th edn., London, 1924), p. 643.
10. ibid., pp. 154–5.
11. ibid., ch. 5 *passim*, pp. 253–4 and 556.
12. ibid., pp. 118–9, 172, 205, 436 and 647–50.
13. ibid., pp. 117–8, 392–3, and 647–50.
14. ibid., p. 259.
15. J. S. Black and G. W. Chrystal, *The Life of William Robertson Smith* (London, 1912), p. 185. Barbour, *Whyte*, pp. 171 and 217.
16. Barbour, ibid., pp. 216 and 219.
17. ibid., p. 82.
18. ibid., p. 157.
19. ibid., pp. 287–8.
20. ibid., p. 382.
21. ibid., p. 117.
22. ibid., p. 194.
23. ibid., pp. 647ff.
24. ibid., pp. 194, 241–8.
25. ibid., pp. 601, 656–7, 173, 273 and 381.
26. ibid., p. 389.
27. ibid., pp. 516–22.
28. ibid., pp. 522–4.
29. ibid., p. 526.
30. ibid., p. 512.

VII

Postlude: After the Revolution

How durable was the revolution whose story has just been told? Even a tentative answer to that question calls for a brief introductory survey of the twentieth-century Scottish scene – secular as well as religious.

That Britain's Victorian prosperity, and the optimism which accompanied it, were beginning to fade had become obvious some time before the end of the nineteenth century. In agriculture, the swamping of the home market by American and Canadian grain helped to produce a crisis which set in during the eighteen-seventies and lasted until the outbreak of the 1914–18 war. Although Scotland suffered less than other areas of the United Kingdom, the Highlands and Islands were severely hit, and it has been observed that the extent of deer forest doubled between 1883 and 1912.[1] In industry, equal damage or worse was done by the economic advance of Germany and the United States; and here Scotland, with its preponderance of heavy industry, proved especially vulnerable – as it continued to be right on into the eighties of the twentieth century. By 1914, the best days of Scottish coalmining, engineering and shipbuilding were wellnigh over. In politics, the imperial confidence of former days seemed on the wane. Many remarked upon the less ebullient spirit of the Diamond Jubilee celebrations as compared with those of the Golden Jubilee ten years before, and the early disasters of the

Boer War were a chastening experience for Imperialists and Little Englanders alike. Nor could much encouragement be extracted from the years which followed the accession of the new sovereign: years whose many-sided violence – strikes in the docks and the mines and on the railways, suffragette outrages and Irish troubles – led one recent historian to see them as marking "The Strange Death of Liberal England".[2] Trust in the special destiny of the British people was seriously eroded, as was the assurance that they would never fall victim to the disorders troubling other nations. A new world had come into existence, a world which (among other things) seemed much less favourable to Christianity and the Christian Church than its predecessor had been. The story of Scottish religion in the twentieth century is largely concerned with the attempts made by churchmen either to counter or to adapt to the multifarious challenges of an almost uniquely difficult time.

Such statistics as were available certainly militated against ecclesiastical complacency. The Census of 1851 had been a shock, but the surveys undertaken south of the Border by *The British Weekly* in 1886 and by *The Daily News* in 1902–3 were still more depressing; and although the Scottish situation was not so desperate little joy could be extracted from the discovery that even the smaller country contained more than one and a half million persons who lacked any church connection – something like $37\frac{1}{2}\%$ of the population. In Protestant eyes, moreover, matters were made worse by the knowledge that the centuries-old balance of religion in the country had been substantially altered by the coincidence of a large Roman Catholic invasion from Ireland with a considerable Protestant emigration from Scotland. The picture did not become any brighter if, instead of counting heads, one sought to take the spiritual temperature. The eminent church leader, John White, did this around 1930, and spoke of the change he had witnessed from "an unquestioning acceptance of the orthodox message of the Church" to "a secular rationalism, Hedonism, and the New Psychology". During his student days (1883–92), the Church had apparently been strong in the land; but a great and (he believed) sudden transformation took place about that time, and it soon found itself in the Slough of Despond. The young minister of Shettleston (1892–1904) discovered that "the new rationalist was out-thinking the old champion of orthodoxy"; and the onslaught on belief, which had intensified while he was at South Leith (1904–11), reached its height in his early years at the Barony of Glasgow (1911 onwards). As White put it, "All the forces that had been attacking religion and the Church seemed to gather strength."[3] Guided by the lights of natural science and the newer disciplines of psychology, anthropology and comparative religion, and following the lead of popularisers like H. G. Wells and George Bernard Shaw, the successors of the Victorians were exchanging faith and commitment for suspended judgement and scepticism. The supernatural, they felt, had been largely discredited: it was displaced by immanentism and a host of this-worldly expectations. Though less deeply affected than its southern neighbour by the agnosticism and ethical relativism of the new world-view, Scotland also was undergoing a sweeping transformation. In William Ferguson's words, "The rock on which Scottish presbyterianism had stood for centuries fell before the onslaught of the scientific spirit of the nineteenth century. The intellectuality of its faith, once its great strength, was now a grievous weakness; for it had rejected sacramentalism and so could not stress a mystic means of grace as a solatium. The sanctity of the sabbath and the habit of church-going remained; but undeniably religion was no longer the very pith and core of Scottish life."[4]

The horrors and miseries of the First World War further accelerated the advance towards a completely secularised society. They also, however, awakened the Churches – which, in P. T. Forsyth's vivid phrase, had been behaving like picnickers on the slopes of a temporarily dormant volcano – to the gravity of the situation and their failure to deal adequately with it. One sign of the new awareness may be found in the number of books published during or immediately after the conflict which sought to analyse the faith (or lack of it) of Britain's young combatants, and to assess their relationship to organised Christianity. Probably the most striking of them was *The Army and Religion: An Enquiry and its Bearing upon the Religious Life of the Nation*, which appeared in 1919 under the sponsorship of the Y.M.C.A. Although largely written by Principal David S. Cairns of the United Free Church College in Aberdeen, this bulky volume was based upon reports from chaplains and servicemen which had been subsequently collated by a large interdenominational committee; and the semi-official character of the work made its conclusions all the more remarkable – and telling.

Ordinary men, according to Cairns' informants, were in a state of mingled ignorance and perplexity where religion was concerned. Nearly all believed in God and immortality, but only in a vague and confused manner. "The great fact of the war", declared the committee near the outset of their report, "has come crashing into the midst of the dim and instinctive theism which is the working faith of perhaps the majority of the youth of our nation, and it is proving wholly insufficient for the spiritual need of the men who have hitherto held it."[5] Later on, they repeated this analysis in greater detail. "The weakness in the whole religious outlook of these men", they opined, "is that their thought of God is not fully Christianised.... On one side is God – 'the great and terrible God' dimly believed to be good, Whose Providence directs and governs all things, and Who seems to be held responsible for the war. On the other is the remote Jesus of history, the 'gentle Jesus' of the hymns of childhood, who, like His Church, is out of touch with the rough and terrible realities of camp and battlefield, and who has no power to redeem them or the world. Is not the war a standing proof of His weakness as of that of the Churches which represent Him? And since He has no power, what hope elsewhere is there for them, or for the world, of realising a nobler life? The temptation lies near – 'Let us eat and drink, for tomorrow we die.'"[6] One desideratum, obviously, was a more robust and sensitive apologetic. But the circumstances also called for fresh attention to the whole business of Christian education. Men's thoughts of Jesus Christ were revealed to be hazy and muddled; belief in His continuing presence through the Holy Spirit had virtually disappeared; the faith was regarded by most as a negative rather than a positive thing; and a "materialistic" view of life had become dominant. "Most of the men" (so ran the report) "have never really understood the things they have been taught.... It is a very frequent thing in our evidence to find the need for 'interpretation' insisted upon, the explanation of what Christ and His salvation really mean. This implies that Christian truth is at present taught in a foreign tongue which has been learned by rote but never understood. Hence in the great convulsion of the war it has been simply dropped, as something quite without use, and out of all relation to the urgent facts, 'just as on a forced march a Bible will be left out of a kit-bag by a man who does not understand or love it', or else retained only as a mascot."[7]

Not the least alarming feature of the situation was the criticism to which organised religion was subjected by men on whom it had lost any real hold. "If we put all the evidence together", wrote Professor John Baillie some years after the war, "one main charge stands out in the very boldest relief, and that is that there is a lack of reality about the religion of the Christian Church, and a conspicuous unrelatedness to the real problems of human life."[8] And Cairns himself presented this damning summary of the indictment: "The point of all the criticisms is that the Church has not independent life or a spiritual message, but is deeply tainted with the materialism of the world."[9] It has to be admitted that much in the behaviour of churchmen during the great conflict lent support to such accusations. Just as Scottish ministers had warmly defended their country's participation in the Crimean War and (in general) looked on the Boer War with approval, so between 1914 and 1918 they were frequently guilty of the sin of jingoism. "We have entered into the War fully conscious as a nation that if we did not enter into it we would stand as criminals before God," declared Dr. Wallace Williamson in the 1915 Assembly of the Auld Kirk; while Professor James Denney went so far as to tell the Free Church General Assembly that "If a Christian cannot take sides in it and strike with every atom of his energy, then a Christian is a being that so far as this world is concerned has committed moral suicide."[10] Though understandable, their attitude left little room for the finer Christian emotions. Few, for example, were prepared to tolerate conscientious objectors; and J. R. Fleming reports that Sir George Adam Smith, whose moderatorial address to the United Free Assembly in 1916 had contained the assertion that "To make peace fundamental or final in our religion is not to follow the order either of Christ or of His apostles", was soon after "quoted from a rather browbeating tribunal, to the confusion and silencing of a trembling youth who sought exemption on the score of religious principle".[11] There were, of course, other and humaner voices to be heard – prominent among them the exiled Presbyterian scholar, John Oman – but many pronouncements made by men of religion during those scarifying years were marred by a sorry amalgam of chauvinism, sentimentality and self-righteousness. Perhaps saddest of all, these failures of the war years cast a shadow backwards upon the ideas and activities of churchmen in the decades immediately before the conflict. As one discerning historian has put it, "The churches had been keeping step with the social gospel of popularly interpreted Christianity, instead of formulating that interpretation for the British people", and it was this which made it so difficult for them to "give to.the nation in war anything more than they had given in peace".[12]

The period between the wars brought little brightening of this sombre scene. Long-established traditions (church-going and Sabbath observance among them) continued to give ground before the onward march of technological progress and social change. Improvement in communications – faster trains, more frequent and more comfortable; the revolution brought about by the electric tram, the motor bus, and above all the private car; the coming of air transport – hastened the decline of rural society, where ancient pieties tended to be most strongly entrenched. It also undermined the hold of custom by introducing people to a new and vastly different way of life and enabling them to escape more easily from that which they no longer desired to follow. And it diminished the authority of the older generation, whose experience seemed increasingly limited and whose ideals of reverence, thrift, temperance and self-denial began to look more like superstition than wisdom. At a very practical level, the spread of new forms of lighting by gas and electricity lengthened the working day and encouraged men and women to indulge more varied interests when their work was done. Cinema, radio and the popular press had clearly taken over from the pulpit as the principal educator and entertainer of the masses, while organised sport displaced religion (and politics) as the dominant preoccupation of their leisure hours. With the collapse of the old sanctions, moreover, kirk session discipline became a thing of the past; easier divorce, and the introduction of efficient methods of birth control, created a fresh pattern of sexual behaviour. Social idealism began to seek expression more and more outside the institutional Churches. Throughout the twenties and thirties, therefore, one finds the pronouncements of Church leaders to be replete with denunciations of the materialism and crass this-worldliness of contemporary society. "The difficulty", remarked Professor H. R. Mackintosh in his moderatorial address to the General Assembly of 1932, "does not lie in modern science, which is to be accepted fearlessly and freely, but in something very different – the modern temper or attitude to life .... The initial assertion, 'I must live my own life' governs all, and true fellowship is made impossible.... Human beings are standardised and dealt with by mechanical rule. The inhuman industrial machine sweeps employer and employee indiscriminatingly into its power. Economic forces more and more crowd out brotherly enterprise and human fellowship. And those whose worship we guide have to live, week in week out, in a society enslaved by the delusion that things, not persons and personal relationships, are what really matter."[13]

A fear often expressed by thoughtful Christians at this time was that the Churches were well on the way to losing – if they had not already lost – two vitally important groups in society, the workers and the intellectuals. As far as the workers were concerned, the fear may not have been altogether well-founded. One suspects that it was more readily entertained by outside observers than by those whose occupations took them as a matter of course into the homes and work-places of the industrial masses. Nevertheless it is difficult to read, for example, the Assembly debates of the depression period, and to note how much more time was spent by the fathers and brethren in discussing the Maintenance of the Ministry Fund than in examining the plight of the nation's unemployed, and in how gingerly a manner they handled all questions of social justice, without feeling that official Christianity had little to offer the oppressed but pious platitudes, assurances of strictly non-political sympathy, and bland exhortations to grin and bear it. This, certainly, was the way in which many of the industrial workers themselves – and not only those who with Willie Gallacher, John Maclean and James Maxton were making the reputation of "Red" Clydeside – reacted to ecclesiastical deliverances during those bitter, destructive years.

Nor is there any denying that the proletarian mythology of the inter-war period has assigned a part which is far from heroic to the clergy and their more faithful followers. A recent study of *Churches and the Working Classes* in Victorian England closes with the remark that "in the twentieth century the crucial contest for the attention and allegiance of the English working classes would be conducted between politics and pleasure, with religion offering no serious challenge to either".[14] Scotland was, of course, different in many respects from its southern neighbour; but the sad story of the epoch between 1918 and 1939 went far towards making the prediction true for it also.

As serious as the alienation of the working classes was the steadily more perceptible estrangement of the intellectuals. It could be argued that the tide of secularisation had been flowing ever since the middle decades of the previous century, for religious tests in the universities went in 1855, the established Church lost its legal powers over the parish schools in 1861, and the national system of education took over in 1872. The status of schoolteachers as compared with ministers had, moreover, been rising for two or three generations; and by the outbreak of the First World War there were signs that they – together, perhaps, with journalists – had ousted the clergy from the position of being the nation's intellectual leaders (Coleridge's "clerisy"). Long before the end of the Victorian age, too, traditional Christian orthodoxy, its confidence and authority undermined by attack from various quarters, was obviously on the defensive. Its foundation-doctrine of the inerrancy of Holy Scripture had crumbled under the hammer-blows of literary and historical criticism; its teaching on Providence appeared highly unconvincing in the light of evolutionary theory as expounded by men like T. H. Huxley and Herbert Spencer; and since the days of George Eliot and John Stuart Mill even its ethics – and the ethics of its God – had seemed to make a poor showing when compared with the humane and lofty standards of contemporary moralists and littérateurs. The wheel of history had apparently come full circle, so that if Joseph Butler could have listened to Britain's intelligentsia any time from the eighteen-eighties onward he might well have repeated his famous complaint of one hundred and fifty years earlier: "It is come, I know not how, to be taken for granted by many persons that Christianity is not so much as a subject of inquiry; but that it is now at length discovered to be fictitious. And accordingly they treat it as if, in the present age, this were an agreed point among all people of discernment; and nothing remained but to set it up as a principal subject of mirth and ridicule, as it were by way of reprisals for its having so long interrupted the pleasures of the world."

While the traumatic experiences of the 1914–18 war almost certainly accelerated the advance of unbelief, they were also responsible for a significant change of mood among the opponents of Christianity. There was, at least in some quarters, a marked decline of the old confidence. As has often been pointed out, to men looking back from Aldous Huxley's *Brave New World* and T. S. Eliot's *The Waste Land* their Edwardian predecessors seemed still to believe in "inexpugnable certainties" on which it had been possible to fall back when all else failed. "The world was 'a vale of soulmaking', freedom was well worth its price for the gains in character it brought, personality in each individual human exemplar was of indefeasible right, and the moral order ruled unshaken in its majesty."[15] Now, however, it was precisely these things that were being challenged, and men had to struggle anew for a certainty which in most cases eluded them. Yet it cannot be said that this change in the intellectual climate brought any marked benefit to the Churches: if anything, they too caught the infection of doubt and hesitancy. And besides, a new aggressiveness made its appearance in other parts of the anti-Christian camp. Inspired partly by atheistic Communism and partly by Freudian psychology, Britain's enlightened middle class found the religion of the Churches either ridiculous or irrelevant – or both; and the most influential mentors of the age were H. G. Wells, D. H. Lawrence, Bernard Shaw, J. B. S. Haldane and Bertrand Russell. Of course, it would be absurd to suggest that the whole story of Christianity in Scotland between the wars is of decline and drift. The reunion of the Church of Scotland and the United Free Church in 1929 was an occasion for general rejoicing, and there were other hopeful signs. But the overall picture was peculiarly cheerless. Even from the standpoint of the nineteen-seventies and eighties, agonising and tormented as they are, it looks as if few periods in Scottish history can have been more difficult and discouraging for the Churches than that in which faith reeled from the impact of one great war, nerved itself belatedly for another, and in the interim endured the soul-destroying effects of a seemingly endless economic depression.

The Second World War was possibly less of a shock to organised religion than the first had been. Men had long since abandoned the more irrational aspects of late-Victorian optimism, and there was fairly general awareness of the problems confronting mankind. Nevertheless, the distresses, tensions and excitements of the years between 1939 and 1945 were very great; and their effect on the life of the Churches, as on that of society as a whole, was to undermine still further whatever certainty and stability remained after all the social and intellectual upheavals of the previous three or four generations. Religious trends which had been noticeable in the inter-war period were, therefore, continued and often accelerated in the years which followed. The atomic threat, and knowledge that "the Bomb" had first been dropped by a professedly Christian nation, contributed to widespread ethical cynicism. The Christian ideal of family life, together with the traditional standards of sexual morality, temperance and thrift, enjoyed ever-diminishing respect. The welfare state took over more and more of the social work once undertaken by the Churches. Steadily increasing mobility – symbolised, especially from the sixties onwards, by the weekend cottage, winter holidays on the ski-slopes and summer holidays in Spain – multiplied the obstacles encountered by ministers and kirk sessions in their efforts to build up some continuity of religious instruction, supervision and fellowship. As the forties drew to a close, it became apparent that the B.B.C. had "abandoned its initial attempt to insist that the tenets of orthodox Christianity were the final authority in matters of religion, philosophy and ethics";[16] and when, a decade later, television began to dominate people's leisure hours its standards were observed to be those of humanism rather than of Christianity. Rationalists and humanists subjected the 1944 Education Act, with its religious provisions, to severe criticism. Such firm evidence as was obtainable suggested increasing ignorance of the Christian faith, and even increasing alienation from it, on the part of the average person. All the Churches reported that the number of young people being admitted into membership was dwindling rapidly, and a "teenage counterculture" arose which seemed to reject practically all the values traditionally associated with Christian civilisation. To complete the picture, there was quite certainly no sign of the oft-heralded "revival of religion" for which churchmen had been longing ever since the last of the Moody and Sankey visits.

Something of a rally took place during the nineteen-fifties – the product, it seems, of various causes. These included the discerning analysis and recommendations of the Baillie "Commission for the Interpretation of God's Will in the Present Crisis" (1941–45); Dr. Billy Graham's All-Scotland Crusade (1955) and the allied Tell Scotland movement; some disenchantment, in certain quarters, with the Marxist analysis of things; and what Dr. Ferguson has called "a more classless form of pastoral activity" by Church Extension charges in the new housing estates.[17] But it was hardly sustained, and by the seventies the situation had again worsened appreciably. A few figures tell their own story. Between 1931 (two years after the Union of the Churches) and 1951 (when post-war recovery was at last becoming perceptible) membership of the Church of Scotland fell slowly from 1,280,620 to 1,273,027 – and that despite a rise in the total population from 4,842,980 to 5,095,969. Between 1951 and 1961, a period of distinct hopefulness for the Scottish Churches, it had risen to 1,290,617. But thereafter the decline was uninterrupted, and at an accelerating pace. Losses suffered each *year* after 1961 roughly equalled the gains made each *decade* between 1941 and 1961; and in 1971 the number of church members was lower than it had been at any other time in the twentieth century. In 1967 there were over 13,000 fewer on the rolls than in the previous year; in 1968, over 18,000; in 1969, over 23,000; in 1970, over 24,000: in each case, more than the entire population of a town the size of Lanark, Galashiels, St. Andrews, Fraserburgh or Montrose. By the end of the following decade the annual losses showed signs of levelling out at around 15,000, but in 1978 the total communicant membership of the Church of Scotland had fallen below one million for the first time since the Union of 1929. Taken in conjunction with other evidence, these statistics epitomised a state of affairs which for once seemed to merit the overworked epithet critical.

Most historical movements eventually run out of steam, and in the daunting state of affairs described above Scotland's religious revolution understandably failed to sustain its earlier momentum. There was, however, no dramatic reversal of the chief developments of the late-Victorian period. In the main, the present century has been marked by a quiet consolidation, a more or less eager acceptance, of what the two preceding generations had achieved   – though certain aspects of the

Victorian legacy seem to have fared rather better than others. The remainder of this study will concern itself with the somewhat diverse fortunes of theology, worship and social attitudes in the post-revolutionary age.

With the secularisation of society in general advancing by leaps and bounds, it was perhaps hardly to be expected that twentieth-century Scottish Christians would show any strong inclination to question the Victorians' abandonment (gradual and regretful though it had been) of the Puritan ethos. The more relaxed and broadminded life-style adopted by men like Norman Macleod, Thomas Davidson and Alexander Whyte became if anything even more obvious among their successors, so that at the time of writing the *mores* of such diverse groups as conservative Evangelicals, admirers of the Iona Community, and men in the Scoto-Catholic tradition are barely distinguishable.

A similar continuity is evident between the social attitudes of the 1880–1914 period and those developed later in the twentieth century. We have seen how social concerns within the Churches had deepened, and social criticisms intensified, during the decades which spanned the death of the old Queen and the accession of her son. The process continued without much slackening into a new age. Indeed, the First World War, that shatterer of Victorian complacency, may have served to stimulate even more strenuous thought and action. In 1916, the Auld Kirk set up a commission to examine the moral and spiritual issues raised by the conflict, and the investigations which followed inevitably highlighted areas of disharmony and injustice in the life of the nation. By 1920 the commission had grown into a permanent Church and Nation Committee. Meanwhile the United Free Church's much older Church and State Committee, which at one time had been almost ex-clusively concerned with the issue of establishment, began to give increased attention to such matters, adding its insights to those of the already existing Social Problems Committee. The confluence of all these streams took place when the Union of the Churches in 1929 brought about the creation of a much-enlarged and even more active Church and Nation Committee. Nearly every year thereafter seemed to mark an enhancement of that body's importance as new topics (not all of them peculiarly Scottish) came within its constantly extending field of interest, while ever greater publicity was given by press and radio to its annual reports and to the debates in Assembly which these reports aroused. As Professor Burleigh — himself once convener of "Church and Nation" – has pointed out in his *Church History of Scotland,* the range of topics dealt with by the committee at one time or another has been almost incredibly wide. Included in his list are: "pacifism and the doctrine of the just war; atomic warfare and the hydrogen bomb; international relations and the cold war; refugees; questions of colonial policy, colour bar, the rights of colonial peoples and Central African Federation; Christianity and Communism; industrial relations; housing and health; marriage, divorce, and remarriage of divorced persons; broadcasting and television; rural depopulation in the Highlands and Lowlands of Scotland and other matters peculiarly affecting Scottish life and interests; betting and gambling and Lord's Day Observance."[18] Gone indeed were the days when only "spiritual" matters were conceived of as having a claim upon churchmen's attention, and when a critical scrutiny of the social order was likely to be denounced as subversive or even atheistical!

Like its predecessor, the Second World War precipitated a tremendous upsurge of questioning and heart-searching in the Scottish Churches. Of this, the most important single consequence came in 1940, when the General Assembly appointed a special "Commission for the Interpretation of God's Will in the Present Crisis". Under the exceptionally gifted convenership of Professor John Baillie, it declared its

intention 'reverently to guide the Church in the interpretation
of the Holy Will and Purpose of God in present day events,
and to examine how the testimony of the Church to the
Gospel may become more effective in our own land, overseas,
and in the international order".[19] The full Commission
handled the fundamental problems of its remit, together with
questions relating to international reconstruction after the war,
while subcommittees examined church life and organisation,
education, marriage and the family, and social and industrial
life. Reports were submitted to the Assembly each year from
1941 to 1945. Three of these subsequently appeared as
pamphlets under the titles of *God's Will in Our Time, The
Church Faces the Future,* and *Home, Community and Church,*
and a volume of extracts was published in 1946 as *God's Will
for Church and Nation.* The Commission's work, which was
warmly welcomed both in Scotland and abroad, may be taken
as typical of responsible and forward-looking thought within
the Kirk during the years of crisis. Its general attitude, and in
particular its message on social matters, is clearly conveyed by
some sentences from its report concerning "The Nature and
Extent of the Church's Concern in the Civil Order".

"Christians have often failed", writes Baillie, "to
distinguish adequately between the religious and political
spheres, and have thus misled the Church into making
pronouncements on questions which it only imperfectly
understood. But we hold it as certain that the greater harm has
come about through the opposite error – through the
indifference of Christians to the maladjustments of that civil
ordering of society in which they like others have a part, and
the consequent failure of the Church to bring its own light to
bear upon the problems so created. If it were merely that
Christians were so exclusively absorbed in heavenly things as
to be indifferent to the earthly ills of themselves and their
neighbours, that alone would spell a serious falsification of the
true Christian temper; but it is to be feared that many of us

must plead guilty to the even more damaging charge of complacently accepting the amenities, and availing ourselves of the privileges, of a social order which happened to offer these things to ourselves while denying them to others. It cannot be denied that during a period when the crying injustices of the existing order were being brought prominently into the light, the Church as a whole seemed content to leave this task to those outside its fellowship or to isolated voices within, instead of itself providing the necessary volume of righteous and enlightened zeal. Arriving only as a late-comer in this most necessary field, it largely failed to bring its Gospel to bear at the right time upon a situation that continued to develop with such tragic speed.... There can be little doubt that it is to the failure of Christians to realise and act upon these social implications of the Gospel that the present weakness of the spiritual life of our land must in no small part be attributed. We long for a revival of spiritual religion, but there are many who suspect the spirituality to which we call them of making too ready a compliance with a social order that for them means only hunger, slum conditions, unemployment, or sweated labour.... Selfishness is of the very essence of the sin from which, in any revival of religion, men need to be redeemed; but what if there be no particular form of this sin from which we more need to be redeemed today than a complacent indifference to the social evils that surround our comfortable lives?"[20]

The reports of the Baillie Commission certainly played a part in bringing about that massive and portentous swing in British opinion as a whole which acclaimed the Beveridge Plan in 1944, and ushered in the era of the welfare state with the inauguration of the National Health Service in 1948. But of course they were also very much the products of that same revolution. Indeed, it can be contended that in them, as in many aspects of its existence during the last two centuries or so, the Church reflected rather than shaped the most influential thinking of the nation. Moreover, there is still room for debate as to whether the Baillie Report and those other manifestations of social criticism which have been detailed here really amount to anything more than a very minor strain in the story of twentieth-century Scottish Presbyterianism. Some would say that to examine Assembly pronouncements and the record of Assembly debates at any time between 1900 and the present, and particularly in days of social unrest or political crisis, is to realise the intimate kinship that has existed, and still exists, between the Church and the established order of things. How suspicious (they remark) are most churchmen of any kind of social change, how closely tied to the attitudes and interests of the more prosperous classes, how excessively deferential to the monarchy, the nobility, the landed gentry, and the forces of "law and order", how wary of organised labour and every conceivable brand of Socialism, how inclined to view social reform as being in some way hostile to personal evangelism, how eager to appeal to authority for the enforcement of their sectional concerns and opinions in such matters as dress, drinking habits, public entertainment and education! The fairness or otherwise of such an indictment is debatable. But one suspects that, the detailed and wide-ranging character of the Church and Nation Committee's recent pronouncements notwithstanding, the high level of social thought which was evident in the Baillie Report has hardly been sustained during the subsequent quarter of a century. Indeed, to talk (as Donald Smith has done) of "The Failure and Recovery of Social Criticism in the Church of Scotland, 1830–1950" is perhaps to be more optimistic than is altogether warranted by the history of the Kirk since Victorian times.

Patterns of worship in Scotland after the religious revolution clearly reflect the relative strengths and weaknesses, at one time or another, of the various parties and groupings within the Churches. Despite the advances made by men of "Scoto-Catholic" outlook in the late-Victorian period, there can be little doubt that Liberal Evangelicalism was the dominating influence during the decades immediately before and after the First World War. The attitudes and convictions of Davidson and Robertson Smith, of A. B. Bruce, Marcus Dods and George Adam Smith had entrenched themselves strongly in the academic world, and by 1914 they were shared to an impressive degree by most of Scotland's theological teachers. But the pulpits also had been taken captive. Down to and even beyond the mid-point of the century, therefore, a host of able and influential preachers – men whose message was echoed and whose style was imitated by a numerous band of admirers both in Britain and in North America – proclaimed a faith which owed a good deal more to the insights of Biblical criticism, literary and historical, and to the world-view shared by teachers as diverse as John Tulloch, Robert Rainy and Robert Flint, than to the traditional formulations of orthodox Calvinism. Such were Walter C. Smith, G. H. Morrison, John Kelman, J. R. P. Sclater, Hugh and James Black, W. M. Macgregor, John A. Hutton, Norman Maclean and A. J. Gossip in the earlier period, and R. E. McIntyre, George Johnstone Jeffrey, Ernest Jarvis, Adam Burnet, James S. Stewart and Murdo Ewen Macdonald in recent times. Generally speaking, these men sat rather loose to questions of church order, expected little from the state and the national recognition of religion, put considerable emphasis on social as well as individual righteousness, and were above all concerned to commend the Gospel in terms which their contemporaries could understand. Their most obvious kinship was probably with Reformed and Lutheran Christianity on the Continent of Europe, the English Free Churches, and mainstream American Protestantism rather than with the Anglican Communion – and the kind of services which they conducted bore the imprint of their theology and churchmanship. The sermon continued to be the central, supremely important element in worship, though prayer, praise and the reading of Scripture were no longer described (oddly) as "the preliminaries". For prayers to be read was still exceptional, and the predominant influence from the past was obviously the Westminster Directory rather than Cranmer's Book of Common Prayer. Ritual, vestments and church furnishings bore few traces of the Catholic inheritance. The rôle of the minister was conceived of as prophetic rather than priestly. It would have been difficult to say that the sacraments – Communion above all – were the focal point round which everything else in public worship revolved.

But if Liberal Evangelicalism probably continued to be the most important single strand in ecclesiastical life (and worship) right down to the nineteen-fifties, it was not without its critics. Prominent among these were representatives of the so-called "High Church" tradition: the associates and followers of men like James Cooper, John Macleod and the Wotherspoon brothers in the Scoto-Catholic activities of the Scottish Church Society. Always very much a minority party, they nevertheless wielded considerable influence – its culminating point, so far as theology was concerned, being the first clause of the Articles Declaratory of the Constitution of the Church of Scotland in Matters Spiritual (1921, 1926), which they pushed through against the initial reaction of John White and Lord Sands.[21] Their policy of concentrating upon limited objectives and securing control of one or two key committees, Public Worship and Aids to Devotion in particular, won them a number of successes. Ministering often in large, prestigious churches of the cathedral or collegiate type; devoted to seemliness and dignity in worship, and by no means averse from a little pomp and circumstance; seldom noted for their preaching ability but deeply concerned to magnify the part played by the sacraments in parish life; zealous for church unity, and especially for closer relations with the Church of England, whose doctrine of apostolic succession through ordination by bishops they matched with the doctrine of *successio presbyterorum*; clerical in temper, and inclined to speak much of "clergy" and "laity" and the representative as opposed to the ruling function of the eldership: these men tended (unlike their Anglican counterparts) to be strongly conservative in politics, and in theology they came to have a good deal in common – not least through their stress on the importance of continuity in religion – with the neo-orthodox of the Barthian school. Among their leaders might be reckoned Oswald Milligan, minister at Corstorphine Old to the end of the nineteen-thirties and convener of the committee which produced the 1940 *Book of Common Order*; Charles Warr, whose ministry at St. Giles', Edinburgh lasted from 1926 to 1954; Nevile Davidson, minister at Glasgow Cathedral from 1935 to 1967; and Ronald Selby Wright, who ministered at the Canongate, Edinburgh until as recently as 1977, and was Scotland's best-known chaplain to the Forces during the Second World War. The group's most noteworthy publications included Wotherspoon and Kirkpatrick's *Manual of Church Doctrine*, W. D. Maxwell's studies in the history of worship, Geddes Macgregor's *Corpus Christi: the Nature of the Church according to the Reformed Tradition,* and R. S. Louden's *The True Face of the Kirk.*

The principal contribution of Scoto-Catholicism to the life of the Church, however, was incontrovertibly *The Book of Common Order,* which the General Assembly's Committee on Public Worship and Aids to Devotion published "for the guidance of ministers" in 1940. *Prayers for Divine Service* (1923) and the *Book of Common Order* (1928) were the little volume's immediate predecessors in the pre-Union Church of Scotland and the pre-Union United Free Church respectively; but of course it also stood in line with *Euchologion* and other products of the late-Victorian liturgical revival. Though not a prescribed liturgy (being merely "authorised" and not imposed by the Assembly), it soon put its mark upon the worship of the whole Kirk. More and more ministers – some fully convinced of its superior merits, others simply taking the line of least resistance – either adopted it in its entirety or copied the general pattern of its services. Its implications and long-term significance are perhaps best realised by comparing its salient features with those of Knox's Liturgy (1562/64) and the Westminster Directory, the great monuments of Reform and Puritanism. The 1562 Book contained private prayers for the ordinary worshipper, whereas the only private prayers included in the 1940 Book were vestry prayers and suchlike for the clergy – a difference which suggests that while the former was designed for the use of members as well as ministers the latter had none but ministers in mind. 1562 contained a *Reformed* confession of faith, 1940 the Apostles' and Nicene Creeds only. 1562 assigned an inordinately large place to penitential discipline, 1940 gave it almost no place at all. 1562 included rules on fasting, 1940 passed the whole subject over in silence. 1562 focused attention on men's interior dispositions, 1940 concerned itself also with the externals of the ecclesiastical institution. 1562 was "so framed" (in the judgement of one authority) "as to make responsive worship impossible",[22] 1940 almost the exact opposite. 1645 went out of its way to affirm that "Festival days, vulgarly called Holy-days, having no warrant in the Word of God, are not to be continued", 1940 devoted a whole section to "Prayers for the Seasons of the Christian Year". 1645 declared that "no place is capable of any holiness under pretence of whatsoever dedication or consecration", 1940 included orders "for laying the foundation stone of a church", "for the dedication of an organ", and "for the dedication of church furnishings and memorials". Perhaps most revealing of all, 1645 offered detailed counsel on preaching while 1940 left the subject completely untouched.

Opinion will no doubt continue to be divided as to the merits or otherwise of the 1940 Book. What seems to be fairly certain, however, is that it both reinforced and consolidated the gains made by Scoto-Catholicism since mid-Victorian times, as well as marking the highest point of the reaction against certain aspects of the Protestant and Puritan inheritance. Nor – if officially authorised publications are a guide – has the worship of the Church of Scotland experienced any notable change of direction during the last fifty years or so. *The Church Hymnary: Third Edition* (published in 1973) and *The Book of Common Order* (published in 1979) both continue along the lines laid down by their predecessors of 1927 and 1940 respectively, and the Aids to Devotion Committee remains true as ever to the principles which have guided it over several generations.

At the same time, there have been signs in recent years of a growing reluctance, at least in some quarters, to accept the achievements of the liturgical revolution with either docility or delight. For this change various reasons may be adduced, including the fact that the residual Moderatism of the pre-1929 Auld Kirk, which had not a little to do with the rise of the Scoto-Catholic movement, has shrunk almost to vanishing point. More important, however, is the transformation gradually being effected among those whose forerunners had been Moderatism's fiercest opponents. Even before the Second World War preachers were following theologians in a new reluctance to sound the notes characteristic of Evangelicalism since Robertson Smith; and there can be little doubt that from the late forties onwards the prevailing temper in the Church has ceased to be unambiguously and exuberantly liberal. The most striking example of this was the increasingly conservative emphasis of Tom Allan's memorable ministries at North Kelvinside and St. George's Tron in Glasgow between 1946 and 1964; but after his death the trend became even more pronounced. By the seventies, a minister who had succeeded in attracting an exceptionally large congregation, especially if it included a significant number of young people, was more than likely to stand pretty far to the right of centre (theologically speaking); while the mood which he fostered would owe less to the ecumenical optimism of "Edinburgh 1910" or the eirenic broadmindedness of the inter-war Student Christian Movement than to the piety of the Scripture Union and the Inter-Varsity Fellowship – as well perhaps as the Keswick Convention, "Bible Belt" American preachers like Billy Graham, and a Pentecostalist emotionalism hitherto unknown in the Scottish Presbyterian tradition.

The implications of all this for worship hardly need to be spelled out. It would be a wild exaggeration to suggest that the achievements of the liturgical revival are presently in imminent danger of being rejected by large numbers of Scottish worshippers. Yet there are grounds for suspecting that a considerable and possibly increasing minority would welcome a reversal of at least some of the trends whose history over several generations has just been traced. *The Church Hymnary: Third Edition* is quite often compared to its disadvantage with other compilations (either its forerunner of 1927 or works of a more popular or Pentecostalist flavour); and real indignation has been aroused both by its bowdlerising of the Psalter and by its doctrinaire assumption that "you make worship Christian if you scatter Trinitarian formulae over it with a pepper-pot".[23] When the National Church Association published a *Reformed Book of Church Order* in 1977, it did so with the frank intention of challenging that revised version of the 1940 Book which the Aids to Devotion Committee were to bring out two years later. Whether such discontent will grow or diminish during the remainder of the present century is impossible to forecast, and in any case the historian should beware of donning the prophet's mantle. The wisest comment would seem to be along the lines of that with which Professor J. M. Barkley ended his recent survey of "The renaissance of public worship in Scotland": "those who have entered into and reaped the harvest of this renaissance must remember that no

P

form of public worship can ever be considered final in detail. History and experience of the God of history do not stand still."[24]

Turning finally from social attitudes and liturgical practice to theology, and in particular to the view which Scottish churchmen took of Bible and Confession in the post-revolutionary period, we have a rather more eventful story to tell. Yet when the present century began there were few discernible signs of any serious challenge being offered to the liberal-Evangelical dominance which had changed the face of religion in Victoria's later years.

What might be called the new orthodoxy was marked by three outstanding characteristics: deference to the methods and findings of natural science, wariness of all credal and confessional statements, and devotion to the use of literary and historical criticism in the study of the Bible. On the first, it should perhaps be said that Scotland's leading theologians in the period 1870–1920 were more sceptical concerning the extreme claims then made for science, and more aware of the dangers attendant upon exclusive absorption in its pursuits, than their conservative opponents were willing to admit. But it is also true that they never tired of affirming their belief that the discoveries of biology, chemistry and physics, if properly understood, would only reinforce the Christian interpretation of the universe; and few if any of them were inclined to repudiate the main principles of evolutionary theory.

As for the relationship of liberal Evangelicalism to creeds and confessions, the currents of thought which had brought about the Declaratory Acts of 1879 and 1892 – and the Church of Scotland Act on the Formula of Subscription (1910) – continued to flow. Professor W. A. Curtis' inaugural lecture at Aberdeen in 1903 asserted that the doctrinal details of the Confession could "no longer be claimed to represent the spontaneous beliefs of the great majority of our preachers and teachers";[25] and four years later his view found support in an important little volume, published in Glasgow, which had as its title *Creed Revision in Scotland: its Necessity and Scope.* Though not drawn from any one school of thought, the contributors – a distinguished group including James Moffatt, John Herkless, Alan Menzies, E. F. Scott and R. H. Strachan – were in pretty complete agreement on a number of things. To begin with, most of them clearly believed that the Confession's best days were over. As J. H. Leckie (biographer of Fergus Ferguson, one of the moving spirits behind the 1879 Declaratory Act) put it: "The fact of dominant force today, aggressive and vivid, is that the professed creed of the Church does not any longer, *as a system,* have any particular relation to its religious life. The Westminster Confession is not expounded in our Theological Colleges. You may search the libraries of many divines and find no copy of it there. It was read for the first time by many official Presbyterians when the decision of the House of Lords in the Church case gave it a new and painful interest. No man writes his sermons with conscious regard to its venerable propositions, nor does any theological professor compose his books in the light of its authority. The central thoughts, also, of the Confession are no longer the central thoughts of living faith. The doctrine of Predestination, which is the keystone of the Westminster arch, holds no vital place in the belief of the modern man; while, on the other hand, the idea of the Divine Fatherhood, though it is the centre of real faith today, finds no adequate expression whatever in the ancient creed of the Presbyterian Church."[26]

Furthermore, most of the writers in *Creed Revision* considered the Declaratory Acts to be a rather unsatisfactory, stopgap solution of the confessional problem. "A Declaratory Act", said Leckie, "can never be regarded as more than a merely temporary expedient. It bears on its face the signs of its mortality. It is, indeed, a useful relief to conscience in a time of transition, a device for preserving self-respect in a season of suspense. But this is all. It is a temporary bridge that shakily hangs between 'Formula' and 'Fact'. Sooner or later the bridge must be taken away, and the Church must set itself to make the 'Fact' and the 'Formula' solidly at one."[27] Behind many of the essays there also lay the conviction, peculiarly characteristic of the age, that conduct mattered very much more than creed. "We get upon a wrong track", wrote D. M. Ross, "when we make a body of doctrine, no matter how intrinsically good it may be, the bond of union for a church. To do so is to give undue weight to intellectualism in religion, with the result that mere orthodoxy – the mere acceptance of doctrinal beliefs – tends to be exalted at the expense of the religion of heart and life. Is it not evident from the Gospels that what Christ laid stress on was not men's beliefs about the spiritual world but their own spiritual attitude towards God and their fellows...? And when we turn to St. Paul we find that amid all his splendour of theological thinking he is ever laying the main stress on the 'law of the spirit of life in Christ Jesus'.... The New Testament seems to suggest, then, that the Church, in revising its relation to the Creed as a bond of union, should be less concerned about attaining a satisfactory summary of doctrine than about the spiritual attitude of its ministers and office-bearers and members. Not only so, but the New Testament presents us with a creed – and a creed whose sum and substance is the confession of the spiritual lordship of Jesus. There is theological doctrine, of course, in the New Testament – several types of doctrine, indeed – but the bond of union is not acceptance of a compendium of doctrine but the acceptance of Jesus as Lord. Is it not here, then, that we ought to take our stand?"[28]

In the light of these views, the advocates of confessional change propounded their recommendations for specific action. Some desired a fairly drastic rewriting of the Westminster documents, contending with James Moffatt (the future translator of the Bible) that "the Church, as she is true to the authority of faith, is morally bound... to move in the direction of revision, cautiously and reverently, but none the less with sympathy".[29] Others favoured the production of an entirely new creed. "We have as many learned Doctors of the Church today as in any bygone time," declared Leckie. "The difficulties to be faced are not greater than those that confronted the Westminster divines or the men of the Reformation. Is our courage less than theirs, or is the old fire dead on the altar?" And he continued: "One thing at least is sure – It has never been the way of the Church to hold her peace in critical times of thought. The Christological controversies issued in the Nicene and other ancient Creeds. The Reformation conflicts created the various Protestant symbols and the Decrees of the Council of Trent. The Puritan thought and spirit produced our Confession of Faith. For each great moment there was utterance; to each clear question of the mind the Church responded with her Credo. It is thus that she has proved herself a living force in living times; and thus that she must prove herself today."[30] Yet others would have preferred to impose no confessional formula whatsoever. Chief among them was E. F. Scott, later a well-known New Testament scholar. "May it not be fairly argued", he asked, "that the whole system of creeds, deeply as it has rooted itself in the Church, is alien to the true idea of Christianity?" And his conclusion was as follows: "The modern revolt against the system of creeds does not arise... from any disloyalty to the Christian faith. We may claim, rather, that it means a reversion to the true idea of Christianity, as we find it in the New Testament and in the teaching of Christ Himself. The truth must needs reveal itself differently to every honest seeker, and the Church can have no right to dictate to him what he is bound to believe. It can assist him in his seeking; it can bring him into fellowship with others who are also striving, in their different ways, to reach a knowledge of the truth. But it oversteps its rights when it imposes its own formula in place of the personal creed which each man must discover for himself.... In dispensing with a written creed it will, we believe, lose nothing that is worth preserving, and will only affirm more clearly the true principles of the Christian faith."[31]

Interestingly enough, as things turned out, the radicalism of *Creed Revision* did very little to alter the official attitude to Westminster; and no advance beyond the Declaratory Acts and the Church of Scotland Act on the Formula falls to be recorded. Why this surprising inactivity? One explanation is that the innovators failed because they were utterly unrepresentative of the Church as a whole; but their distinction and their numbers alike make this rather hard to believe. More plausible is the suggestion that the years immediately after 1907 saw a powerful deflecting of ecclesiastical energies into new channels: from 1908 the reunion conversations, from 1914 the task of coping with the enormous problems created or uncovered by the First World War, from 1929 onwards adjustment to Union, the agonies of the Depression, another global conflict, and the painful period of reconstruction which succeeded it. Some waning of theological interest and expertise may also have played its part. Whatever the reason, the high hopes entertained by Moffatt and his colleagues were never realised; and when the time came for the Kirk to clarify its theological position in the Articles Declaratory of 1921 the most effective force was not liberal Evangelicalism but the Scoto-Catholic group led by Cooper and the Wotherspoons. An opportunity had been missed (so some would say) which might never return. In the half-century after the 1929 Union – and particularly since the Barthian explosion of the nineteen-thirties and the resurgence, in the wake of the Second World War, of a deeply conservative theology – all attempts to alter the Church's confessional stance have run into very considerable difficulties; and at the time of writing it is not the Confession but the "conscience clause" which seems to be under threat.

Even more determinative of liberal Evangelicalism's general character than its approach to natural science or creeds and confessions was its attitude to the Bible; but here also the significant issues had all been raised (and very often discussed at great length) long before the twentieth century began. By 1900, scholars could talk with some confidence about the "assured results" of literary and historical criticism of the sacred books. Interested laymen were becoming familiar with scholarly theories concerning the non-Mosaic authorship of the Pentateuch, the non-Davidic authorship of many of the Psalms, and the non-apostolic authorship of the Gospels. In theological colleges and divinity faculties an evolutionary account of Israel's religion was becoming the rule rather than the exception. Preachers as well as professors were beginning to abandon the literal interpretation of many a Biblical narrative. Open acknowledgement of a diversity of attitudes among the New Testament writers was being more and more frequently made. The so-called "Quest of the Historical Jesus" had come to be as eagerly pursued in Scotland as elsewhere. And a host of well-respected scholars – including George Adam Smith, J. E. McFadyen, A. R. S. Kennedy and A. C. Welch in Old Testament studies, and Marcus Dods, James Denney, William Milligan, Alan Menzies, H. A. A. Kennedy and James Moffat in New Testament – were at work applying the new principles and methods to every part and aspect of Holy Scripture. By the outbreak of war in 1914, Scottish writers had built up an impressive body of literature in this whole field: commentaries, scholarly or popular, on every book of the Bible; translations of foreign classics, often in series bearing the imprint of T. and T. Clark; several world-famous dictionaries and encyclopaedias under the editorship of the indefatigable James Hastings, United Free Church minister at St. Cyrus; and the first instalment of James Moffatt's pioneering translation of the entire Bible into modern English (or Scots, as some humorists were to suggest).

Despite all this activity, early twentieth-century Presbyterianism seldom succumbed to unbalanced or excessive enthusiasm for the new ideals. A. B. Bruce's posthumously-published article on "Jesus Christ" in the *Encyclopaedia Biblica* (1901) may have gone some distance along a road more often traversed by German scholars of the period, but even it – as one discerning English commentator has remarked – did no more than hint at a definite break with orthodox Christology.[32] In any case, few of Bruce's academic contemporaries were as venturesome as he. While Bruce grew more radical with advancing years, his Glasgow colleague James Orr developed in the opposite direction, winning widespread respect on both sides of the Atlantic for his forceful but generally level-headed conservatism. And James Denney, one of the finest Biblical theologians Scotland ever produced, pursued a notably middle-of-the-road course. He could shock James Cooper with his proposal, made in *Jesus and the Gospel,* that "the symbol of the Church's unity might be expressed thus: I believe in God through Jesus Christ His only Son, our Lord and Saviour".[33] But he was no reductionist, and a careful avoidance of extremes marked almost everything that he wrote. In his *Expositor's Bible* commentary on Second Corinthians, for example, he contrasted the Pauline gospel with all literal or legalistic perversions of "the spirituality, the freedom, and the newness of Christianity", and went on: "In a Protestant scholasticism this glorious Gospel ... is lost when 'a learned ministry' deals with the New Testament writings as the scribes dealt with the Old; it is lost also – for extremes meet – when an unlearned piety swears by verbal, even by literal, inspiration, and takes up to mere documents an attitude which in principle is fatal to Christianity.... It is not with the 'letter' one can hopefully address unbelieving men; it is only with the power of the Holy Spirit at work in the heart; and where the Spirit is, there is liberty."[34] Under the direction of men such as Denney, Scottish theology before the First World War may have been confident; but it was hardly hubristic. Yet something not unlike nemesis was on the way.

In the aftermath of the First World War, liberal Evangelicalism continued as a living tradition, though probably with rather less of its former exuberance and productivity. But as the twenties gave way to the thirties, and the storm-clouds of an even more terrible conflict began to darken the sky, new influences from the Continent of Europe gradually transformed the theological scene. In particular, churchmen became acquainted with the names of Karl Barth and Emil Brunner, and with what has at different times been called "the Theology of Crisis", "the Dialectical Theology", and "the Theology of the Word of God". They were thereby introduced to a temper and attitude very different from that which had prevailed among them for something like half a century. Dogmatic rather than apologetic, it started not from man – his predicament, his virtues, his self-consciousness – but from God and the divine Word of judgement and forgiveness. It asserted a complete discontinuity between the Christian revelation and human life even at its best. Supernaturalistic, authoritarian, strongly church-centred, it was addicted to paradox and contemptuous of the unredeemed intellect; stressed the transcendence rather than the immanence of the divine; and violently opposed a number of modern "isms", including psychologism, historicism, and subjectivism. In short, it was bent upon questioning, if not reversing, the dominant tendencies of Christian thought as they had developed in Britain throughout the nineteenth century. Scotland, like other parts of the world, was deeply divided in its views of the new phenomenon; and no estimate of the durability or otherwise of the late-Victorian revolution in religion would be complete without a brief concluding review of how Scottish theologians reacted to the Barthian movement. Roughly speaking, they fell into four groups: those who were only superficially influenced and therefore continued the liberal tradition without much change; those whose entire outlook was affected but who in the end withheld their whole-hearted approval; those who may be described as real if cautious admirers; and those in whom we can discern the unqualified zeal of out-and-out converts.

The most attractive exemplar of the first group was David S. Cairns, from 1907 professor of Apologetics and Systematic Theology at the United Free College (after 1929, Christ's College) Aberdeen, and author of *Christianity in the Modern World* (1906), *The Reasonableness of the Christian Faith* (1918), *The Faith that Rebels* (1928), and *The Riddle of the World* (1937). An admiring disciple of the Marburg theologian Wilhelm Herrmann, Cairns typified early twentieth-century liberalism in his overriding concern to commend the Faith in terms which men familiar with psychology, sociology and the natural sciences could understand and appreciate; but there were few to equal the infectious warmth of his piety, his ability to stir youthful audiences, his enthusiasm for the early manifestations of the ecumenical movement, and his unusually attractive literary style. Though perhaps disqualified by age from responding positively to the new theology of the thirties (he had been born as far back as 1862), Cairns certainly did his best to grapple with its criticisms of the tradition to which he belonged. In the end he remained unconvinced. An appendix to his last substantial work, *The Riddle of the World,* focused attention upon what he considered the most alarming aspect of the Barthian message. "Barth", he declared, "repudiates altogether every form of 'natural theology', holding that sin has destroyed the image of God in man, and so prevented men from gaining any real knowledge of God either from His works in Nature, or His voice in conscience. Nor can there be any real knowledge of God apart from the Bible revelation in any human being. The saints and prophets of heathendom, Socrates, Gautama, Plato, were unvisited by any revelation of Him or His message. Nor can the true missionary recognise any real point of contact in the noblest representative of heathen religion to whom he comes. As there is in such a man no real knowledge of God there can be no real point of contact."

To such an outlook, Cairns' reaction could hardly be other than hostile. "It is much easier", he remarked, "to understand how in the heart of a great struggle with a threatened national apostasy from Christian faith a prophetic spirit like Barth's should have reached such a position, than to justify it. There does not appear to be any adequate ground for it in Scripture.... Much of our weightiest and most efficient modern missionary testimony is against it.... It surely gives a most dreary view of human history that in all the countless ages before the Old Testament revelation began, and in all the immense populations of the unevangelised world, the Universal Father never spoke to anyone of the ruined human race and showed him something of Himself." And so the argument terminated in the following questions, each with its own implicit answer: "Can any true and final revelation be recognised as such that does not corroborate something that is there before? Can there be a revelation that is not corroboration? If we have no glimmerings within us of the knowledge of God, how can we recognise His Son as the fulness of His glory? Can the Divine Image in man really be destroyed without the destruction of the essential personality?"[35] The value of Cairns' contentions will be variously assessed; but not a few who met him or read his books came to regard his long life of patient, resourceful and sensitive dialogue with unbelief as one of the most effective counters to Barthian intransigence to be met with in their time.

Of all those on whom the new conservatism exerted a powerful but perhaps not finally decisive influence, none had a more remarkable academic career, or achieved wider recognition at home and abroad, than John Baillie, who held chairs in the U.S.A. and Canada before returning to Scotland

and becoming professor of Divinity in the University of Edinburgh, principal of New College, Moderator of the General Assembly of the Church of Scotland, and a president of the World Council of Churches. Born in the Free Church manse of Gairloch in 1886, he was exposed in early years to the rigours of traditional Calvinism; but study of philosophy at Edinburgh University and theology at New College, along with summer semesters at Marburg and Jena, introduced him to a very different thought-world – the world of ebullient pre-war liberalism. Like his brother Donald (whose training was on almost identical lines), he responded with enthusiasm. Yet he also had his reservations, and on going to the chair of Systematic Theology at Auburn Seminary, New York, he seems to have decided to act as mediator between two extremes: "a conservative biblicism which is suspicious of all modern scientific conclusions" and "a liberal modernism which is equally eager to assimilate every new scientific suggestion as the messianic deliverer of religion from its bondage to custom and tradition".[36] The consequence was that while in America he appeared a conservative among liberals; in Scotland, some years later, a liberal among conservatives. Yet the general movement of his thought – as least after the publication of his first three volumes, *The Roots of Religion in the Human Soul* (1926), *The Interpretation of Religion* (1929), and *The Place of Jesus Christ in Modern Christianity* (1929) – was pretty steadily towards a greater traditionalism. Of the years around 1930 he wrote later: "I remember being vaguely haunted by the feeling that, exhilarating as the thought of this period had been, it was now approaching something like a dead end. It seemed as if there were nowhere much further to go along the paths we were then pursuing. As things fell out, however, we had not long to wait before we found ourselves being headed off in a totally different direction.... The turning point is most conveniently marked by the publication of Karl Barth's *Epistle to the Romans* in 1918."[37] Other thinkers as well as Barth –

Kierkegaard, Buber, Brunner and Tillich among them – helped in the transition to what may be called a temperate neo-orthodoxy, and by 1931 he could publish an article with the revealing title, "The Predicament of Humanism".[38]

Despite all this, however, it is clear (as one of his students at Union Seminary, the young Dietrich Bonhoeffer, regretfully noted)[39] that Baillie never completely yielded to the new Swiss and German fashions. Although practically all the references to Barth in *And the Life Everlasting* (1934) were favourable, this was no longer the case in what may be Baillie's most important work, *Our Knowledge of God* (1939), where issue was joined on just such matters as had troubled the ageing Cairns. The passage of time served only to deepen his misgivings, and in the years immediately after the Second World War he began "to move beyond his earlier neo-orthodoxy on the basis of a renewed confidence in reason".[40] The closing pages of the posthumously-published Gifford Lectures, *The Sense of the Presence of God* (1962), therefore contained not only the last but also perhaps the strongest expression of his resistance to Barthian teaching. After quoting from Gustaf Wingren's "cogent and indeed merciless refutation of Dr. Barth", in which the Swedish theologian had remarked that "Barth has the ability to a very large degree of being able to employ the language of Scripture in a system that is totally foreign to the Bible", Baillie commented: "I should probably not myself have been quite so outspoken as Dr. Wingren, but I am in full agreement with him none the less."[41] With all his indebtedness to the great Swiss master, Baillie was never really a member of the Barthian school; and his most memorable utterances seem always to be of a mediating kind. "I believe", he declared in the late fifties, "any effective and significant post-Barthian movement must go *through* Barthianism, not repudiating the remarkable contribution which it has made to all our thinking but entering fully into its heritage, while at the same time correcting its deficiencies and also recovering for us much that was of value in those early ways of thought which were too brashly jettisoned."[42] One is sometimes inclined to think that the fascinating transition from *The Roots of Religion* and *The Interpretation of Religion* to *A Diary of Private Prayer* (1936), *Invitation to Pilgrimage* (1942) and *The Sense of the Presence of God* (revealing titles, all of them) was due less to Barthian theology than to the long-term influence of the traditional piety of Scottish Calvinism. Baillie loved to recall his childhood initiation into the profundities of the Shorter Catechism: may it have been the teaching and example of a West Highland manse which helped to steady him on that curious journey from the liberalism of the twenties to the neo-liberalism of the fifties?

One of Baillie's senior colleagues when he returned to Edinburgh in 1934 was H. R. Mackintosh, another Edinburgh-trained philosopher who (after a few years in the pastorate) had been appointed by the United Free Church to the chair of Systematic Theology at New College as early as 1904. While still quite a young man, Mackintosh made his reputation with a massive study of *The Person of Jesus Christ* (1911); and he enhanced it with *The Christian Experience of Forgiveness* (1927) and the posthumously-published *Types of Modern Theology* (1937) – each of which has become a standard work on its subject. Although well into middle age when the Barthian bombshell exploded on the theologians' playground (he had been Baillie's teacher before the First World War), Mackintosh viewed the new movement with considerable favour, and the closing sentences of his last work have often been quoted. "At the moment", he wrote of the great Swiss thinker, "he stands in the midst of his theological work, which cannot but take years to complete. Nothing more enriching for the whole Church could be thought of than that the time for completion should be given him, if God will, and that more and more his living influence should pass from land to land."[43]

In the light of such a statement, Mackintosh has

sometimes been regarded – not surprisingly – as little short of a Barthian convert. "His early thought", wrote J. W. Leitch in *A Theology of Transition: H. R. Mackintosh as an Approach to Barth,* "swung constantly to and fro: rebelling against later orthodoxy, not least as represented in certain elements of the Free Church tradition, and just as much against the Hegelianism which sought to replace it – finding in Ritschl the corrective of both which he sought – reacting against the Ritschlians in turn – finding in other writers, and above all in the things his Free Church upbringing had taught him, the arguments by means of which he sought to correct them.... He listened to most and he learned from many...: he listened with the Bible in his hand... and his thought, swing as it might, was firmly anchored here. But that is not all.... In the last years of his life, helped chiefly by Barth, he broke through the maze of nineteenth-century thought and found himself on the way to a position which was undoubtedly nearer to the Confessions and Catechisms of his Church than to Ritschl, but nearer to the apostolic Christianity he had all along sought to express than to either. Here he stood closer to Barth than he had ever done to Ritschl, so that he would seem to represent the remarkable – and indeed unique – spectacle of one who, starting as at least in some sense a Ritschlian, finally completely changed his direction and found himself in close proximity to Barth."[44] The case is not entirely convincing, however. Although Mackintosh deserted Ritschlianism, and found increasingly little good to say of Hegel, there was something about even his latest work which raises doubts as to his true-blue Barthianism. His *Types of Modern Theology* (as J. K. Mozley has pointed out) looked with disfavour on certain aspects of Kierkegaard's thought which tended to win approval from the early Barthians – the description of God as "absolutely unknown", for example, the assertion that the image of God in man was altogether destroyed by the Fall, the tendency to define **the human and the divine** by contrast with each other, and the call for crucifixion of the intellect as the means of entry into the Kingdom of God. Even his adulatory appreciation of Barth himself contained some searching criticisms.[45]

What can be said without fear of contradiction is that, as both Leitch and Mozley recognise, Mackintosh was in the last analysis a *Biblical* theologian. In Mozley's words, "Mackintosh would have found it unnatural to approach any religious questions, however speculative, except by attention to the guidance given in Scripture. His orthodoxy was rooted in Scripture; to pass outside of the control of the Word of God in the Bible, and to treat as outside the range of Scripture problems to which, whether definitely or by implication, it claimed to possess the solution, would have seemed to him an essentially unreasonable course." At the same time, alongside his scriptural orthodoxy Mackintosh also retained – to quote Mozley again – "the generous interests of a receptive and sensitive mind", which is why he was "well qualified to appraise the value of modern theological movements, and to discriminate between the truth that was being affirmed or reaffirmed and the form in which expression was given to it".[46] In the end, it is perhaps difficult to better the verdict of Mackintosh's close friend and biographer. "His theological outlook", Professor A. B. Macaulay tells us, "may perhaps be described as that of either a 'right-wing' liberal or a 'left-wing' conservative.... He held Professor Karl Barth in high esteem, and sympathised warmly with the Swiss theologian's evangelical fervour. But he had imbibed too much philosophical wisdom from Pringle-Pattison for the fact to escape him that, if the result of the reduction of reality necessarily involved in the process of man's apprehension of it has the effect of vitiating the truth of ordinary knowledge, the same reduction must attend the process of his apprehension of revelation and have the effect, therefore, of vitiating the truth of the knowledge supposed to be reached by faith."[47]

The very year – 1937 – in which Mackintosh's latest book made its appearance also saw the publication of the first by a young Scottish minister, George S. Hendry. Hendry subsequently emigrated to the U.S.A. and became one of the most distinguished dogmatic theologians of the English-speaking world; but his early importance was as a Barthian without the reservations which we have discerned in Mackintosh. "I share the conviction with some others", he affirmed in his preface to *God the Creator*, "that Scottish theology has to find its true affinity with the theology of continental Protestantism rather than with that of England and America."[48] It soon became clear what was meant, for the predominant influences in the pages which followed were Martin Luther and Karl Barth. As Hendry put it in his closing chapter, "The theological movement which is associated with the name of Karl Barth marks the end of the age-old acquiescence of theology in its Babylonian captivity to modern thought and the beginning of a new apprehension of the Godhead of God. The issues which Luther raised have again become vital for theology."[49] There is no need to trace the whole argument of a forceful and stimulating work. Suffice it to say that in his denial of any through road from philosophy to the knowledge of God, his emphasis on the incomprehensibility of God's dealings with the world, and his assertion that "The essence of Protestantism is the recognition of the all-sufficiency and exclusiveness of the revelation of God in His Word – not, as it is often caricatured, the right of private judgement or freedom of thought",[50] Hendry proclaimed himself a true disciple of the men who in Bonn and Zürich and elsewhere were overturning the achievements of theologians over more than a century, and endeavouring to lead the Churches back behind Ritschl and Schleiermacher and the Enlightenment to the great Protestant pioneers and to the well-springs of their thinking in the Bible itself.

Hendry's book announced to the world that Barthianism

had at last established a firm bridgehead north of the Tweed. Not a few Scottish divines saw reason to agree with his sardonic remark that "The history of Protestant theology is the history of the gradual relaxation of that tension [i.e., between Christian faith and the principles of philosophy] which Luther had restored.... God must now pass a test set by human thought before He can be accorded permission to be God."[51] Not a few rejoiced, as he himself did, that "Although this has been the major trend of Protestant thought, however, it does not compose the whole of its history. There has always been a minority, a remnant who did not bow the knee to Baal." Not a few shared his opinion that "It is the most hopeful feature of our time that this protest has been raised anew with forcefulness and a dignity which have secured for it a hearing even where it has not won assent."[52] Even as he wrote, there were various signs that the faithful remnant was on the increase. Scholarly older men like John McConnachie of Dundee gave added respectability by their adherence, and the last generation of divinity students to leave college before the Second World War provided a number of valuable recruits. In the forties and fifties the movement began to supply teachers for the theological faculties as well as ministers for the parishes. Professor G. T. Thomson of Edinburgh published his translation of the prolegomenon to Barth's *Church Dogmatics* – volume I, part I – as early as 1936; and a decade later the succeeding volumes began to come out in English, lending their aid to the revolution (or counter-revolution?) which by then was well under way. In June 1948 the *Scottish Journal of Theology* made its appearance under the joint editorship of J. K. S. Reid and T. F. Torrance. By these and other means the new views gradually percolated through the Kirk. The successive reports of the Special Commission on Baptism (which the Assembly set up in 1953) may almost be regarded as the party's manifesto, the establishment of the Panel on Doctrine in 1960 as its greatest triumph. When, in the late sixties, voices began to be raised in favour of a new – and conservative – confessional statement, it seemed likely that their support would come from the same quarter. By 1970 the achievements of neo-orthodoxy were many and various.

At the same time, however, it was also becoming apparent that Barthianism would never form more than one of several strands in the thinking of the Church of Scotland. The majority of its leaders and teachers were hardly committed disciples even during the fifties, when the wind was blowing strongest from Basel. John Baillie's younger brother Donald, for example, who held the chair of Systematic Theology at St. Andrews from 1934 until his death twenty years later, always held somewhat aloof: a fact which made its own impression on all who (with Principal Taylor of Aberdeen University) considered him to be "the very pattern of the Christian scholar", and (with Professor Rudolf Bultmann of Marburg) acclaimed his *God was in Christ* (1948) as "the most significant book of our time in the field of Christology".[53] The state of affairs round about 1960, therefore, was that whereas ministers who had been up at university during or just before the Second World War quite frequently favoured the neo-orthodox position, those who were either senior or junior to them generally refrained from going so far. Indeed, some of the abler students of divinity were being drawn not to Barth but to the neo-liberalism of Bultmann and his interpreters at Glasgow, Ian Henderson, John Macquarrie and Ronald Gregor Smith. As for interested church members, the enthusiasm which their Victorian and Edwardian predecessors had felt for the liberal Evangelicalism of Robertson Smith, A. B. Bruce and Marcus Dods was seldom, apparently, given to the new movements; and where theological concern did exist it very often tended to find satisfaction in the old-fashioned scholastic Calvinism of Holland and North America rather than in anything emanating from Karl Barth's Switzerland or Rudolf Bultmann's Germany.

Theological fashions come and go more quickly now than in the late-Victorian period, and only a very rash prophet would dare to predict what the remainder of the twentieth century holds for the intellectual life of the Church of Scotland. It may be that traditional understandings of Bible and Confession will recover their old predominance. It may be that increasing polarisation of views will become the order of the day, with ever more intransigent forms of Biblicistic fundamentalism confronting ever wilder forms of "this-worldly" radicalism. It may be that some as yet unforeseen interpretation of things will win through to complete supremacy. On the whole, however, it seems most likely that the *via media* presently trodden by all but a few of Scotland's theological teachers will continue to attract the greater number of thinking men and women within the Church. Should this be so, then the fairly cautious liberalism – or open-minded conservatism – which has marked Presbyterian thinking for more than a century will have given fresh evidence of its continuing vitality, and yet another generation will acknowledge its indebtedness to the revolutionaries of the Victorian age.

Notes to Chapter VII

1. W. Ferguson, *Scotland: 1689 to the Present* (Edinburgh, 1968), p. 332.
2. G. Dangerfield, *The Strange Death of Liberal England* (London, 1936).
3. A Muir, *John White* (London, 1958), pp. 440–41.
4. Ferguson, *Scotland*, p. 339.
5. *The Army and Religion: An Enquiry and its Bearing upon the Religious Life of the Nation* (London, 1919), p. 30.
6. ibid., p. 30.
7. ibid., pp. 264–5.
8. J. Baillie, *The Roots of Religion in the Human Soul* (London, 1926), pp. 11–12.
9. *Army and Religion*, p. 187.
10. J. R. Fleming, *A History of the Church in Scotland, 1875–1929* (Edinburgh, 1933), pp. 96–7.
11. ibid., pp. 97–8.
12. G. S. Spinks, *Religion in Britain since 1900* (London, 1952), p. 66.
13. *Proceedings and Debates of the General Assembly of the Church of Scotland, 1932* (Edinburgh, 1932), p. 396.
14. K. S. Inglis, *Churches and the Working Classes in Victorian England* (London, 1963), p. 336.
15. Spinks, *Religion since 1900*, p. 68.
16. ibid., p. 229.
17. Ferguson, *Scotland*, p. 409.
18. J. H. S. Burleigh, *A Church History of Scotland* (London, 1960), p. 416.
19. *God's Will for Church and Nation: Reprinted from the Reports of the Commission for the Interpretation of God's Will in the Present Crisis as Presented to the General Assembly of the Church of Scotland during the War Years* (London, 1946), p. 7.
20. ibid., pp. 34 and 49.
21. Muir, *White*, esp. chs. X and XI.
22. T. Leishman, "The Ritual of the Church of Scotland", in R. H. Story (ed.), *The Church of Scotland, Past and Present*, vol. V (London, n.d.), p. 327.
23. Letter by J. A. Whyte in *Life and Work* (December, 1981), p. 37.
24. J. M. Barkley, "The renaissance of public worship in the Church of Scotland 1865–1905", in D. Baker (ed.), *Renaissance and Renewal in Christian History* (Oxford, 1977), p. 350.

25. Quoted in J. K. Mozley, *Some Tendencies in British Theology* (London, 1951), p. 146.
26. *Creed Revision in Scotland* (Glasgow, 1907), p. 54.
27. ibid., pp. 56–7.
28. ibid., pp. 95–6.
29. ibid., p. 9.
30. ibid., pp. 59–60.
31. ibid., pp. 74–8.
32. Mozley, *Tendencies in Theology,* p. 109.
33. J. Denney, *Jesus and the Gospel* (London, 1908), p. 398.
34. J. Denney, *The Second Epistle to the Corinthians* (London, 1894), pp. 125–6.
35. D. S. Cairns, *The Riddle of the World* (London, 1937), pp. 365–6.
36. D. S. Klinefelter, "The Theology of John Baillie: A Biographical Introduction", in *Scottish Journal of Theology,* vol. 22 no. 4 (December, 1969), p. 427.
37. Quoted, ibid., p. 428.
38. ibid., p. 429.
39. D. Bonhoeffer, *No Rusty Swords* (London, 1970), pp. 85–6.
40. Klinefelter, "Baillie", p. 433.
41. J. Baillie, *The Sense of the Presence of God* (London, 1962), pp. 255–6.
42. Quoted, Klinefelter, "Baillie", p. 433.
43. H. R. Mackintosh, *Types of Modern Theology* (London, 1937), p. 319.
44. J. W. Leitch, *A Theology of Transition* (London, 1952), pp. 33–4.
45. Mozley, *Tendencies in Theology,* p. 141.
46. ibid., p. 140.
47. H. R. Mackintosh, *Sermons, with a Memoir by A. B. Macaulay* (Edinburgh, 1938), pp. 24–5.
48. G. S. Hendry, *God the Creator* (London, 1937), p. viii.
49. ibid., pp. 154–5.
50. ibid., p. 28.
51. ibid., pp. 153–4.
52. ibid., p. 154.
53. D. M. Baillie, *The Theology of the Sacraments and other Papers, with a biographical essay by John Baillie* (London, 1957), p. 35 and n.

Index